AF599049

THE WAY OF CALLIGRAPHY

All my research is associated with practice. Solving practical problems in return for a sober and objective mind is the ultimate goal of my research.

I believe that all ideas and theories since the ancient times are not created in a vacuum. They must be made up of numerous concrete objects, and must be simple, practical, and feasible. This is the main idea behind this book.

"Man is the measure of all things, of those things that are, that they are, and of those that are not, that they are not." Surrounded by countless jewels and gems on the ground, I am looking for a piece of string to link them together. The words of the ancient Greek philosopher Protagoras are the string that I am looking for.

—Sun Xiaoyun

www.royalcollins.com

THE WAY OF CALLIGRAPHY

Sun Xiaoyun

RC

Books Beyond Boundaries

ROYAL COLLINS

The Way of Calligraphy

Sun Xiaoyun

First published in 2023 by Royal Collins Publishing Group Inc.
Groupe Publication Royal Collins Inc.
550-555 boul. René-Lévesque O Montréal (Québec) H2Z1B1 Canada

ISBN: 978-1-4878-1038-2

To find out more about our publications, please visit www.royalcollins.com.

About the Author

SUN XIAOYUN was born in Nanjing in August 1955. She is the Honorary Curator of the Jiangsu Art Museum, Representative of the 17th and 18th National Congresses of the Communist Party of China, member of China Federation of Literary and Art Circles (CFLAC), Vice Chairman of Jiangsu Provincial Federation of Literary and Art Circles (SPFLAC), Vice President of the Jiangsu Provincial Women's Federation, Chairman of the Chinese Calligraphers Association, Deputy Director of its Semi-Cursive Script Committee, Deputy Dean of the Calligraphy & Seal Cutting Institute of the Chinese National Academy of Painting (CNAP), Chairman of the Jiangsu Calligraphers Association, and Chairman of the Nanjing Calligraphers Association. She is also National First-level Artisan, Level-2 Professor, doctoral supervisor, and master supervisor. She is entitled to State Council Special Allowances. She won the Chinese Calligraphy Lanting Award, the highest prize in Chinese calligraphy art circles, and the Jiangsu Provincial Government's First-Group of "Zijin Culture Medal."

She is one of the Talents of the First Four Groups of Projects of the National First Publicity and Cultural System, Advanced Worker of the National Culture System, National Literary and Art Worker of Professional Excellence and Moral Integrity, Expert Directly Contacted

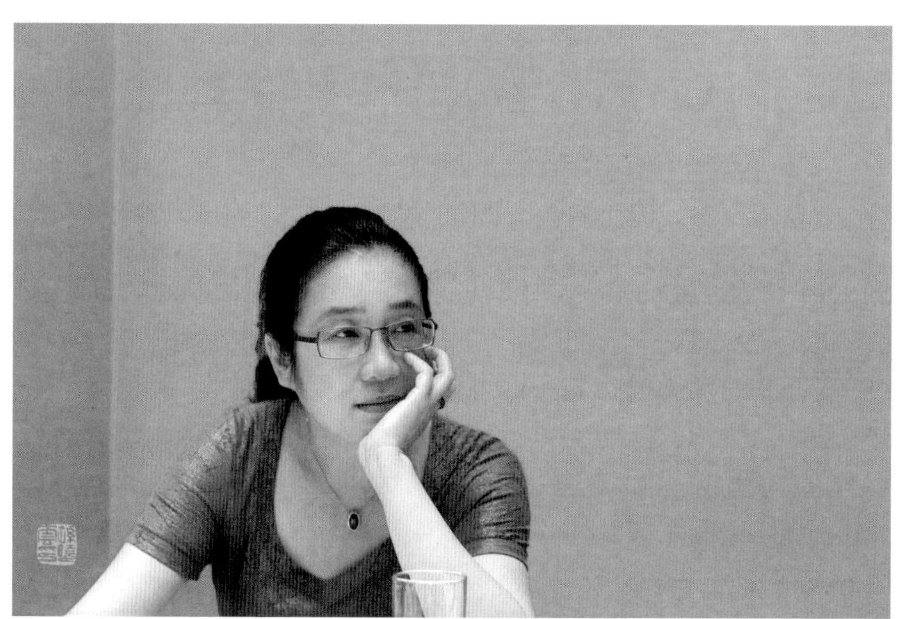

by the Central Government, the first group of Literary and Art Workers of Professional Excellence and Moral Integrity in Jiangsu Province, Young and Middle-Aged Expert with Outstanding Contributions in Jiangsu Province, Goodwill Ambassador of the Red Cross Society of China Jiangsu Branch, Nanjing Top-10 Cultural Icon, torch bearer for the Beijing Olympic Games, and Provincial & Ministerial Level Model Worker.

Her calligraphic works have won the National Calligraphy Award seven times, and she has been funded by the Publicity Department of the CPC Central Committee and the Publicity Department of CPC Jiangsu Provincial Committee to hold "Sun Xiaoyun's Painting and Calligraphy Exhibition" and "*The Tao in Chinese Calligraphy: Sun Xiaoyun's Calligraphy Exhibition*" in the National Art Museum of China (NAMOC), Jiangsu Art Museum, Italy, and France, among other places. In addition, she has held more than twenty personally-themed calligraphy exhibitions around the world. The Rongbaozhai Publishing House has published *The Collection of Sun Xiaoyun's Calligraphy & Painting*, and Selected Works of Sun Xiaoyun's Calligraphy, and People's Fine Arts Publishing House published The Collection of Chinese Contemporary Master Calligraphers: Sun Xiaoyun, et al. The "Sun Xiaoyun Calligraphy Award Fund" was established. She successfully organized the "Following the Original—International Symposium on the Study of Ancient Calligraphy Creation," and edited and published the namesake collection of papers.

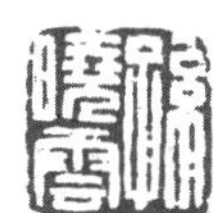

Preface

It has been 44 years since I picked up calligraphy. Passion for it seems to grow in me.

It may be attributed to my family influence and strict calligraphy training since childhood. When I was a child, my mother never bothered herself with my homework, but checked my calligraphy every day. I saw her writing with a pen on draft paper when she was 20, and it was awesome. My father even said that it was why he was drawn to her.

From primary school to senior high, the blank space in each of my books was thickly covered with words and drawings. Writing blackboard newspapers, big-character posters, and posters of other kinds were all my jobs at school. In my fourth grade in primary school, I worshipped the terrific blackboard writing of my Chinese teacher Ms. Liu, who came from Henan Province and had a long and slender face. When my family was driven out of the Community of Military Region (an army compound where servicemen and their families live) in the 1960s–1970s, grandma went to school to help me with my transfer procedures. Ms. Liu sighed and said how reluctant she felt that I had to leave. She must be in her 80s or 90s now, but I am not sure if she is still alive.

In the 1960s–70s, my parents were both locked up and I had not heard from them for a long time. In order to hide their lockup from my uncle and some relatives, I wrote to them by imitating my mother's handwriting. I even wrote to my uncle by mimicking my grandma's tone, ending the letter with two shaky words "母示 (mother's instructions)." My uncle said that he pinned my letters in his mosquito net and read them every day. The letters had "fooled" him for several years. I was then only 14 or 15 years old.

My grandfather, Zhu Fukan, was a paleographer, epigrapher, calligrapher, and painter. He came from Yin County in Zhejiang Province, the same town as my grandmother. The grandfather of my grandmother was Zhang Meiyi, courtesy name Rangsan or Jian Sou. He was the aide and staff to Xue Fucheng, President of Shanghai Association of Ningbo Natives, and two-time principal of Shanghai Nanyang Public School. The year before last, I surprisingly exchanged my handwriting for two of his manuscripts, most of which were rules on stone rubbings from an inscription and drafting. The first one was a letter to Master Hongyi (the celebrated artist Li Shutong). Meanwhile, I got the manuscript of *Numismatics* by Zhang Jiongbo (who opened the Minghua Bank in Shanghai then). A son of Zhang Meiyi, he was a numismatist of the Republic of China. His manuscript was filled with meticulously written small regular script, or xiǎokǎi (小楷), with English written horizontally from time to time. Last year, I found a fan written by my grandpa when he was 32 years old. The handwriting was prudent and seasoned, full of the style of inscriptions on ancient bronzes and stone tablets. He signed off as "秦戡 (read as Qin Kān, the name my grandfather used before he was 40 years old)," and I had no idea who the vendor of the painting was.

The offspring from a family practicing martial arts must know a thing or two about Kungfu or at least do a somersault; children reared in a family of opera artists usually can sing several excerpts of opera; it therefore seemed natural for me to pick up calligraphy as a kid. When I began pondering some calligraphy problems, I also thought: why should a woman like me undertake a man's mission? It's too difficult and exhausting. Yet still I couldn't help it. I have to write every day, and think every day, just as I drink coffee every day. I am addicted to it. Of course, I've found joy in it, because I've experienced the meaning of "discovery."

I took the college entrance exam twice but failed at both. It's a shame that I don't have a college degree and many things have therefore been affected. Fortunately, it hasn't affected my study or research, nor has it affected my writing.

This book, *The Way of Calligraphy*, was written from January to August 1998. The days of writing passed serenely from the bitter winter to the scorching summer. Usually, I would make a cup of coffee after lunch, and start the computer through a haze of steaming coffee. Only a fluorescent computer screen could be seen except for a table heaped with books that were filled with paper notes.

The writing went on smoothly, I should say. Before setting pen to the paper, I spent ten minutes composing an outline of twenty themes which did not change much after completing the book. I'd been asking myself those questions for many years. I felt somewhat abashed that not until I was 43 did I put my thoughts on paper.

In the 1980s, all I was thinking was calligraphy. I kept a diary all day, turning over and over, trying to write something, but I couldn't find the right form and appropriate tone. I was not adept at the theories of history. I remember that during history class in middle school, I dozed off most of the time, failing to remember emperors' reign titles of dynasties, famous names, and whoever did what at when. That was a total mess to me. Then in my early 30s, I tried to write some theoretical articles and showed them to my friend. I remember the look in his eyes when he replied the next day: "A calligraphy diary is the best you can write."

I know myself too well. I am only interested in visible, tactile, and practical things. I am fascinated by things and details related to people's functions, physiology, and psychology. It's the same with calligraphy. My biggest wish in childhood was to become a doctor or a detective. I am a big fan of the TV program *Discovery*. The reasoning and investigation in it are based on tiny details that often go unnoticed. From these details people deduce the fundamental truth and decide what is possible (impossible) according to their own circumstances.

I don't want to be a theorist on calligraphy, nor could I do it well. All my research is associated with practice. Solving practical problems in return for a sober and objective mind is the ultimate goal of my research. I have become accustomed to changing the periods in my book into question marks, and then, after pondering and practicing, I draw the full stop myself. I believe that all ideas and theories since ancient times are not made in a vacuum. They must be made up of numerous concrete objects, and must be simple, practical, and feasible. This is the main idea behind this book, and you may consider it my belief in writing.

I want to repeat the saying of the ancient Greek philosopher Protagoras as is already quoted in the book: "Man is the measure of all things, of those things that are, that they are, and of those that are not, that they are not." Surrounded by countless jewels and gems on the ground, I was looking for a piece of string to link them together. The words of the Greek philosopher were the string I was looking for.

Thanks to the string, I roughly make a necklace like this: the origin and termination of Chinese calligraphy and brushwork and why they were lost; what is "bāfēn shū (八分书, broad chancery style)" and "kǎizé (楷

则, model in calligraphy)," what is "shì (势, strength/released energy)" in calligraphy, how to interpret "five movements with fingers when holding the ink brush," what the several ancient parables such as "wūlòuhén (屋漏痕, literally means water stains on the wall; comparing the brushwork to the rainwater running down the wall of the house)," "zhéchāigǔ (折钗股, literally means twirling the hairpin; describing the strokes that are bending but retain a touch of mellowness)" and "envisaging the artistic effect before putting pen to paper" yìzàibǐxiān (意在笔先, refers to graphic interpretation of "brushwork," relations between writing tools, postures, and the development of calligraphy), and relations between "zhāngcǎo (章草, a specific kind of cursive script)," and the termination of calligraphic evolution.

In this book, I also put forward the concepts of "měihuà (美化, beautification)" and "lìhuà (隶化, change into clerical script)," the division of four stages of "wánfǎ (完法, completing the method)," "shàngfǎ (尚法, upholding the method)," "biànfǎ (变法, changing the method)" and "wúfǎ (无法, no method)," the essence of the "tièxué (帖学, study of calligraphy books)" and "bēixué (碑学, study of stone inscriptions)," decoding the writing styles of major calligraphers in history, what is the meaning of "common origin of calligraphy and painting," what is the so-called "painting of man-of-letters," the boundary between calligraphy and painting, etc. In my view, this is not a textbook, but a book to "seek" the "origin" of ancient calligraphy.

Since a diary is the best I can write and I have written it for nearly 40 years, I have mastered it quite well and decided to use the first person to tell readers my experience and confusion in learning calligraphy, i.e., which problems I have encountered from what perspective and approach, and the problems I've solved. I particularly added personal experiences to make the book more readable. The readers' feedback after its publication in 2000 proved that my approach did work.

I'm lucky. First, I grew up in a scholarly family where I could receive proper training since childhood. And I have practiced calligraphy much longer than my peers. Second, I live in such a developed information age, being able to see all the treasures of imperial painting and calligraphy, historical material, and even cultural relics underground that I could not see or find in the past. Third, I live in an era of diversified, open, and free art. Stone inscription tablets and model books coexist; one can choose either tablets or model books based on his own needs; and I can rest assured to deliver opinions and impart knowledge. Fourth, I can work in such a serene, leisurely, and professional environment as the art academy, and have been tremendously praised, deeply encouraged and selflessly supported by so many seniors, peers, and friends.

孙晓云

SUN XIAOYUN

Nanjing, on the night of December 19, 2002

Contents

CHAPTER 1

It Is Better to Turn "China" into Calligraphy

In English, china with lower case c refers to high quality porcelain originally unique to China while China with upper case C is the country in East Asia. In addition to silk, it is porcelain that is associated with Chinese civilization in the imagination of ancient Westerners. Today, both silk and porcelain can be made all over the world. They are so elaborately and exquisitely produced that they are even superior to those made in China. Therefore, I am afraid that silk and porcelain can no longer stand for Chinese civilization.

Thus, the symbol of Chinese civilization and the uniqueness of Chinese art must be the calligraphy that has been in existence from time immemorial. Instead of translating 中国 into China, it's better to turn it into Calligraphy.

In China, calligraphy was once called "Model Calligraphy." In the era of imperial examinations, good handwriting was the primary requirement for the promotion of numerous scholars. Since the Han dynasty, it has been the strict demand that only talented women and men with lofty ideals are able to meet. A history of calligraphy is the records of not only numerous talented people who have made pains-taking efforts to practice calligraphy year after year but calligraphers in different times who applied themselves sedulously to both teaching and studying calligraphy as well. Such a scenario has been under way for around three thousand years.

Shortly after the prosperity of literature and art in the 1930s, China entered into the Anti-Japanese, the Civil War, "the Anti-rightist," and "the Cultural Revolution," during which calligraphy had not been popular for around 40 years. It is in 1955 when I was born.

My mother was born in a scholarly family and wrote with a beautiful hand. When I was three years old, with great passion, I copied "Chariot, Horse, Cannon, Elephant, Soldier, Pawn, General" while watching my father play Chinese chess. My mother started to teach me how to frame characters, as she discovered that I copied these characters quite well. From then on, I have never stopped practicing calligraphy.

When I was very young, there were only *Xuanmi Ta* by Liu Gongquan and *Shisan Hang* by Wang Xianzhi available for me to imitate. When I grew a little older, there were few ancient inscriptions in the bookstore, as they were thought to be the "feudal dregs" and thus must be swept away at that time. On the bookshelf was *Chairman Mao's Poems* by contemporary calligraphers. What impressed me most was Zhou Huijun's cursive script of *Selected Poems by Lu Xun* which I had studied over and over again. Later I learned that she imitated the scripts by Mi Fu, a renown calligrapher in the Song dynasty. I got to learn Zhou Huijun earlier than Mi Fu.

"Swallows, which nested in front of distinguished families in the old days," have already "flown into the homes of ordinary people." Today, it is quite likely that the calligraphy books are the greatest in number and widest in variety in bookstores. There are various versions of histories of calligraphy, theories of calligraphy, epigraphy works, and getie—the earliest collection of various calligraphies which have been edited and printed time and again. These books, printed in inferior quality, are immensely oversupplied.

Sometimes, I would stand in front of the shelf, reading a book at leisure for hours. More often than not, I murmured to myself that what should be written about our predecessors had already been done, that what should be thought about our predecessors had already been done, and that what should be commented on our predecessors had already been done. But it is strange that later generations have never stopped writing, thinking or talking about calligraphy. They even have no intention of writing less, thinking less, and talking less.

Though I have never inquired as to their thoughts, I know how I thought. I felt perplexed, a result of my writing and pondering. In order to get out of perplexity, I have no choice but to continue to write and ponder. I would like to let people know what I was confused about and how I got rid of the confusion by my voice. Of course, I could keep silent. And I once refrained myself from making my voice heard. Consequently, I really did not want to say anything at all.

In 1997, one friend asked me, "Will you regret it for the rest of your life"? To my surprise, I was at a loss.

Now I am writing to propound my ideas. After all, I am no different from others.

CHAPTER 2

Three Incidents That Perplexed Me

When it comes to my massive perplexity in calligraphy, it seemed that had not suffered it when I was a kid.I attributed the perplexity to three incidents which all took place in 1978.

I was working at a military club as a "librarian." Time and again, I was in charge of shopping for books, in which I took absolute delight. I bought lots of books of ancient rubbings published after the "Great Cultural Revolution." I often read them in the library by myself. In those days, I was so confident and courageous that I took my first facsimile of *Preface to Wang Xizhi's Sacred Teachings* for display. Unexpectedly, I was thought to have been trained to copy *Preface to Wang Xizhi's Sacred Teachings*. The problem came when I copied from *Book Charts,* composed by Sun Guoting (Picture 1).

Book Charts is the calligraphy by Sun Guoting. The dots are so varied that I was not able to copy them in any way with my practical experience and common sense despite all my efforts. When I imitated in a natural way, the brush was not supposed to produce such unpredictable strokes except that I "retouch" or trace them at a snail's pace.

That made me doubt if Sun Guoting used the tool I have and the way I write now. However, the content of *Book Charts* makes clear that Sun Guoting is an admirer and true voice of Wang Xizhi and Wang Wei.

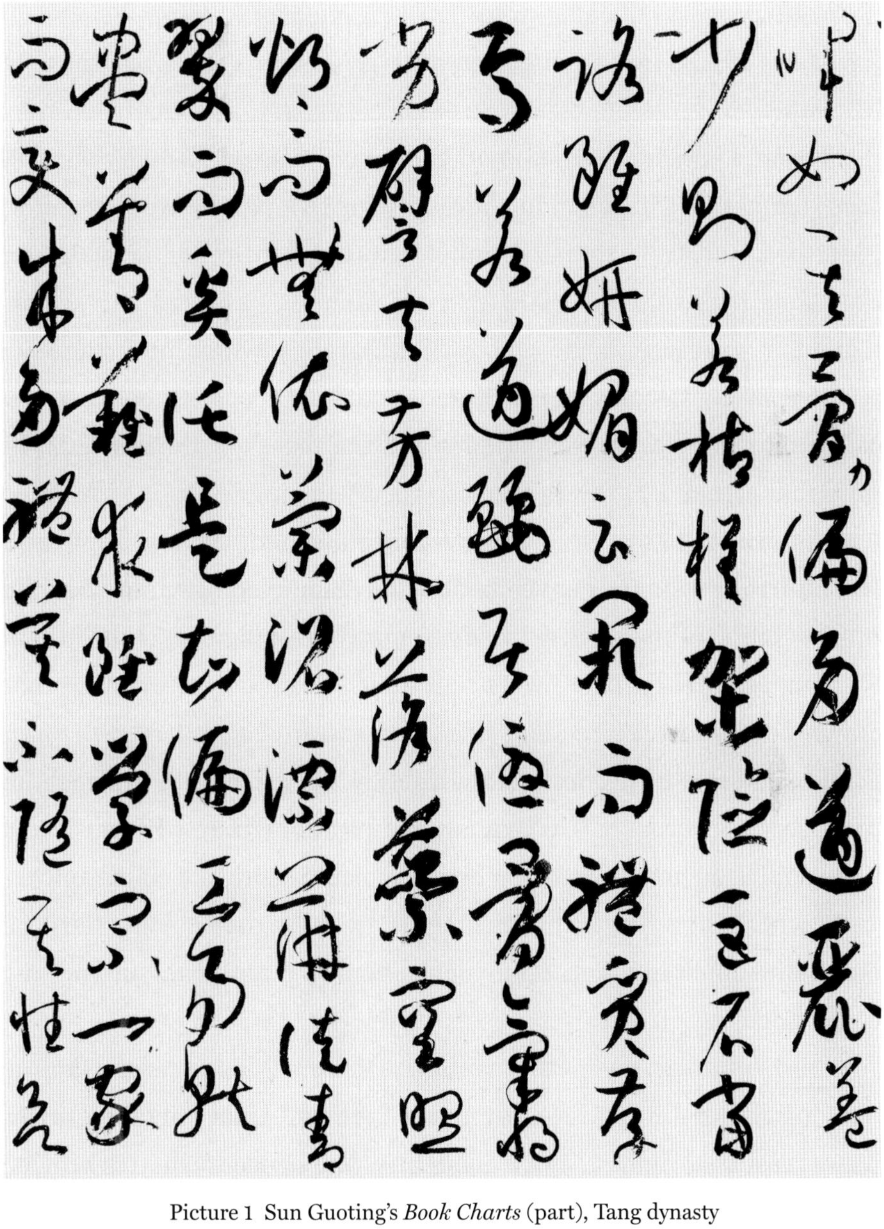

Picture 1 Sun Guoting's *Book Charts* (part), Tang dynasty

Were the works of calligraphy by Wang Xizhi and Wang Wei, which have been looked up to generation after generation, really like those of Mr. Sun?

Second, I bought *A Selection of Calligraphic Essays Through the Ages* (two volumes) in Duoyunxuan, the institution that purchases, distributes, publishes, and collects calligraphy, painting, and other artworks in Shanghai. It was the last set with more than ten damaged pages. This is my first exposure to the theory of calligraphy, which unfortunately resulted in my sleeplessness. There was a wide disparity between my calligraphy practice and experience and the theory of the ancients. In my opinion, their lengthy and tedious theories counted for little. And the well-known sayings that have been handed down for thousands of years had little to do with my engagement with calligraphy. After studying the interpretation of the theories made by our contemporaries, I took them with a grain of salt. There were numerous questions in my mind that crawled out from all directions like small insects. Later, I read *Renjian Cihua*, a literary criticism work written by Wang Guowei, in which he proposed the concept of "Ge," namely not intuitionistic or obscure. It was quite similar to how I felt when I read ancient theories of calligraphy.

I firmly believed that the arguments made by the ancients must be based on something. Yet, no evidence could be found to support my conviction.

Third, my uncle, my mother's brother (Picture 2) returned to Nanjing not long ago after he was redressed as a "rightist." I was only three when he was cast as a "rightist." Such an identity had been attached to him for twenty years. All I knew was that his calligraphy was even better than that of my mother.

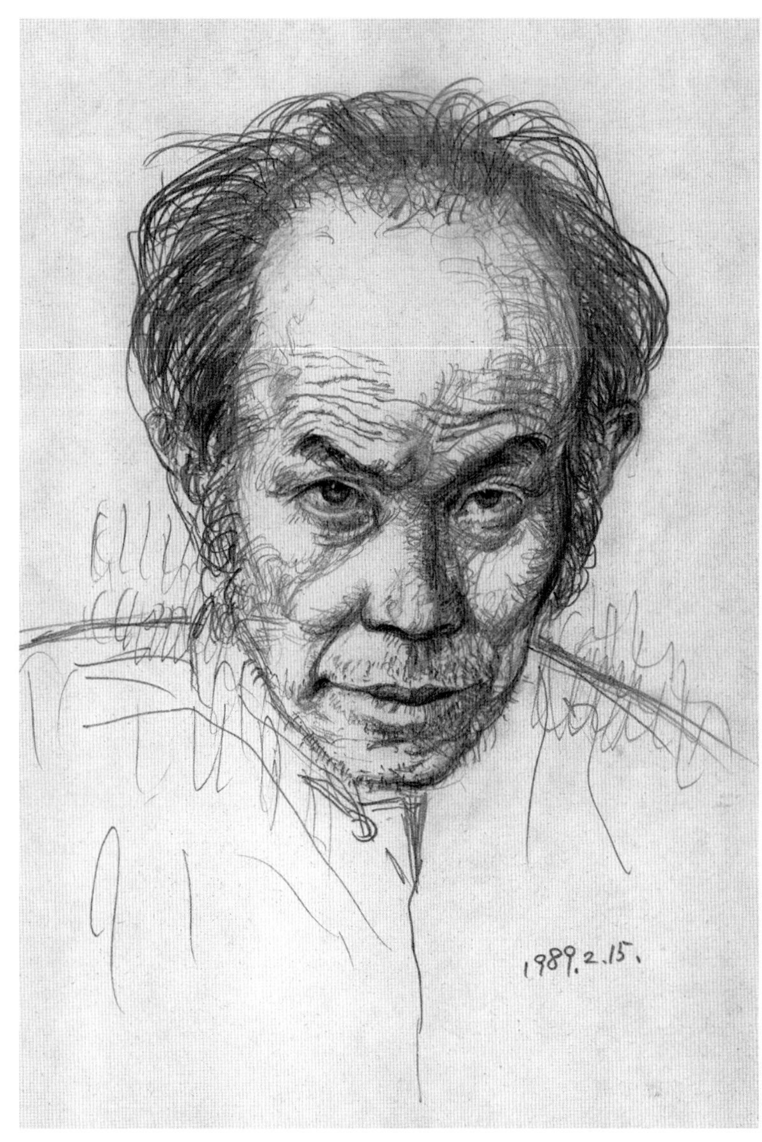

Picture 2 Sun Xiaoyun's painting of her uncle

That day, I kept on talking excitedly to him about art theories. My uncle, who had been lying silently, suddenly shook his head when I spoke of the figures of calligraphy and painting and opined: "They are entirely different things." Interestingly, he mispronounced one of the characters, which he actually never corrected.

However, 23 is a hyper age. I went on to talk a lot about calligraphy, certainly including *Book Charts* by Sun Guoting. At length, my uncle unveiled an unexpected trump card by opening *Book Charts* and doing a demonstration with a brush. "Take a look, it should be written in this way. It looks like this." It turned out that Sun Guoting wrote it that way. That's how my maternal grandfather taught him, which I had never thought about.

At that moment, I wanted to smoke.

Our first meeting in twenty years ended in unpleasantness. To be exact, the meeting came to an end with my utter bewilderment. It was the first time in my life that I did not feel confident in myself at all. All of a sudden, I felt empty though I did not openly admit that my uncle was right. A wall that I had built with great effort ever since my childhood collapsed overnight.

Was I really wrong? Why was I not able to figure out? How should we think about the history of calligraphy? How could we sort out the development of calligraphy over thousands of years? What was the road awaiting me to take?

In the years that followed, I did not practice my handwriting at all. Instead, I spent quite some time drawing. After my failure to be admitted to the Military Art Academy, I entered Jiangsu Traditional Chinese Painting Institute to further study for two years. I remained increasingly puzzled along with my exposure to "Chinese Paintings," "Ink Paintings," and “the method of writing with brushes,” which frankly still baffled me. It might be said that the way to use the brush was obscure and unintelligible to me. My perplexity put me such an agony that I thinned down to around 88 pounds, the lowest weight since I became an adult. It took me many years to understand that perplexity is a passion and a great driving force.

CHAPTER 3

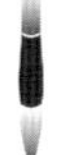

"Let's Go Back to the Beginning of Our Conversation."

In 1985, I was transferred from the army to Nanjing Calligraphy and Painting Institute on the recommendation of Mr. Wei Tianchi, a calligraphy professor at Nanjing Normal University. From then on, I have been a calligrapher by trade.

In those years, I kind of contemplated calligraphy obsessively, regardless of whether I was walking, cycling, eating, and even sleeping. Once I got on what I had pondered, I just wanted to have someone to share with, in addition to immensely rejoicing in it. One of my friends, who succumbed to the temptation of a table of good dishes I prepared, was often dragged in to be my listener. And one cigarette after another, we kept smoking.

I had lived such a persistent and excited life for four years. I got into the habit of writing diaries when I was nine. Eventually, there is now a jumbo box of diaries. Looking through the diaries of those years, I suddenly realized that they were not diaries at all. Instead, day in and day out, all I wrote were theoretical articles on calligraphy. In retrospect, at that time it was quite likely that I looked awful as many people tried to avoid me. To this day when thinking of my friends, I still feel both guilty about my obsession and grateful to them for being my dedicated listeners as well.

In 1989, I wrote an article entitled "To Harp on the Old Tune Regularly," which was published in a calligraphy journal in Henan Province. A couple of days ago, I took out the journal to find that here is exactly what I would like to say:

"To date, there are three kinds of aesthetic interpretations of calligraphy "conventions": First, the aesthetic interpretation is made from the perspective of western aesthetics, philosophy, psychology, and geometry; second it is made from the perspective of the unique spirit of Chinese Taoism, Buddhism, Zen, and Japanese calligraphy; and third, it is made from the perspective of inductive narration against the background of historical theories of our previous dynasties.

"I wonder if there are any additional perspectives from which we expound on calligraphy aesthetics. We should puzzle things out for ourselves rather than getting our puzzles resolved from piles of books or with direct references to and blindly believing in the great calligraphers.

Take solving equations for instance. To solve an equation and find an unknown number, there must be one or several known numbers. People tend to focus on looking for unknowns, and forget to go after among the known."

"We should achieve following results through our efforts. First, we can fully explain how the theory and practice of ancient calligraphers are consistent. Second, there is certainly a link between the theories we come up with and how we practice. Thirdly, the theory of calligraphy will be instructive and enlightening to the further development of calligraphy . . ."

At that time, it might be said that I laid myself out to voice my opinions in a roundabout way for fear that I would be misunderstood or a target for criticism. As a matter of fact, the ancients put it, "Get to the root" which is exactly the how and why.

The classic Daoist text *Zhuangzi* has the following words:

Zhuangzi and Huizi were strolling about on the bridge over the Hao River. Zhangzi said with a sigh, "How leisurely and light-heartedly fish swim in the river. That's their joy."

Huizi asked curiously, "How do you know that they are carefree as you are not a fish"?

Zhuangzi replied instantly, "You are not me. How can you know that I don't know that they are carefree"?

Huizi rejoined, "I'm not you. It's true that I have no idea what you have in your mind. However, you are not a fish. You don't know the joy of a fish, which is absolutely certain."

Zhuangzi defended, "Let's go back to the beginning of our conversation. Now that you inquired "How do you know that fish are carefree," you have admitted that I knew that fish were carefree. In other words, you deliberately asked me this question. As a matter of fact, it was on the bridge that I figured that out."

Let's go back to the beginning of our conversation!

CHAPTER 4

To What Does "Simplicity and Ease of Writing" Precisely Refer?

In retrospect, Chinese calligraphy is not only scripts but regarded as an independent art form as well. Accordingly, it is necessary for us to look at the history of calligraphy from more than a single perspective.

First of all, I would like to stress that this article will not touch upon philology.

As is known to all, the origin of Chinese characters was quite similar to that of Western characters in the period of painted pottery (approximately 8,000–3,000 years ago) in that they were both pictographic characters written with "brushes." However, they later went their separate ways. The Western characters evolved into alphabetic writing and brushes were replaced by hard pens whereas with the full play of brushes, Chinese characters developed into the contemporary square characters which are roughly grouped into six categories, namely self-explanatory characters, pictographs, pictophonetic characters, associative compounds, mutually explanatory characters, and phonetic loan characters. It is hard to verify when and why the Chinese and Western characters diverged. Yet, one thing is for sure whether in China or in the West:

The purpose and need for inventing characters are the same, namely, for keeping records and conveying information.

They also share their design and nature in the course of their evolution, namely for the sake of comprehensiveness, easy identification, convenient and fast writing, and aesthetics.

They both cease to evolve because both the writing tools match so perfectly with people's expression of their thoughts and their physiological conditions of hands that it is convenient for people to write in a regular and fixed manner.

It makes sense for us to look at the Western character with the help of the above assertions. However, the problem arises if we look at the Chinese character in the same way. It seems that something doubtful is missing.

People had finished inventing characters and all the radicals had been definitely coined before *The Motivations of the Characters* by Xu Shen. In other words, Chinese characters had been formed before the appearance of the small seal script. And yet, the styles of calligraphy kept evolving till the period of Wei, Jin, South, and North Dynasties during which the regular script eventually took shape. That is to say, it is ever since then that Chinese calligraphy or the shape of Chinese characters ceased to evolve yet has been carried forward to this day. According to the history of calligraphy development, it is clear and definite that only when the regular script took shape over time in the Eastern Han dynasty did there be calligraphic theories.

Here is the problem.

Undoubtedly, calligraphic styles evolve in response to people's need for simplicity and ease of writing. It is an obvious fact that drawing a circle is easier and faster than drawing a square. Drawing circles seems to come naturally to a three-year-old baby whereas it has to be taught to draw squares. The turning stroke is roundish in the seal script while it is square in the regular script. In addition, the dot was made standard. Take "Yong (永) with eight strokes" which actually represents the general strokes in Chinese calligraphy. It is truly more laborious and difficult to write these strokes. But both the ancient and contemporary theories of calligraphy plausibly explain that the evolution is for the sake of "simplicity and ease of writing."

At that time, I was almost driven mad by the puzzlement.

Emperor Qin Shihuang's character policy led to the establishment of official scripts of the Chinese written language. And it was in the Qin dynasty that the small script was adopted for the purpose of standardizing the script. And history is powerless to stop the appearance of the official script which was evolved from the small seal script. The Zhangcao script, a specific kind of cursive hand of Chinese calligraphy which appeared in the Eastern Han dynasty when Han Zhang, namely Liu Da (lived AD 56–88, reigned AD 75–88) was on the throne, was not created by the emperor. The influence of Cai, Su, Mi, and Huang's styles of calligraphy in the Song dynasty is far greater than that of Emperor Song Weizong's calligraphy, which features thin strokes. Thus, it can be seen that no emperor could use his power to stop the evolution of calligraphy. Likewise, the evolvement of calligraphy is independent of any will. There is no doubt that "simplicity and ease of writing" will inevitably suspend further progress from the perspectives of human nature, development patterns, and reasonableness.

However, it is not simple and easy to write the regular script.

To what does "simplicity and ease of writing" precisely refer?

CHAPTER 5

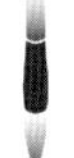

The Blind Men and the Elephant

Let me start with the regular script.

Today, when it comes to the regular script, we will immediately associate it with Ouyang Xun, Zhu Suiliang, Liu Gongquan, and Yan Zhenqing, who are all noted calligraphers in the Tang dynasty Actually, the conception of the regular script the ancients had differs from that held by our contemporaries. The regular script was known as "Formal Script" or "Standard Script" in the Wei and Jin Dynasties, during which the regular script grew mature. It is in the regular script that regulations were made how to write dots, horizontals, verticals, left-falling stokes, right-falling strokes, turning strokes, and hook strokes. Later generations have been following these regulations and this is how the name of "regular script" came into being, that is, a model of handwriting. Now that characters have developed to be models, they are mature and will remain stable. Without doubt, there is no era like the Tang dynasty, which witnessed the most complete and rich display of artistry of the regular script.

Taking the regular script, which matured in the Tang dynasty both as the model and the orthodox style, people have been encouraged to study and copy from it for generations. Children who learn to write in the regular script must practice hard every day. And both literati and calligraphers are good at it. As a matter of fact, the regular script had become mature about 500 years before the Tang dynasty.

Ge Zuo Stone Tablet (Picture 3), collected in the Nanjing Museum, is a famous stele from the Three Kingdoms Period. In the stele are twelve impressive characters in the regular script.

In the Municipal Museum of Nanjing is stored *The Epitaph of Wang Minzhi* (Picture 4) inscribed by Wang Xizhi's family. The inscriptions are regular scripts with a little touch of the official style.

In the summer of 1998, the tomb of Gao Song, a famous official of the Eastern Jin dynasty, was unearthed in Nanjing. Among the relics, there were two brick epitaphs of regular scripts (Picture 5), both of which prove not only the existence of the regular script before the Eastern Jin dynasty but also the authenticity of Wang Xizhi's calligraphy with irrefutable facts. Gao Ershi, who argued with Guo Moruo about the authenticity of the ink in *the Preface to Lanting Collection* in those years, can lie peacefully in his grave.

It should be noted that in the history of calligraphy, when the regular script came into being, one form of the regular script termed "Bafen script" was mentioned time and again.

The creator of "Bafen script" was Wang Cizhong from Shanggu in the Eastern Han dynasty. It is strange that we cannot find the corresponding plates in the inscriptions of the past dynasties, and there is no clear definition in the calligraphy theory of the past dynasties, which keeps later generations in the dark. Then what exactly does this "Bafen script" look like?

Who is Wang Cizhong? It has nothing to do with me. What I really care about is what indeed "Bafen script" looks like?

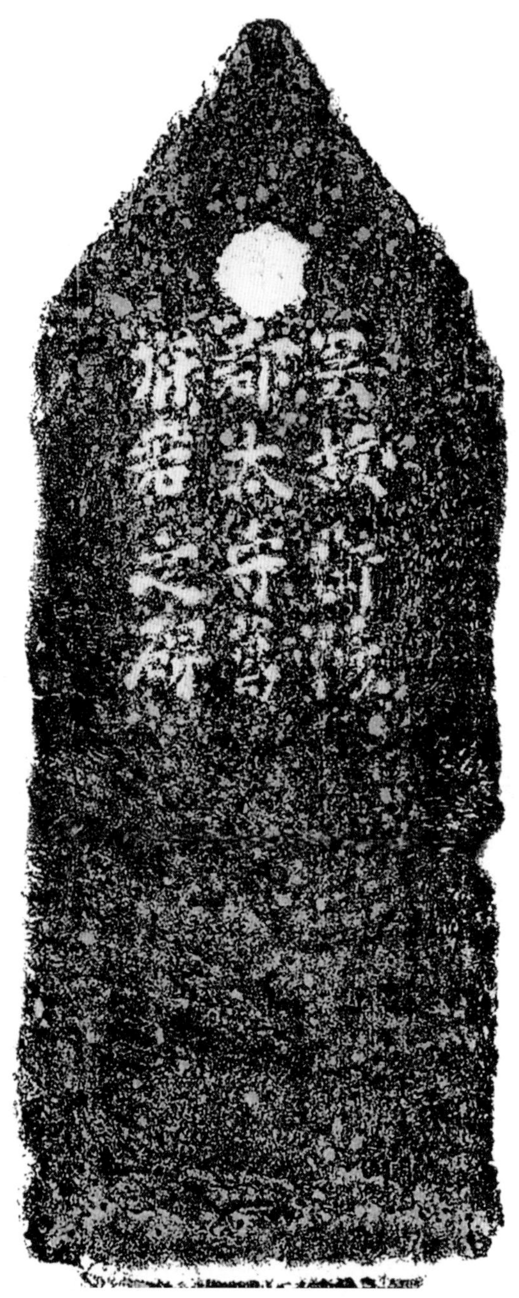

Picture 3 *Ge Zuo Stone Tablet*, Kingdom of Wu

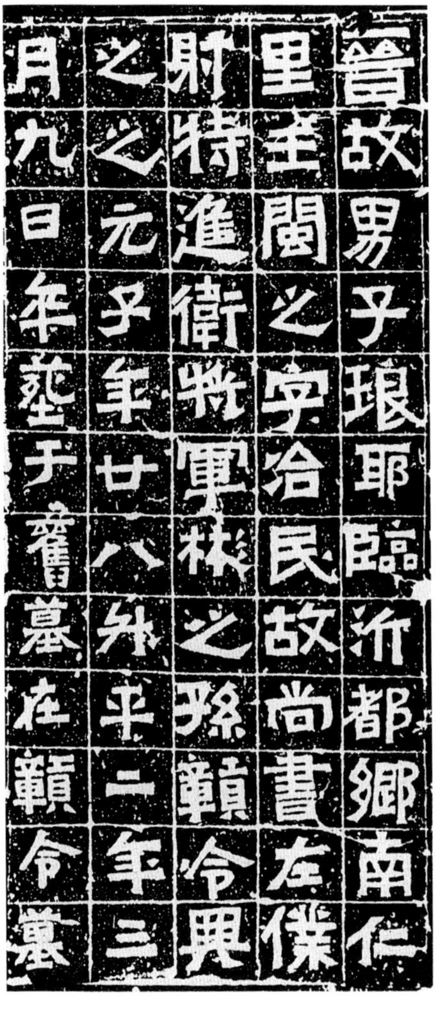

Picture 4 *The Epitaph of Wang Minzhi* (part), Eastern Jin dynasty

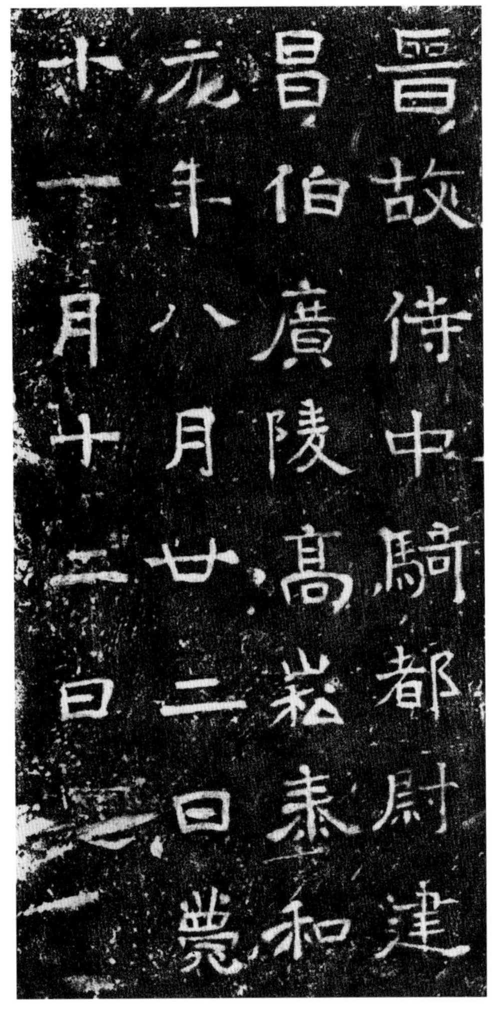

Picture 5 *The Epitaph of Gao Song* (part), Eastern Jin dynasty

In those days, I was so determined in trying to figure out what actually "the Bafen script" looked like that quite a lot of books became dog-eared owing to my referring to them over and over again. By stringing all the doubts and questions together laboriously, finally I worked out what "the Bafen script" was.

There are three explanations about "the Bafen script" in the calligraphy history:

The first is that "the style is a fusion between approximately two-tenths of the official script and eight-tenths of the small seal script." The second is that there is a clear distinction of all the parts of a character in terms of the brushstrokes just like the shape of character "八" (bā, eight): the right and the left. The third is that the character should be eight fens (a unit of length, and one fen is one-third of a centimeter) in size.

The former is about the choice made between the official script and the small seal script, which shows both the reason for its appearance and the shape of characters as well, though vaguely. The second is actually the emphasis placed on the neat and orderly strokes. The latter obviously talks about the size of characters.

The three interpretations are a bit like the famous image of the blind men and the elephant, each trying to understand an elephant solely by touching it. I took time to convene the three parties to communicate clearly, only to find that they were concerned about the same issue.

Above all, I will not allow the second view to pass unchallenged. It is most cryptic yet most crucial.

CHAPTER 6

My Doubts about the Existence of "Yǒng (永) with Eight Strokes"

When it comes to the method for using the brush, "Yǒng (永) with eight strokes" (Picture 6) is the earliest one we came into contact with and the most familiar one we got with as well. As a matter of fact, this method is known to all who have had even a slight acquaintance with calligraphy.

This method, taken its rise from the official script, was created by Cui Ziyu of the Eastern Han dynasty (AD 25–220). It is said that Wang Xizhi

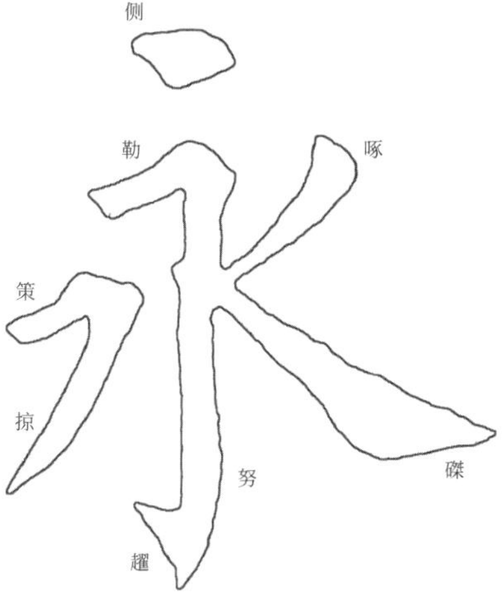

Picture 6 Yong (永) with eight strokes

practiced calligraphy assiduously for many years. Because of his focus on imitating "Yǒng (永) with eight strokes" for 15 years, he could write all the characters well.

When I was a girl, I found that the front page of the copybook was usually printed with the character "永" in bright red. In addition, there was always an explanation of each stroke. The copy I made of "永" could pass for being authentic but I had never had an eye on the explanations at all. I kind of lived in ignorance when I was young. However, I really achieved something to write home about by studying the copybooks once again when I grew older.

In "Yǒng (永) with eight strokes," the dot is a "slanted dot," the horizontal is like a "rope for reining in a horse," the vertical is like a "crossbow in place," the hook is that "the feel of writing the hook is the same as that of our jumping," the upper left horizontal is like "a whip spurring the horse," the lower left falling is like "smoothing one's hair," the upper right falling is like "the way in which a bird pecks at food, and the lower right falling is "the feeling of the surgeon opening the skin with the scalpel."

It is obvious that the dot, horizontal, vertical, hook, left-falling, and right-falling are the shapes of strokes, while the latter are the course of actions which, in effect, is the manner of moving the brush when people write.

By looking it up the dictionary, I found that these words which describe these actions all connote that the actions are performed with courage, resolution, and rapidity.

These brush movements were regulated into rules around 2,000 years ago. Ever since then, there appeared the theory of calligraphy, or "the techniques of calligraphy" that all the calligraphers have been talking about.

"The techniques of calligraphy" have always been enigmatic and wrapped in mystery. There are quite a lot of records in history books. Here are two instances.

Zhong You, a native of the Eastern Han dynasty, "had lived in the seclusion of his own home for 16 years." However, when he saw Cai Yong's calligraphy work in Wei Cheng's home, "he made an earnest request for the work which was not granted," and then he "thumped himself on the chest with a mallet, resulting in his spitting blood." After Wei's death, Zhong You "robbed his tomb" and finally got it.

At the age of 12, Wang Xizhi found that his father hid his former generation's calligraphy theory in his pillow. "He took it secretly to read." In his later years, he untiringly taught his son Wang Xianzhi his theory of calligraphy *On the Strokes of Characters* by saying "keep it to yourself, keep it in secrecy, do not show and share with your friends."

After reading it for the first time, I thought to myself: The ancients were really making such a fuss about it. They would not have to go that far.

However, the more I read, the more firmly I believe that something that has kept our ancients arguing about for generations must be worthwhile. It is undoubtedly such an art of high skill which is exceedingly difficult to learn with ineffable beauty that it fascinates the ancients to not only practice and study but collect and treasure as well.

There is no doubt about the existence of the techniques of calligraphy.

There's only one possibility why we think the techniques are imaginary, why we are made puzzled by them, why we think they are of no great importance—the techniques of calligraphy are no longer in use.

CHAPTER 7

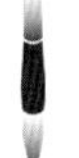

Let Me Start with the Ways to Hold the Chinese Brush

When it comes to the technique of writing, we have to start with the ways to hold the Chinese brush.

We all know how to hold the brush, as there are pictures which illustrate the postures of holding the Chinese brush with the right hand on the first page of all the calligraphy elementary courses and copybooks for calligraphy. People who practice calligraphy are familiar with the postures as they are with chopsticks.

Han Fangming, a calligrapher in the Tang dynasty, summed up five ways to hold the brush:

1. "Hooking the shaft" (Picture 7). "The index finger and the middle finger hook the brush shaft, and actually all the five fingers are involved in holding the shaft." The key is that the strength of the fingers will be exerted rather than that of the palm when one writes. When the five fingers work together, the strength is concentrated on the shaft with each of

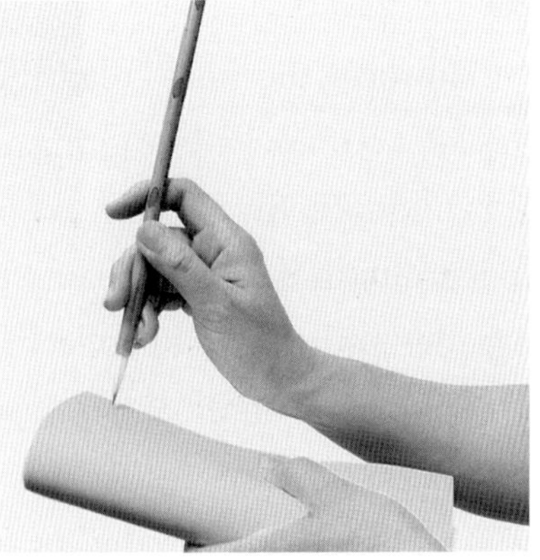

Picture 7 Hooking the shaft

the five fingers playing their separate roles. This certainly facilitates people to do demonstrations and explanations when teaching calligraphy as well."

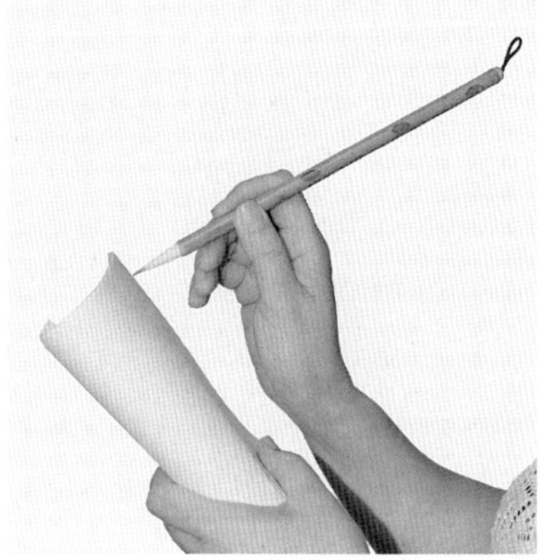

Picture 8 Hooking the shaft with three fingers

"This is regarded as the ideal posture." This, of course, is the method that we are most familiar with. The upward index finger is like a goose holding his head high, from which comes the legend of Wang Xizhi's love for geese, as a matter of fact. The method of hooking the shaft with the index finger and the middle finger has long been hailed as the "classic" by calligraphers of all ages.

There is another method called "Hooking the shaft with three fingers" (Picture 8). This method differs from the former in that only the thumb, the index finger and the middle finger are involved in holding the brush. The thumb is on the left side of the shaft, and the index finger is on the right side. The two fingers meet. It seems that there is a long and narrow gap between the thumb and the index finger, so it is also called "phoenix eye." Actually, it is the very way we hold pencils and pens. According to Han Fangming, "When people write calligraphy in this way, the writing lacks force and vigor due to the insufficiency of strength."

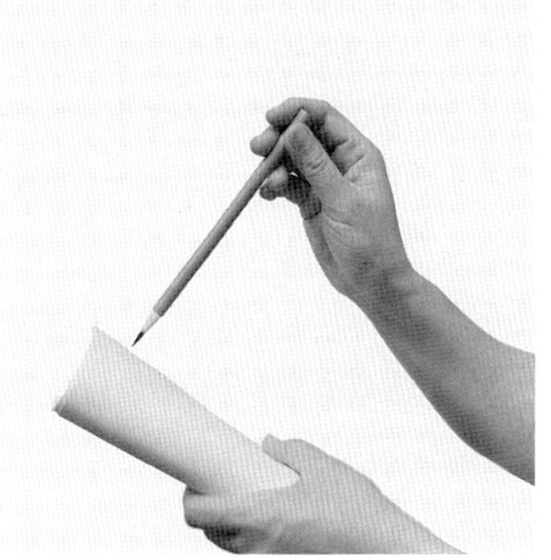

Picture 9 Gripping the shaft

2. "Gripping the shaft" (Picture 9). Five fingers are used to grip the end of

the brush shaft. People can write quite fast by hanging the brush. It is usually used to prepare a draft. Today, people often use this method. However, people are not encouraged to use this method as the characters written in this way appear to have no proper frames.

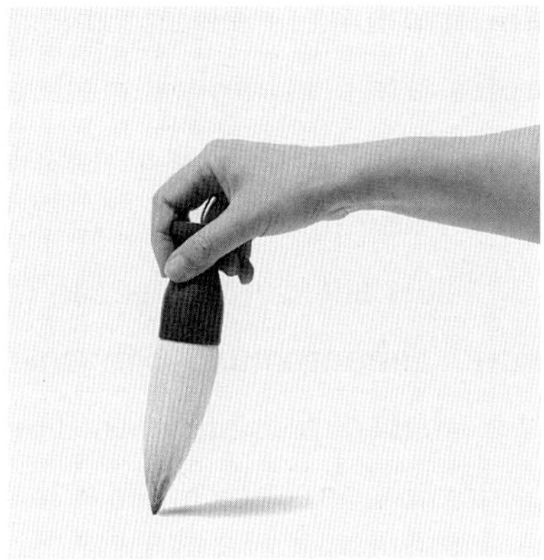

Picture 10 Pinching the brush

3. "Pinching the brush": (Picture 10). It is similar to "gripping the brush." This method is peculiar to cursive scripts in jumbo size or stamps. Nowadays, there is a kind of brush similar to a bucket. Its shaft is thick and short, with a flat and round top. It is named "pinching brush," in other words, to pinch it all the five fingers are involved.

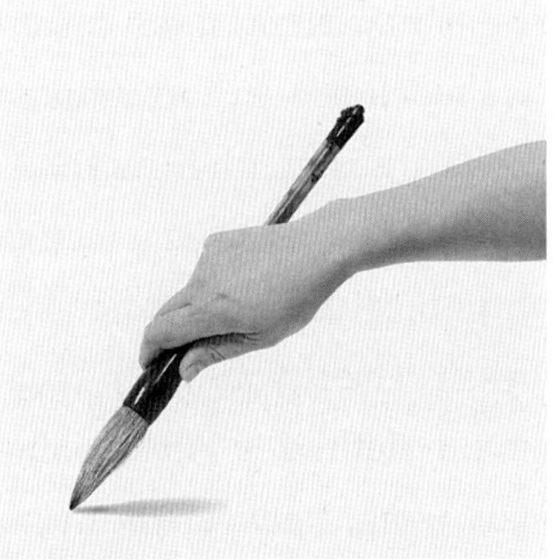

Picture 11 Holding the shaft

4. "Holding the shaft" (Picture 11). The palm is bent in a form of fist in which the shaft is held, hanging the wrist in the air to write with the strength of the elbow. If you are strong and vigorous, you may write in this way. But that is not the way calligraphers do.

5. "Taking the shaft" (Picture 12). The brush is placed in the middle of the first two sections of all the four fingers (the index, middle, the ring, and little fingers), with the thumb pressing it. It is not much different from "holding the shaft." That is not the method calligraphers use either.

Only the first method is commonly used by ancient calligraphers. It is not only classic but scientific and pragmatic as well. It is hailed as an ideal posture. Therefore, this is the only authentic and model way of holding the brush and has been passed down to later generations.

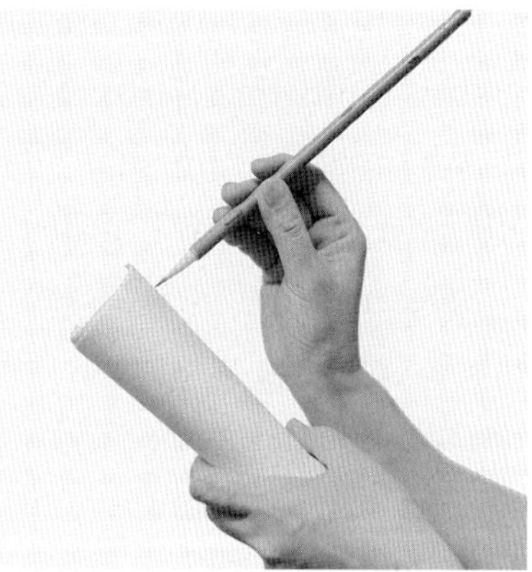

Picture 12 Taking the shaft

The ancients were also very particular about where they should hold the shaft. According to Wei Sheng (272–349), a female calligrapher in the Eastern Jin dynasty and the teacher of Wang Xizhi, people should hold the shaft at the point two cun and one fen from the top if they write the regular script and they should hold the shaft at the point three cun and one fen from the top if they write cursive script. Two cun in the Han measurements is equivalent to a little more than one cun today, so three cun is no more than two cun in contemporary measurements. Thus, there must be something in what Wei proposed.

Like everyone else, I began learning to write calligraphy with "the classic method" and inevitably suffered a lot of pain in the wrist. When I was young, I preferred other methods in the absence of my parents not only because it was much easier for me to handle with them but also because I felt more comfortable with them and suffered less pain in the wrist. To this day, I will occasionally use the brush haphazardly, which is often mercilessly pointed out to my face.

I know that my achievements in calligraphy have little to do with whether I hold the brush in a "standard or regular" way or not. The "classic" method that the ancients hailed can be said to exist in name only, or actually is an empty shell. I am sure that the ancients' method of "hooking the shaft with all the five fingers" is relatively unique to them.

My childhood experience has sobered me up.

It is a pity that the ancients did not have a video, consequently, how they handled the brush is no longer visible. All we can see today are the still postures of how brushes are held.

Because the ancients didn't have video, they couldn't record the process of using the brush. What we can do is to describe them by making use of analogies and pithy formulas.

Fortunately, there are lots of views kept by the ancients which we might as well take a look again.

CHAPTER 8

"Five Fingers" or "Five Characters"

The techniques of writing calligraphy are scattered throughout the history of calligraphy. There are Cai Yong's *Nine Ways of Wielding the Chinese Brush*, Wang Xizhi's *Twelve Writings on Brushwork*, Ouyang Xiu's *Eight Knacks and Thirty Six Methods*, Zhang Huaigu's *Ten Methods of Handling the Brush*, Li Hua's *Two-character Knacks*, Yan Zhenqing's *Twelve Meanings of Brushwork* by Zhang Changshi, to name but a few. They are all familiar to us.

There is still a lot more. Consider, for example, "the five-character technique of writing," which was handed down by Lu Xisheng in the Tang dynasty. The five characters are "pressing, repressing, hooking, blocking, and propping." It is also called "stirring the lamp-wick," the posture of carrying the writing brush is like someone stirring the lamp-wick. Obviously, the five characters "pressing," "repressing," "hooking," "supporting," and "sustaining" describe the different functions of all the five fingers the right hand. In this regard, it seems that Li Yu, emperor of the Southern Tang dynasty explained in detail:

"There is a seven-character technique of writing which is also known as "stirring the lamp-wick. Together with Zhong You (151–230) and Wang Xizhi (303–361), this technique was started with Madame Wei (272–349), originally named Wei Sheng, a famous calligrapher in the Jin dynasty. This technique was passed down to Ouyang Xiu (1007–1072), Yan Zhenqing (709–784), Chu Sui-liang (596–658), and Lu Ji (261–303). Thought it has been handed down to this day, few people in the world has much idea how this technique evolves ..." Li Yu summarized this technique in the following:

Pressing (with the thumb), to be specific, the force will landat the lower end of the phalanx of the thumb by pressing the shaft as straight as one lifts something very heavy.

Repressing (with the index) refers to the first knuckle of the index finger slightly obliquely clinging to the outside of the shaft.

Hooking (with the middle finger) means that the first and second knuckles of the middle finger bend to hook on the outside of the shaft.

Blocking (with the ring finger) means that the fingernail of ring finger clings to the shaft, resulting in reacting force together with the index finger and the middle finger.

Propping (with the little finger) means that the little finger plays the smallest role as an aid or support to the ring finger.

As the ancients all put it, the seven-character technique of writing created by Li Yu actually originated from the five-character technique of writing by Lu Xisheng. How was Lu's the five-character technique of writing actually interpreted? Unfortunately, I failed to find the answer to this question.

Here comes the issue of two concepts: five fingers or five characters? To be specific, whether pressing, repressing, hooking, blocking, and propping simply associate with the thumb, the index, the middle finger, the ring finger, and the little finger respectively or they are the summary of the collaboration of the five fingers?

Later, in Shen Yinmo's *On Calligraphy*, I found that Mr. Shen had made a clear exposition of the functions of the thumb, the index, the middle finger, the ring finger, and the little finger, which match with "pressing," "repressing," "hooking," "blocking," and "propping" respectively. Obviously, Mr. Shen also referred to Li Yu's theory.

According to Mr. Shen's theory,

Pressing means the thumb pad is pressed to or pressing the right side of the shaft, just like pressing the flute hole with the finger when one plays the flute.

Repressing has the sense of holding fast. The first section of the index finger is used to stick the outside of the shaft obliquely and forcefully. The index collaborates with the thumb to hold the shaft fast."

Hooking refers to "the first and second sections of the middle finger are bent to hook the outer part of the shaft."

Propping "addresses the function of the little finger." "Because the ring finger is weak in strength, it can neither block nor push the middle finger, which hooks the shaft alone. In addition, the little finger will assist the ring finger to support underneath to increase the strength."

I cannot help but think again: how is the exposition connected with the posture of "stirring the lamp-wick"? What does "stirring the lamp-wick" really mean? Why did the ancients always connect the posture of "stirring the lamp-wick" with Lu's five-character technique of writing and Li's seven-character technique of writing? Mr. Shen did not further his elaboration.

I was still puzzled. It seemed that there are still lots of puzzles.

How about putting aside these puzzles for the time being so that we can start exploring the posture of "stirring the lamp-wick"?

CHAPTER 9

The Vivid Posture of "Stirring the Lamp Wick (拨镫)"

As the name suggests, the word has held the same meaning since olden days.

"Dèng (镫)" refers to a stirrup. "Dèng (镫)" is also equivalent to "dèng (灯/燈, meaning lamp)" in the pronunciation in ancient Chinese.

"Bō (拨)" is a hand move of repeatedly stirring back and forth.

When you "stir the lamp wick," you take the brush as you would ride a horse; your thumb will serve as the left stirrup; and the other four fingers as the right stirrup. In ancient times, people tied the reins controlling the horse's head to the stirrups on the left and right, so that they could free both hands to hold weapons. When their two feet "stirred" on both sides, the horse would advance or retreat at their disposal.

When "stirrup" is taken for "lamp" in "stirring the lamp wick," the brush can be compared to the wick. You use your thumb, index, and middle fingers to "stir" the "wick" in order to rotate the brush.

Whatever kind of "stirring," the thumb and the other four fingers must cooperate to roll the "lamp wick" back and forth, so that the brush can be flexibly controlled.

"Stirring the lamp wick" happens to coincide with the ancients' discussion about "turning the brush." For more than two thousand years (from the Han dynasty to the Qing dynasty), diverse theories on calligraphy were recorded by the ancients, especially "turning the brush," which formed a long tradition. Here are a few of the records:

In *Jiu Shi* (*Nine Types of Force*) by Cai Yong in the Eastern Han dynasty, the first type of force is "structure and script style," and the second is "turning the brush."

In the Tang dynasty, Lu Xie said in *Rhymed Formula by the Pond* (Línchí jué, 临池诀): "Whenever you use a brush, turn it freely and flexibly under your control."

Su Shi in the Song dynasty once put it in *On Calligraphy*: "Venerable Ouyang Wenzhong (Ouyang Xiu) told me: you should move the brush with your fingers without moving your wrist. What wise words he said"!

Chen Yizeng in the Yuan dynasty in *Crucial Tips for Members of the Imperial Academy* (Hànlín Yàojué, 翰林要诀) stated that "one should be able to rotate the brush in a smooth and flexible manner."

Dong Qichang in the Ming dynasty summarized in *Essays on Huachan Studio* that "'turn' and 'constrain' are the essential tips for a calligrapher."

The opening sentence of *Pledge on Calligraphy* by Song Cao of the Qing dynasty affirmed: "The method of learning calligraphy lies in the mind. If your mind can turn the wrist, then your hand can turn the brush."

You'll never know the big difference of turning the brush until you give it a try! I dug out the ancient hieroglyphics and early zhuànwén (篆文, seal script) and zhòuwén (籀文, a style of calligraphy in the Zhou dynasty), observed them again, and imitated the handwriting. I was suddenly enlightened that the round and smooth twist of strokes were just a result of turning the brush to the left and right directions! I kept trying again and again, just like Christopher Columbus, who discovered the New World of the Americas.

It turns out that "stirring the lamp wick" is a method of turning the brush back and forth with the right hand regularly. In the method, using five fingers together and forming two hooks takes effect. When turning the brush, "stirring the lamp wick" is the most convenient, steadfast, and effective way to control strokes.

I then thought about how ancients used similes to describe the writing style, such as "a porter and a princess contending to be the first to cross the road" and "the goose paddling on the water." I was puzzled and had no idea what they meant. The answer to the riddle came out: "road" and "goose" are the brush; "porter and princess" and "goose's feet" are the thumb and other fingers on both sides of the brush; "contending" and "paddling" are the twisting of fingers on both sides. This is the same as the posture of "stirring the lamp wick."

What a highly imaginative nation we Chinese are! Our ancestors made metaphors incisively and vividly, without knowing how we successors racked our brains to guess their true meaning!

CHAPTER 10

Real Calligraphy Should Be Written with Brushwork

To tell the truth, I was preoccupied with questions and eager to find out solutions. On the one hand, I was impatient with the verbosity of ancients. On the other hand, I was afraid my impatience might drive the important things in the verbosity away.

Well, I had to turn patiently to re-look at the literal interpretation of "Five Movements with Fingers When Holding Ink Brush," i.e. "yè (擫), yā (押), gōu (钩), gé (格) and dǐ (抵) (pronounced in Chinese)."

"Yè (Picture 13)" has only two meanings, "yèdí (擫笛, pressing down on the flute when playing the musical instrument)" and "yèmài (擫脉, a doctor pressing the patient's wrist exactly on artery or veins when recording his pulse)." You can try holding the brush with two kinds of "yè" movement, with the palm inward, and the index finger, middle finger and ring finger pressing the brush inward.

"Yā (Picture 14)" is the same as "press." It refers to how the thumb should bend the brush from inside to outside with the finger pad pressing the brush, just opposite to "yè" movement.

"Gōu (hook, Picture 15)" is the way the middle finger hooking the outside of the brush. Whether it's about "drawing the outline" or a "hook" stroke, it is moved vertically.

"Gé (Picture 16)" involves the meaning of being obstructed and separated; the move belongs to the sense of reverse.

I looked up all the meanings of "dǐ" and pondered for a long while. "Dǐ" should be taken as "offset" in the backdrop.

In this way, the five Chinese characters do not necessarily refer to the postures in sequence of thumb, index finger, middle finger, ring finger, and little finger. Lu Xie in the Tang dynasty wrote: "The method of using the brush is as follows: expand the thumb, 'yè' the middle finger, restrain the index finger and hide the ring finger, so that the palm is shaped like hiding an egg. That is the essential key to holding the brush." Lu only mentioned four fingers here. It proves that he was not talking about the static state of fingers, but the respective movement of each finger. And the movement of each finger must be coordinated by other fingers. The "essential key" for Lu refers to the method of using the brush by each finger. "Holding/using" the brush refers to movement. And the "movement" is turning the pen.

It is also obvious in practice that only the thumb, index and middle fingers work in the brush-rotation process, particularly when writing small-sized words. Ring finger and little finger don't play the role of turning, but they maintain the stability of hand.

Here is a picture of Japanese Monk Kukai holding brush, who came to China to learn calligraphy in the Tang dynasty (Picture 17). The caption reads: "While rotating/turning the brush in front of the middle finger, align the two little fingers to help support the middle finger ..." Unfortunately, the words in the picture are incomplete. But it proved that in and before the Tang dynasty, the ancients held the brush in this manner. I emphasize the word "turning/rotating," because judging from the picture, it is obviously "single hook" brush-holding and is suitable for

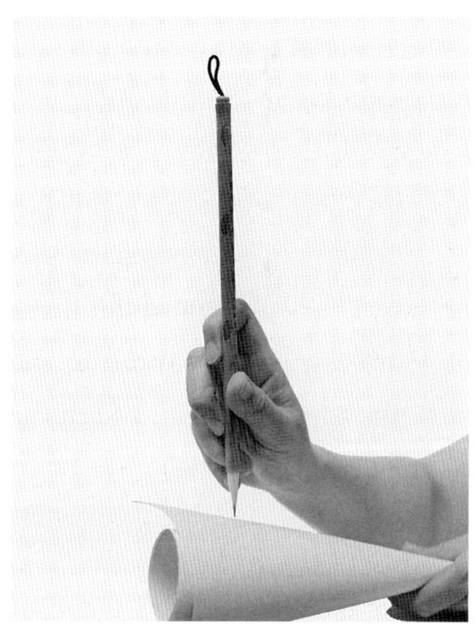

Picture 13 Yè (擫)

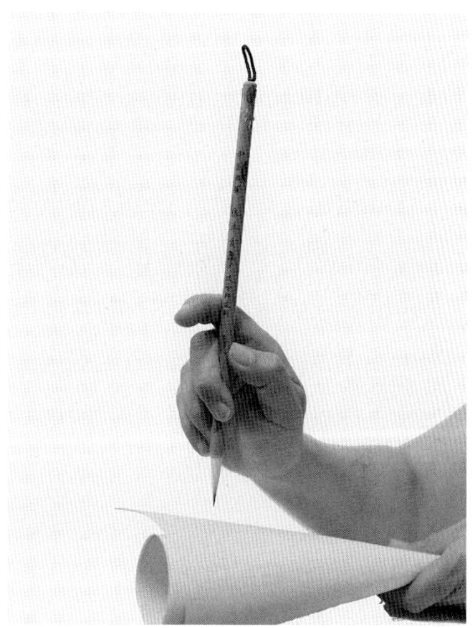

Picture 14 Yā (押)

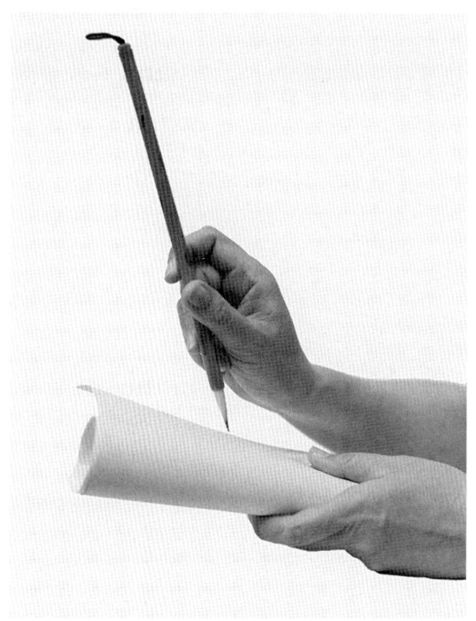

Picture 15 Gōu (钩)

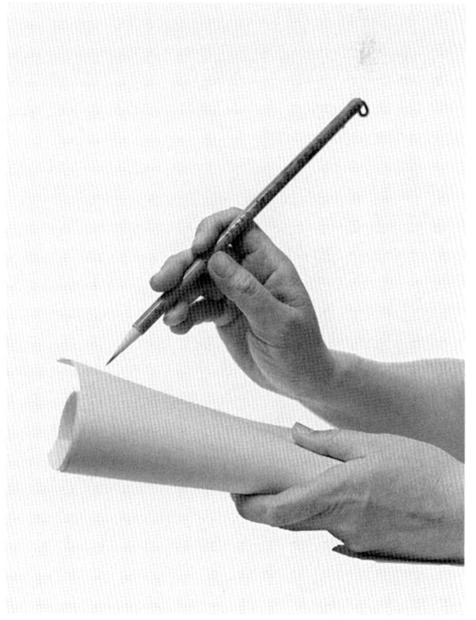

Picture 16 Gé (格)

writing small words. Once you try, you will find out that in "single hook" you can only rotate the brush in a limited range, yet in "double hook" you can do it with more flexibility and stability.

Therefore, when I held the brush using the "classic" method and kept trying, suddenly it dawned on me:

When my hand controls the brush to move back and forth, if it turns right and controls the brush to rotate from top of the thumb to the base of the knuckle, it must be twirled to the top of finger through the coordination of the index finger, middle finger, and ring finger. The hand

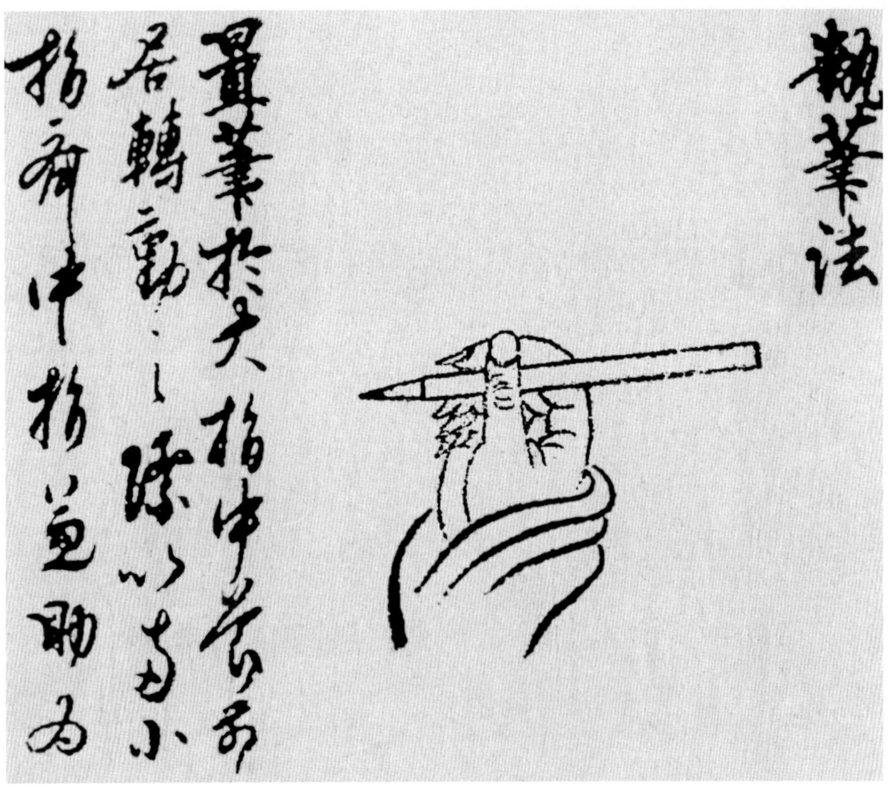

Picture 17 Monk Kukai (Japan) Holding the Brush

is making force in the shape of "yèdí" and "yèmài," and that is why it's called "yè."

If my hand turns the brush to the left, the brush then rotates from the root of the upper joint of the thumb to the top, and the thumb presses the brush, it is called "yā (压, pressing)." "Making one's finger mark on a contract" is to strengthen the force of the thumb, so it is called "yā (押, pressing down with the thumb)."

The term "stirring the lamp wick" is such a vivid expression. "yè" means turning the horse's head to the right, evidently stirring the right stirrup (with index and middle fingers) backwards; "yā" refers to turning the horse's head to the left, which means stirring the left stirrup (using the thumb) backwards.

"Yè" and "yā" are interchangeable. "Yè" starts with "yā," and "yā" also starts with "yè." "Yè" stops at "yā" and "yā" also stops at "yè."

"Gōu (hook)" makes the index and middle fingers first go down. When the "hook" is put in place, the ring finger and the little finger go up; then the move turns into "gé." It is evident, however, that "yè" and "yā" move back and forth horizontally while "Gōu" and "gé" move back and forth vertically.

As for the meaning of "offset," the dictionary says: if one thing is offset by another, the effect of the first thing is reduced by the second which acts in the opposite way. In terms of turning the brush, when you turn to one end, you must turn back, from left to right, from vertical to inverse, to make the brush-turning smooth, so that the opposite effect is required to offset the force anytime.

Therefore, Lu Xisheng advocated "yè, yā, gōu, gé, dǐ"; Li Yu proposed "yè, yā, gōu, jiē, dǐ, jù, dǎo, sòng"; Cui Ziyu said, "*The Eight Principles of Yong*"; Ouyang Xun theorized "the thirty-six methods." All the ancient brush-holding methods are largely identical with minor differences except that everyone held his opinion from individual perspective owing to a unique experience. Their ideas revolve around a central point, namely discussing the skills and methods of brush turning.

The reason why ancients preferred the "classical" method of writing is that the posture is most suitable for turning the brush and most conducive to controlling the horizontal and vertical strokes.

I tried imitating Sun Guoting's Shū pǔ (书谱, *Treatise on Calligraphy*) by adopting the classic method, and it worked.

After so many trials I could finally conclude that:

Brushwork is the "classic" method of using the right hand to hold brush and turning the brush back and forth regularly to flexibly move strokes. Using the brushwork is the so-called "yòng bǐ (用笔, brush holding)." Strictly speaking, only words written with brushwork can be considered "calligraphy." No wonder calligraphy was called "the method/law of handwriting" at the very beginning.

In 1992, when I was teaching calligraphy at the Central Academy of Fine Arts, a student told me, "It makes sense that Japanese call calligraphy 'shūdào (书道, way of handwriting)'. I think it inappropriate that Chinese call it 'shūfǎ (书法, model/method/law of handwriting)'. 'Shūyì (书艺, art of handwriting)' is a better substitute." I asked him why. And he threw up his hands and said, "What is 'fǎ (法, model/method/law)'? And where is 'fǎ' in calligraphy anyway"?

What a thought-provoking question!

CHAPTER 11

Man Is the Measure of All Things

I used to play an ancient Chinese toy when I was a kid—jiǔ liánhuán (九连环, Nine Linked Rings Puzzle). The rules of playing are strict. The puzzle consists of a long loop with a handle on one end that is interlocked with nine rings. The objective is to disentangle all the nine rings from the loop, and the solution takes hundreds of moves, and one careless move will get you stuck there.

Solving a puzzle can be compared to solving the Nine Linked Rings Puzzle. When you untangle one ring, you have to move on to separate the next. It won't proceed even if only one ring gets locked.

However, my puzzle concerning calligraphy was, why did ancient people write via turning the brush? What was the advantage of doing so? And how did that relate to the development of Chinese characters?

History books had little records of the key to my questions. The Banpo Relic Site near the city of Xi'an in Shaanxi Province dated back to six to seven thousand years ago; Yangshao Culture (a Neolithic culture that existed extensively along the Yellow River in China, dated from around 5000 to 3000 BC) emerged five to six thousand years ago, and the hand-painted patterns on colored pottery vessels irrefutably proved the existence of writing brush. Chinese characters remained in a stage of infancy stage then. How could we expect to read historical books of that time? Even if I intended to consult historical materials about the Four Treasures of the Study, I had nowhere to search. I wanted to ask people, but there was no one to ask. I was kind of desperate then. There were "unknown numbers" everywhere.

But there is an indisputable "known number."

In the six to seven thousand years since the appearance of the Banpo Relic Site, people have undergone tremendous changes in their lifestyles such as food, clothing, housing, transportation, and hobbies. The only things that have not changed are the physiological phenomena and bodily functions of human beings. To be specific, we share the same arms (upper arms, lower arms) and hands (palm, five fingers) with ancients living six to seven thousand years ago, and the functions and movements remain the same. My own body, arms, hands, and my physical condition and feelings are the most direct proof and reliable evidence beyond time and space.

I remember Protagoras, an ancient Greek philosopher, once said: "Man is the measure of all things, of those things that are, that they are, and of those that are not, that they are not."

I began to consult a large amount of material and extant calligraphic works, and drew conclusions bit by bit from my own experiment and experience.

CHAPTER 12

The First Motive for the Creation of Brushwork: "Gathering the Brush-tip (裹锋)" and Continuous Writing

Tao Zongyi in the Yuan dynasty (1271 to 1368) wrote in the *Chuo Geng Lu* (輟耕錄 Chuò Gēng Lù *The Records of Stopping Plowing*) that before ancient people made brushes out of animal hair, they "dipped a bamboo stick in lacquer and wrote," implying that the little hair on the tip of the tender bamboo was used as brush hair. In the remote age, people wrapped the outer edge of the brush with some hair; or cut a few splits in a brush head and filled the splits with hair.

At that time, ancients used nothing more than carbon, ink, and lacquer, namely some mineral pigments. In order to get more ink or lacquer on the tip of the brush and draw more strokes at one time (with strokes presented in a thick or thin way at any time), ancient people naturally selected animal hair or plant materials with a similar texture.

Human beings formed their habits and chose their methods when they used tools. This came from practice, with the rule "survival of the fittest." I tried both "no brush turning" and "brush turning" and the results were divergent:

When I didn't turn the brush, I could barely write anything. The brush hair was either too flat or slit, and I had to make the tip of the brush pointy again and again. When I tried turning the brush, the tip of the brush always gathered together and I could keep writing multiple words without having to make the tip pointy from time to time. I could write distinct characters even when the brush hair was split up. This could be considered one of the earliest motives for the emergence of ancient brushwork.

We can observe evident traces of brush turning on inscriptions of bronze ware in the Yin and Zhou dynasties dating back more than three thousand years ago (Picture 18). Or maybe earlier, such as the freehand drawing of irregular geometry (Picture 19) in the painted pottery of Lower Xiajiadian Culture (2200–1600 BC), which later developed into the representative patterns of tāotiè (饕餮, a mythical ferocious and gluttonous wild beast) (Picture 20), yúnléi (云雷, a pattern defined by spirals, sharp turns, and switchbacks) (Picture 21), and kuí (夔, a one-legged monster in Chinese fables) (Picture 22) in bronze ware of the Shang and Zhou dynasties. All of the patterns feature spiraled and cursive lines of symmetry.

Only by turning the brush handle from side to side can the brush hair be gathered all the time, so that such lines can be drawn quickly and evenly. Thanks to the appearance of brushwork, the patterns with traditional Chinese characteristics were created. If you don't believe it, why not give it a try?

Men are wise. The origin of handwriting has embarked on a road of "convenience" since its birth.

There was, of course, a second motive.

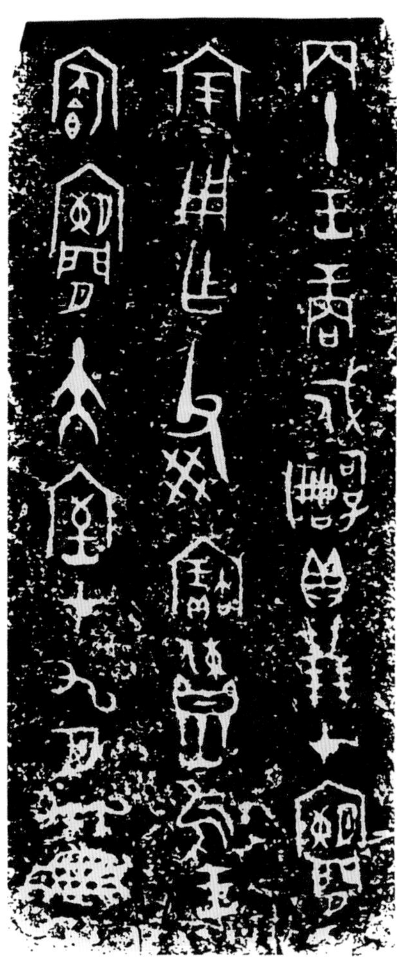

Picture 18 Inscriptions on bronze ware, Yin and Zhou dynasties

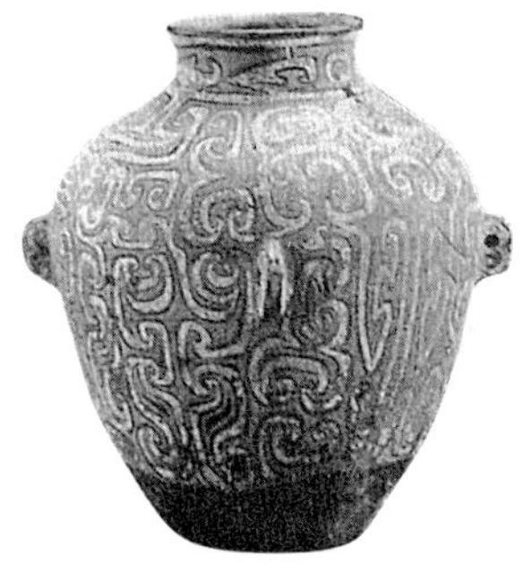

Picture 19 Colored-drawing pottery pot, Lower Xiajiadian Culture (2200–1600 BC)

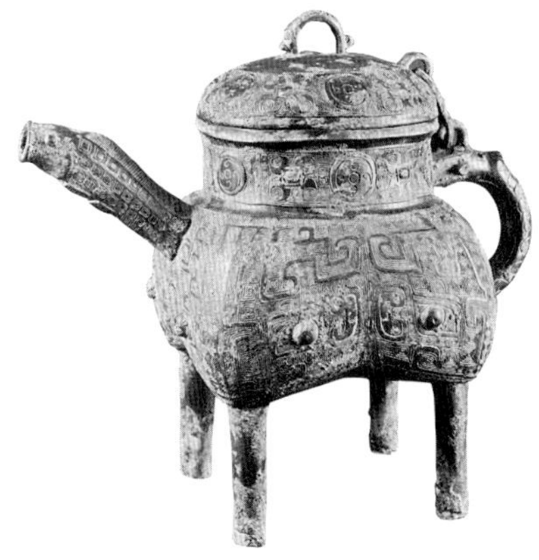

Picture 20 Tāotiè pattern on a bronze wine warmer, Shang dynasty

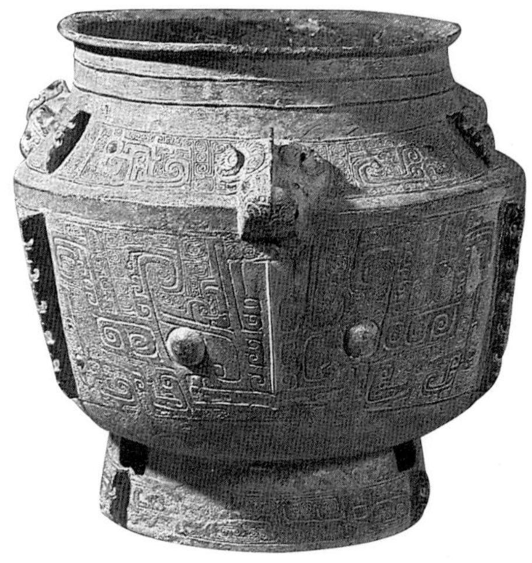

Picture 21 Three-sheep design drinking vessel, Shang dynasty

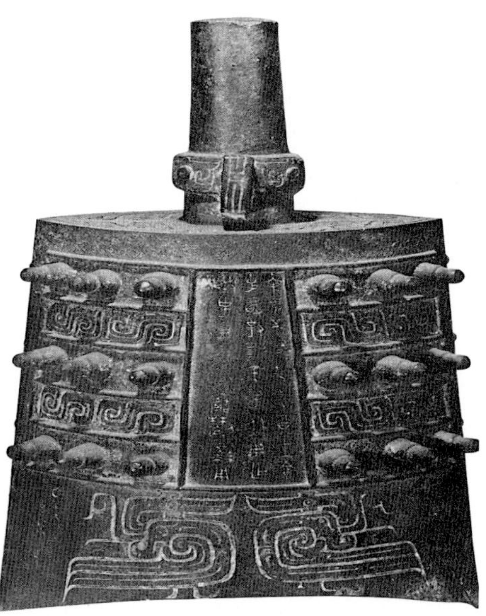

Picture 22 Kuí-patterned chime bell, Spring and Autumn Period

CHAPTER 13

The Second Motive for the Creation of Brushwork: Writing without Support

When phrases such as "席地而坐 xídì'érzuò sitting on the floor" and "窗明几净 chuāngmíngjījìng bright windows and spotless desks" came into being, Chinese people had no experience of using desks or chairs. To be exact, for the seven thousand years since the advent of writing brush, people spent at least 5,500 years sitting on the ground, and later only on bed or tà (榻, similar to a couch).

To ancient Chinese, "sit" means sitting on the knees, with soles of their feet facing up and the buttocks resting on their ankles. Japanese and Koreans still sit in this way. Ancient Chinese even sat like this in bed or on couches. It was not until the introduction of the Hu (a Northern barbarian tribe in ancient China) bed and Hu chair in the Northern and Southern dynasties that people began to sit as we do today. We don't get used to sitting on our knees when we travel to Japan or Korea, but we can't forget that our ancestors used to sit like that.

Legend has it that the zǔ (俎) was an ancient sacrificial utensil or vessel for chopping and displaying livestock. "Jǐ (a small wooden table or chair, 几)" is said to have existed in the Shang and Zhou dynasties. It was at first in a shape of deep squat, the prototype of the later armrest of the chair. In the Jin dynasty, "quān jǐ (圈几, round jǐ)" appeared (Picture 23), which was the prototype of the arm-chair. The zǔ soon developed into the "àn (案, desk)," which was divided into the "long àn" and "square àn." Both of them were low, and they were the products of sitting on the ground. "Long àn" later evolved into "high àn," specifically used for sacrifice and decoration; "square àn" developed into tall square table.

The earliest chair can be observed in the Dunhuang frescoes. But the chair was not popular then and was only used by a small number of aristocrats and monks. From the Tang dynasty to the Five dynasties, all kinds of chairs and stools were produced, which served as the transition from the old custom of "sitting on the floor" to sitting with both feet on the ground. But still, it was limited to the upper class. It was not until the Song dynasty that tables, chairs, and stools were commonly used amongst the masses of ordinary folks.

This is an important piece of historical proof.

Imagine that when an ancient "sat on the ground," holding a pottery or a bamboo slip in his left hand and a writing brush in his right hand, without any support. If he wanted to properly control the brush and use it smoothly, he must keep the upper arm close to the waist, with the

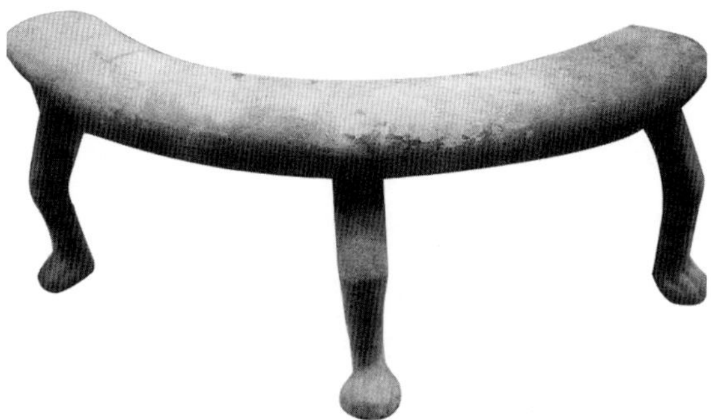

Picture 23 Quān jǐ (圈几, an ancient chair), Jin dynasty

lower arm as support, and the palm that held the brush like hiding an egg. The bamboo slip or other objects to write on should be about one chǐ (尺, about 24 centimeters in the Jin dynasty) away from the writer's eyes and he probably maintained a posture of reading.

I once happened to see a picture of a cultural relic, which aroused my great interest:

This is a pair of celadon-glazed double sitting & writing porcelain figurines dated from the second year of the Yongning Reign of the Western Jin dynasty (Picture 24) unearthed in Changsha, Hunan Province, in 1958. The two figurines sit opposite each other, with a rectangular "jǐ" in the middle and an inkstone, a brush, and a brush holder on it. One figurine seems to be holding several boards, which are clearly "dú (牍, wooden chips)." Ancient chips are made of thin wood, about one *chǐ* (about 24 centimeters in the Han and Jin dynasties) long, so they are called "chǐdú." The other figurine holds a "chǐdú" in his left hand and writes with a brush in his right hand, just in the same posture as he is reading.

This shows that "jǐ" at that time was not used as the support for the elbow or wrist when writing, but only as a table to hold utensils and writing materials. The two porcelain figurines testify to the writing posture of people in the Western Jin dynasty, and to the fact that over several thousand years, Chinese people have been writing in this posture without support for arms or wrists.

In the Northern China, in addition to a table, the *kàng* (炕, a heated brick bed) is used, inheriting the shape of jǐ-shapedtable on the kàng, but people have to sit cross-legged. The "sitting" posture of ancient Chinese has been lost for one thousand years since the birth of the tà (榻, couch) and chair.

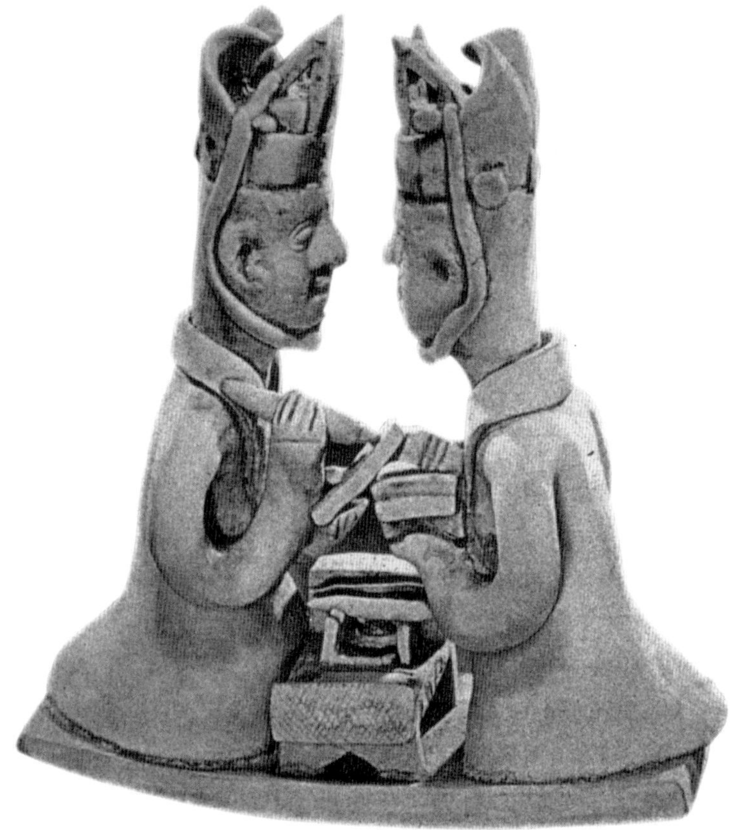

Picture 24 Celadon-glazed double sitting & writing porcelain figurines, Western Jin dynasty

The first time I saw the small characters on bamboo slips in the museum, I was so surprised that I stopped there, observing them for a long time. Bamboo slips are no more than a centimeter wide, and some of them are only seven or eight millimeters in width. Strangely, such small characters were written so smoothly and fluently without a single trace of stroke shivering or brush stalling. Historically, the writing posture was undoubtedly similar to that of the Western Jin porcelain figurines.

We might as well sit on the ground and copy the posture of porcelain figurines of the Western Jin dynasty without any support. The result will be apparent when we try either turning or not turning the brush.

When we choose not to turn the brush, the tip of the brush will bear too much force, making it hard to grasp the handle. The writing posture becomes unstable; the hand easily shakes and the strokes seem sluggish. Just because the left hand holds the wood chip or paper, the support for writing cannot be entirely stable, and the force of the brush tip will scatter the brush hairs, affecting the pace and aesthetic effect.

Turning the brush focuses on twirling the fingers to disperse the force on the brush tip so that the thickness of strokes becomes easier to control, making them round, smooth and fast.

Therefore, other than the reasons mentioned in the previous chapter, the second motive of ancients is to conceive a most convenient and scientific way to use the brush in a state of no support for the right arm and the right hand.

CHAPTER 14

Reasoning Boldly

As can be seen from the previous chapter, in addition to the full play of human physiological functions, every change in human life and daily tools objectively has more or less influence on calligraphy. Human civilization is developing towards convenience and swiftness, with an endless pursuit of practicality and perfection. The development trend keeps pace with calligraphy and accords with the law of nature.

Following the clues of this law, I boldly wondered: could the termination of the development of Chinese characters relate to this?

It is said that people are most efficient when they are lying down, and I happen to have trouble sleeping.

I remember in my tender age, I once witnessed a dialogue on "art" between two painters.

One said, "Art is passion."

The other objected, "Art is skill."

I was obviously in favor of the latter, because skills are real, visible, and learnable. Everyone has passion. But what is passion and what is art? I still couldn't figure them out after thinking about them for nearly twenty years.

Recently, a friend of mine, who designed computer software, came back from the United States to visit her family in China. "We are the same," she said, "both of us are artisans."

I love to hear that.

As long as one thing is a craft, there is something tangible and specific inside. A craftsman must have tools, and is most particular about tools. Craftsmen can talk and communicate with respect to the use of tools for a long time.

Now, let's get started with the tools.

CHAPTER 15

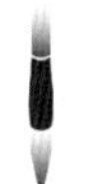

Diameter of the Brush

We no longer know what the earliest brush looked like. After all, I cannot go back to be an ancient, nor can I fantasize the picture. In addition to the physiological functions of men, I could only find the trace of most of the ancient items from real objects.

The writing brush is about the same thickness, length, and size according to the unearthed cultural relics, from the Warring States Period to the early Western Han dynasty. They were all about one chǐ long, that is, 20 centimeters, with the brush hairs (all are rabbit hairs) as long as two centimeters. The difference is that people in the Warring States Period slightly cut four splits in a brush head and filled the splits with brush hair. The hair then was wrapped with flaxen thread and coated with lacquer. The tip of the brush can be changed, which is probably the origin of the literary quotation "退笔成冢 (tuì bǐ chéng zhǒng burying the used brush heads into a tomb). In the Qin dynasty, the brush head was unprecedentedly made into a cavity, and the brush hair was put inside. Zhang Hua in the Jin dynasty said in *Records of Diverse Matter* that "Meng Tian made the brush." Meng Tian was a general of the Qin dynasty, so he probably invented this kind of aforementioned brush.

As the brush hair of the Qin dynasty was embedded into the brush cavity and fixed with lacquer, the head of the brush could be kept perfectly round, upright and stable, showing more advantages over the tangled brush hair. In some cases, the tail of a Qin brush was sharpened, so that it could be easily inserted into the hair and carried around. This is called "zān bǐ, (簪笔, hairpin brush)."

Meanwhile, there also emerged hard brushes, namely bamboo brushes. Ancients cut the heads of brushes into oblique shapes, similar to western ink pens. In my view, "tadpole-shaped text" was probably written with such brushes. Of course, they were not the mainstream.

In 1954, a complete set of writing instruments was excavated from a Warring States Period tomb in the Zuojiagong Mountains, Changsha, Hunan Province. In 1975, more than one thousand bamboo slips were discovered in Twelve Qin dynasty tombs in Shuihudi, Yunmeng County, Hubei Province. They all are the earliest extant brushes. The strangest thing is that the diameter of the brush is only about 0.4 cm, just like a medium-thick wool needle, much thinner than the contemporary small regular-script writing brush.

This is an important clue.

Later I did some experiments. It was a simple rule: from the Warring States Period to the early Western Han dynasty, the thin brush can be turned three times by the thumb side. When handling the brush, the handwriting must be curved, just like the lines of the clerical script. Therefore, the formation of calligraphy style may be caused by the characteristics of the brush. In ancient times, there were only a few writing materials, nothing more than tree bark and bones, and only a small area on the bark and bones was flat. If you wanted to record more things, you had to write the characters as small as possible. The thinner the brush handle, the smaller the word must be when the handle is turned. Moreover, the height of handling the brush is also crucial. The lower the brush and the closer the fulcrum, the smaller the character. This is common sense. At that time, the height of the hand holding the brush was not higher than an inch. Therefore, it's reasonable to say that "people wrote no big characters in the ancient times" due to the physiological nature.

If the diameter of the brush is increased from 0.4 cm to 0.6 cm or 0.7 cm, when you write and turn it, you will find that the strokes written tend to be simple and straight.

Soon I found information about the unearthed cultural relics:

In 1985, a brush of the Western Han dynasty (Picture 25) was unearthed in Taowan Village, Jinping Town, Haizhou, Lianyungang, Jiangsu Province. The diameter of the brush was 0.4 cm. In 1993, a pair of brushes were unearthed from a tomb from the Western Han dynasty in Wenquan Town, Donghai County, Lianyungang, Jiangsu Province with a diameter of 0.7 cm and tapering toward 0.3 cm on one end. Both of them are from tombs of the middle and late Western Han dynasty. The Western Han dynasty saw the transition from seal script to clerical

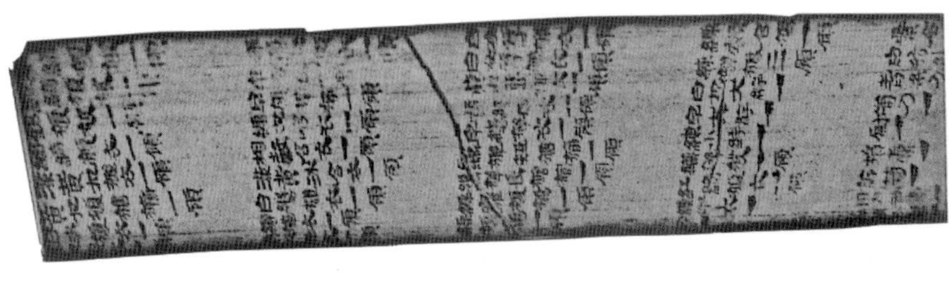

Picture 25 A brush of the Western Han dynasty unearthed in Taowan Village, Jinping Town, Haizhou, Lianyungang City, Jiangsu Province

script. Therefore, brushes in this period were used for writing both seal script and clerical script.

In 1957, a writing brush with a diameter of 0.6–0.7 cm was unearthed from the Number Two Tomb from the Eastern Han dynasty at Mozui Mountain in Wuwei, Gansu Province. As it happens, the Eastern Han dynasty witnessed the formation and development of regular script. Brushes made since then have retained this diameter and size for a long time.

In terms of character form, the strokes tend to be square and straight. But from the perspective of brush use, as I have mentioned in the former two chapters, the support for writing is not stable because the left hand has to hold the wooden chip or paper simultaneously. If the brush is about 0.4 cm in diameter, once the brush hair touches the bamboo or wooden slip, the writer has to turn the brush immediately so that the force is evenly distributed and curvy, making it hard to control the shape of characters. Thus, when the ancients dealt with this situation, they often stopped after writing each stroke and then continued to write the next stroke. And for one single character they turned the brush many times to generate force, in order to writer smooth lines, keep a stable posture, and easily control the shape of the characters. We can observe this phenomenon clearly from State Covenant Unearthed at Houma (Picture 26) of the Spring and Autumn Period.

The brush is most stable in the hand when the diameter of the brush is between 0.6 cm and 0.7 cm. Under this condition, turning the brush can draw a square straight line, and the uniform force can be changed to concentrate on the tip of the brush until the force is exerted to the fullest, or to prepare for the next round of turning the brush when the

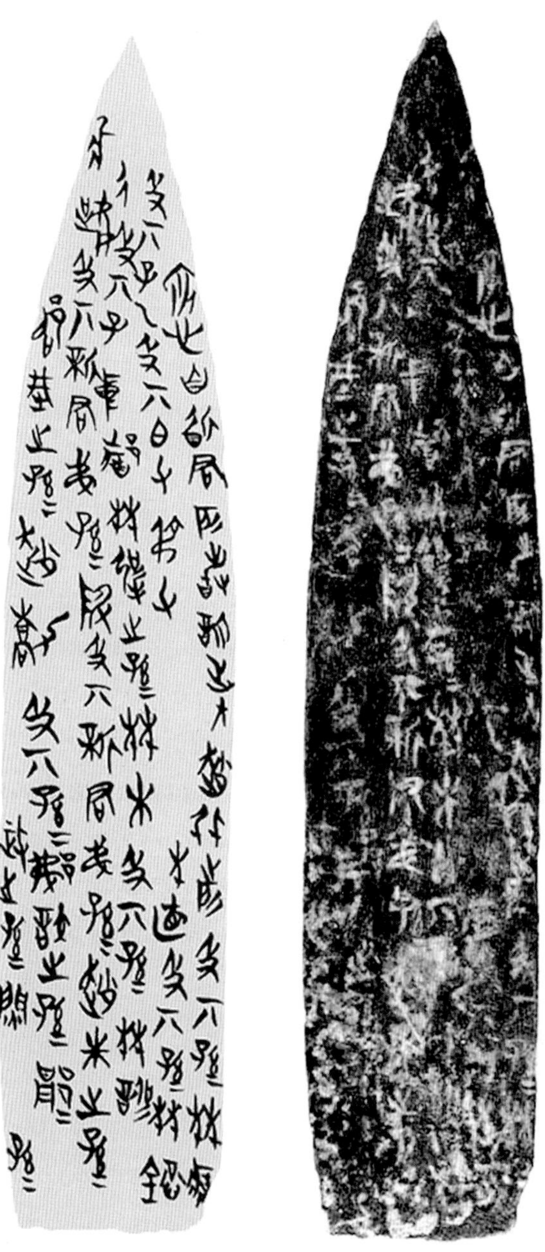

Picture 26 State Covenant Unearthed at Houma (侯马盟书 Hóumǎ méngshū), Spring and Autumn Period

force comes to an end. Ancient people have vividly compared the two typical forces to "a dangling needle" and "dew drop."

I always found it hard to choose the right word to describe this kind of exerting strength. Once, while watching figure skating on TV, I suddenly realized that this force equals the force of gliding. In physics, it is called "accelerating process" and "inertia force." The move of generating force increases the speed of writing. Such kind of force is swift and accurate. In an era when a large amount of official daily work was required to be taken down and no typing tools were available, writing in this manner could accelerate the speed and keep the script clean and tidy.

Later, I read that Su Dongpo compared the force exertion vividly to "punting on the river."

This rule of using the brush is "kǎizé (楷则)," the rule of the model.

If the brush is thickened to more than 1 cm in diameter, the brush can only turn a little more than one round, which means the strokes will be smoother and squarer. That is because the length of the upper thumb is only three centimeters at most, and there are knuckles. The greater number of turns the brush makes in the palm, the more twisty and curvier the lines become. On the contrary, by reducing the number of turns, the stroke will be straighter and one can write larger words. Therefore, some brush handles were thickened after the Tang dynasty. No wonder legend has it that Liu Gongquan, an eminent calligrapher in the Tang dynasty, asked brushmaker Zhuge for a brush. Zhuge gave him as a gift the brush that Wang Xizhi often used, but the brush didn't suit Liu well.

If the diameter of the brush is more than 1.5 centimeters thick, it will be difficult to turn the brush, and the brush will easily slip down.

I cannot help but understand why the ancients took so much effort to make the large brush into a "dǒu bǐ (斗笔, funnel brush)," thick at the bottom and thin at the top (Picture 27). In fact, the brush was designed so to maintain a freely-moving handle. "Dǒu bǐ" has no longer exists these days, but fortunately, its early evidence has been retained.

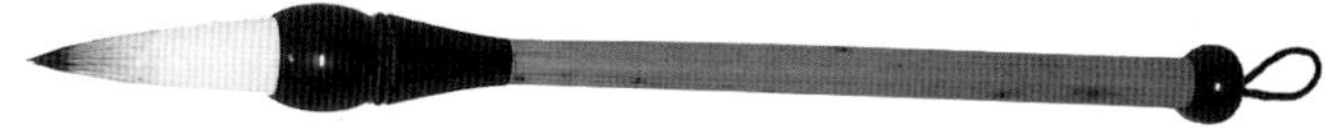

Picture 27 Dǒubǐ, the funnel brush

CHAPTER 16

The Length and Hardness of the Brush Hair

The issue regarding the brush hair cannot be neglected either.

The before-mentioned brush hair from the pre-Qin to Han dynasty are all rabbit hair, also known as tùjiànháo (兔箭毫, literally translated as rabbit arrow hair). It refers to the two slips of hair on the back of a rabbit in autumn, also known as zǐháo (紫毫, the purple hair). Zǐháo is hard, rigid, and erect. As it is erect, it is also elastic. Its elasticity makes it suitable for turning the brush. Cai Yong in the Eastern Han dynasty said in *Prose on the Brush*: "The brush hair has to come from a rabbit's hair in winter." Produced in Xuancheng, Anhui Province, the "Zhongshan Rabbit Horn Brush" was then a household name. Officials of different prefectures in the Han dynasty offered superior rabbit hair to the court. However, the rabbit hair easily goes bad. It is rare and not durable, that's why after the Qin dynasty ancients preferred deer hair. Deer hair gave a similar performance to rabbit hair, and the brush made would not easily go bad. Zhong Yao and Zhang Zhi were said to use rat whiskers as brush hair. I guess rat whiskers must also be hard and rigid.

I was fortunate to have seen in Lianyungang Museum a pair of brushes of the Western Han dynasty unearthed from Donghai County (Picture 28), whose brush handles were already separated from the hair.

The two hairs are 2.3 cm and 3.2 cm long respectively; both of their ends were tightly tied with two circles of thread. However, the brush inserted into the handle are 0.9 cm and 1.1 cm deep respectively. They look so vivid. Though they were buried for two thousand years, the black zǐháo (紫毫 purple hair) is still pliable and firm with the end of the hair thin and pointy. Along with zǐháo, a large number of wooden tablets were unearthed, which are made of expensive and rare *Phoebe zhennan S. Lee* wood, found only in Sichuan and other Chinese provinces. The wood is covered with densely written small words. The words must have been written by a zǐháo brush, judging from the fact that they were buried deep together. It has so far been the best preserved and most convincing piece of brush hair that I have ever seen.

Zǐháo is pliable and strong, and the tip of the hair is thin and pointy to write tiny characters. When we tightly tie the end of the hair and embed it into the brush handle to a depth of one third of the hair, the hair cannot only absorb more ink, but also write many words at one time, and being more stable and firmer to produce bold lines.

The method of making brushes in the Wei and Jin dynasties was still inherited from the Han dynasty. Fu Yuan in the Jin dynasty in *Essay on the Brush* mentioned that "the rare rabbit was selected to make superior brush hair."

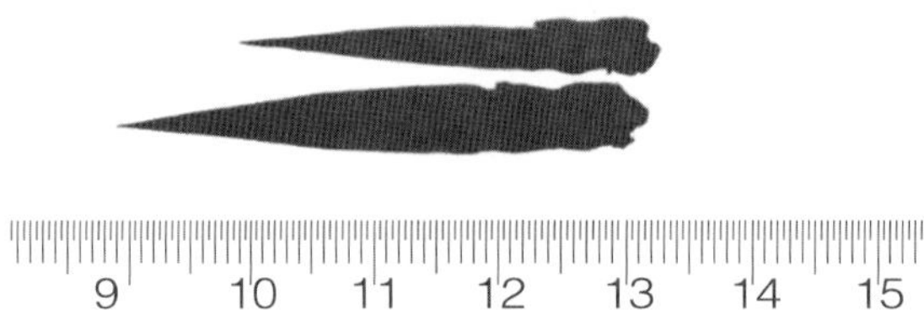

Picture 28 A pair of brushes of the Western Han dynasty unearthed from Wenquan Town, Donghai County, Lianyungang, Jiangsu Province

By the Tang dynasty, the hairs of many animals were used to make brush hair, such as the hair of musk deers, palm civets, horses, rats, foxes, and chickens, as well as human fetal hair. Nevertheless, rabbit hair still remained the top choice because it represented the most authentic and was best suited for calligraphy. The zǐháo (rabbit hair) brush of Xuanzhou, Anhui Province, was exquisitely manufactured with meticulously chosen fine materials. It was as valuable as gold at that time and became an "article of tribute," greatly praised and welcomed by scholars and calligraphers.

Calligraphers in the Song dynasty still used rabbit brushes. Huang Shangu and Su Dongpo recommended the "Zhūgé bǐ (诸葛笔 Zhuge brush)" made in Xuanzhou. The brush was mainly made of zǐháo (purple hair), the *crème de la crème* of rabbit hair.

Lángháo (狼毫 wolf hair, actually made from weasel hair) was introduced from Korea in the Qing dynasty, but it is widely used nowadays.

According to historical records, *Notes to Things Old and New* written by the scholar Cui Bao in the Jin dynasty said that Meng Tian's writing brush "Put deer hair inside and wrapped it with soft goat hair," which was probably "jiānháo (兼毫, a brush that was made by combining hair from two different types of animals)" (Picture 29). As the core of the writing brush, lùháo (鹿毫 deer hair) is hard and stiff. Lùháo then is coated with a soft layer of yángháo (羊毫 goat hair). Goat hair brushes are soft, flexible and absorbent, which together with deer hair achieves a balance

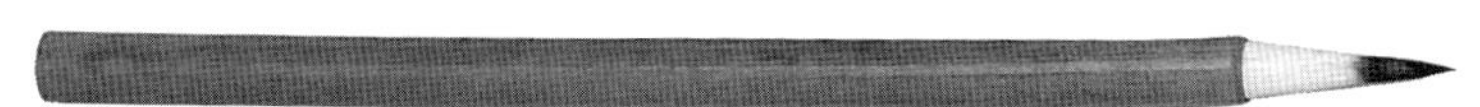

Picture 29 Hair-combining writing brush

between steely and feathery lines. As Wang Xizhi put in *Book of Writing Brush*, the brush can be considered a "it creates lines as straight as a tightened string, as curved as a hook, as round as a compass can draw, and as perfectly square as a T-square can draw."

It is thus clear that the production of brushes was quite exquisite even before the Jin dynasty. This is synchronized with the development of Chinese characters towards straightness, aesthetics, and standardization. In other words, the fact that the brush hair is steely and strong is undoubtedly related to the condition that ancients had no support for their writing. As the old saying goes, "When a workman wishes to get his work well done, he must have his tools sharpened first" or "Calligraphy is subtle, and when you wield the writing brush, it all depends on the fitness of the brush hair."

The history of the writing brush based on rabbit hair lasted for a long time. It was not until the end of the Tang dynasty and the Five dynasties that "sanzhuo-bi" appeared, which was made of pure goat hair. The biggest difference was that it had no core, that is, no hard hair inside. It was soft, so it was not the mainstream of writing brush then.

I felt great joy when I noticed the words "late Tang dynasty and Five dynasties." The emergence of the sanzhuo-bi coincided with the emergence of desks and chairs. Thanks to desks and chairs, the arms, elbows, and wrists could all be supported, so ancients as a matter of course did not need to use the brush core as a support. That's where the soft *yángháo* (goat hair) brush came into being. Historical records reveal that by the Song dynasty, the sanzhuo-bi was prevalent. What a coincidence! That's because desks and chairs were also popularized in the same era!

That makes total sense.

I remember when I was little, the brushes for writing regular script in big and small characters were all made of goat hair. My mother asked me to dip one third of the brush into ink and make it hydrated, just the tip of the brush. She said that was how she was taught by elders to use the brush when she too was a kid.

As time goes by, when I read the ink works of Dong Qichang (Picture 30) in the Ming dynasty, Zha Shibiao, and a large number of calligraphers and painters in the late Ming and early Qing dynasties, I found that usually after they wrote four to five words the ink would dry, and they would dip the ink again. This was often because they wrote large words with a small brush. However, their strokes were round and full, and you'd never guess they were written with small and thin brushes. There was only one possibility to explain the phenomenon, that is, they used a large brush and only soaked its tip into ink, the way my mother taught me.

In Dong and Zha's time, goat hair brush was quite popular. As it lacked a hard core, the brush would be weak and powerless if it were completely soaked. If only the tip of the brush were soaked, two thirds of the brush that was bound with glue would play the role of the hard core. It is a large brush and made of goat hair, so the strokes written are soft and round. Yes, this is the perfect way to use a pure goat-hair brush as a combining-hair brush. What is the aim of doing so? For the convenience and beauty of turning the brush!

In ancient times, all writing brushes were coated with a brush cover, in order to prevent the brush from becoming dry and stiff, so that it could be used again. If the brush was washed repeatedly, its function would gradually be weakened.

There is a good reason to explain why the brush hair was designed into a shape of cone. Try it. It facilitated the brush-turning. Otherwise,

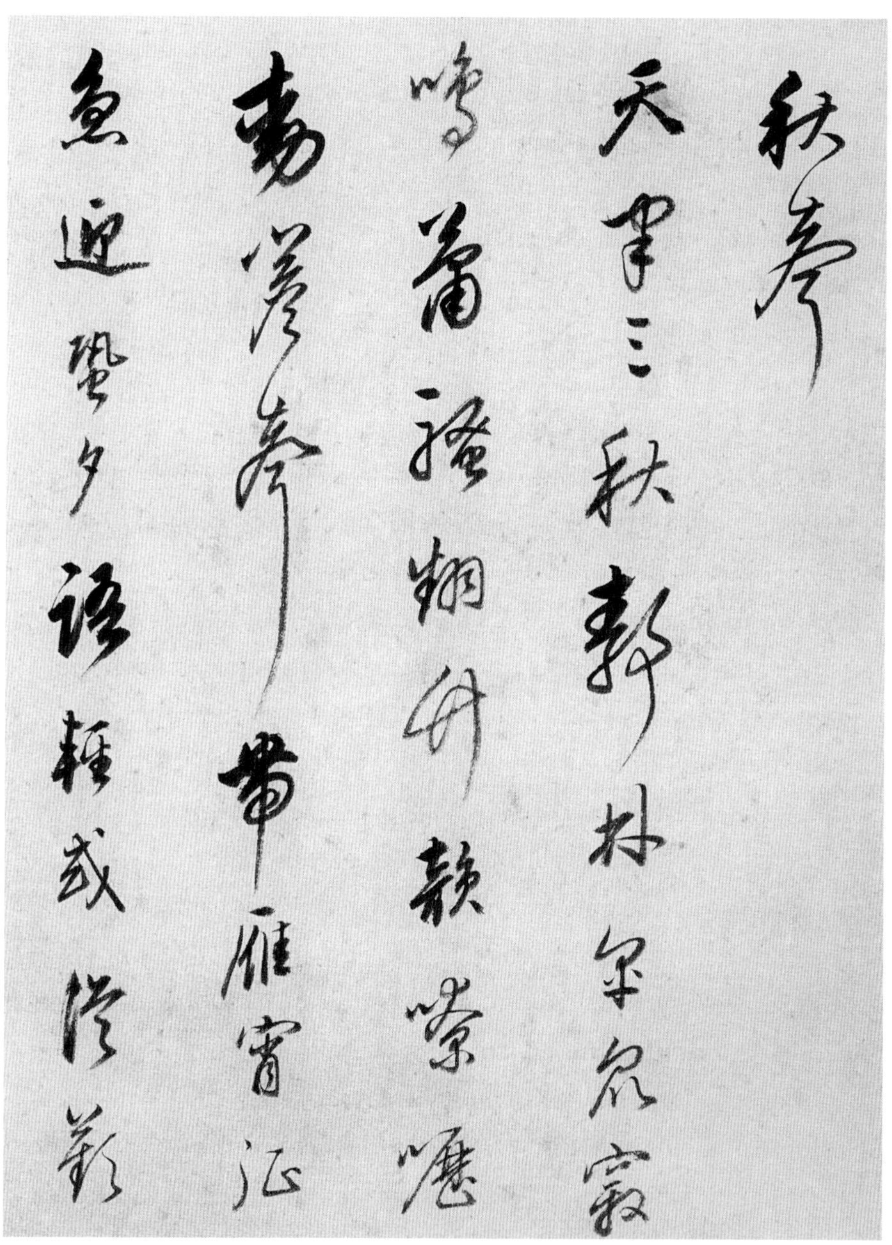

Picture 30 Dong Qichang's *Five-Character Poem* (part), Ming dynasty

it would be more convenient to design the flat brush as westerners do, which allowed calligraphers to write in a straight line.

The making of writing brushes after the Tang dynasty became more sophisticated, in both selecting hair and choosing raw materials. They were beautifully decorated and even worth a fortune. Especially since the Ming and Qing dynasties, a problem that has been increasingly ignored is that the thickness of the brush handle, and the length and hardness of the brush have been gradually inconsistent with the requirements of the ancient method of brush-turning. If even calligraphers do not apply the ancient method, then it really is unnecessary to "choose a brush."

CHAPTER 17

The Origin of Paper and "Move," "Lift," "Hold," and "Dye"

"Cai Lun invented paper-making" in the early second century AD, that is, the Eastern Han dynasty. We were taught in history class as kids, that paper-making is one of the Four Great Inventions of Ancient China. Paper was actually invented much earlier than this. The earliest paper we know is the Western Han Paper unearthed in Baqiao, Xi'an in 1957, known as "Baqiao Paper," Gansu "Juyan Paper" unearthed in Gansu in 1973, "Zhongyan Paper" unearthed in Fufeng, Shaanxi in 1978, and "Lop Nor Paper" unearthed in Xinjiang Autonomous Region in 1993. All of these were paper mainly made of hemp originating from the Western Han dynasty. By the Eastern Han dynasty, straw, bark and rattan were used for paper-making, and paper reached a sophisticated level, "as smooth as a whetstone." Caihou Paper was then famous for its cheap raw material, easy production and tenacious texture.

Before paper came into being, there was "bó (帛)" made of raw silk in the Warring States Period. Single raw-silk fabric is called "zēng (缯)," while double raw silk fabric is "jiān (缣)," and "juàn (绢)" is made of thicker raw silk. According to unearthed materials, remnants of silk and "bó" were found in the ancient tombs of the Yin and Zhou dynasties, indicating that silk-weaving technology reached an advanced level then.

But it was in the Spring and Autumn Period that silk and "*bo*" were explicitly mentioned to be used for painting and calligraphy. In the second part of "*Tianzhi*" (*The Will of Heaven*) of *Mozi*, it was recorded: "Events were written on bamboo slips and silk and carved on metal and stone."

At that time, silk and bó were adopted for writing and painting by aristocrats, while bamboo slips were still used by common folks. Though paper was invented in the Han dynasty, most of the people resorted to paper because they couldn't afford silk, as the saying goes, "silk is expensive while paper is cheap." Generally, aristocrats in the court were used to writing or painting on jiān and bó. It's understandable that the aim of making-paper was to create a cheap and light substitute for silk.

It should be noted that silk must be gelatinized, otherwise the ink will permeate the silk when writing. If the paper were obtained directly from the sink without being processed, the ink would also spread over the paper. This type of paper has been called "raw silk" or "raw paper" since ancient times. Quite the contrary, "mature paper" is a finished product that has gone through "calendering, facing (dragging pulp), filling powder, adding wax and sizing" that features "soft, smooth and clean" surface. Judging from the ink marks of ancient people, the paper used was not saturated at all, or only a little saturated, and the handwriting was smooth and fluent. Ancient people did not write on "raw paper" which was used for funerals and sacrifices. It was not until the Ming dynasty that raw paper was used for calligraphy and painting.

Silk was woven like cloth, about one chi (尺) wide. It is said that the standard length of the Han dynasty weaving cloth was four zhang (丈), and could be cut at will according to the need. As silk was soft, it was rolled around a scroll for people to write upon. The scroll then became a solid support for the silk. As the strokes became short and uneven when the scroll was held in the hand, ancients often mounted the silk on the wall first and then drew on the silk. Due to the limited size of the silk, one had to stitch pieces of silk together to create a mural. Therefore, before table was first adopted in the late Tang dynasty, if ancients wanted to draw uniformed, smooth or longer lines, they must draw them on the wall. The beautifully outlined paintings (created before the Tang dynasty) with strokes of uniformed size all had two words written within the brackets, namely "Song Mo (宋摹, imitated by artists in the Song dynasty)."

Unlike any other dynasties, the Han dynasty was unique. It was an age of maturity and vitality when slips, silk and paper were all used. Evidence can be found in early calligraphy treatises. As Chenggong Sui of the Western Jin dynasty once put it, "Move the slim fingers, lift the weak wrist, hold the plain silk fabric, and dye the brush with ink and write," which was easy to understand:

"Move the finger": the finger only needs to be "moved" when you turn the brush; "lift the wrist": the word "lift" indicates that one must raise the wrist above the height of the elbow. Writing requires "lifting"; writing and painting on the wall both require "lifting." "Hold the plain silk fabric" also implies that white silk is "held" in the left hand. The later popular hand roll came from this. Only by turning the brush can the strokes "dye" on the surface, so that the surrounding brush hairs successively and continuously ink the surface. Each side will neither be too thick nor withered, so that the strokes will appear "round and full."

The "move," "lift," "hold," and "dye" vividly depict the writing posture of ancient people.

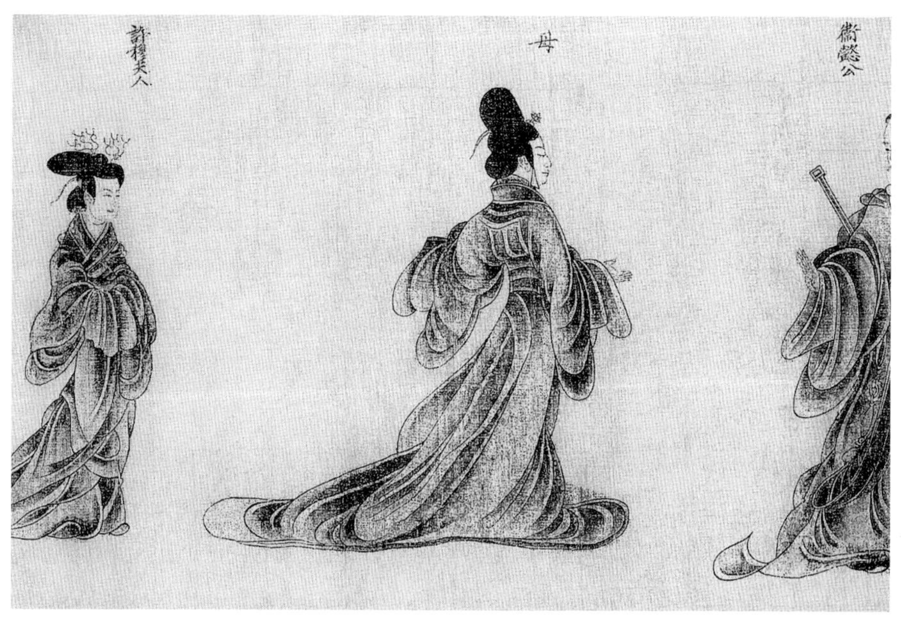

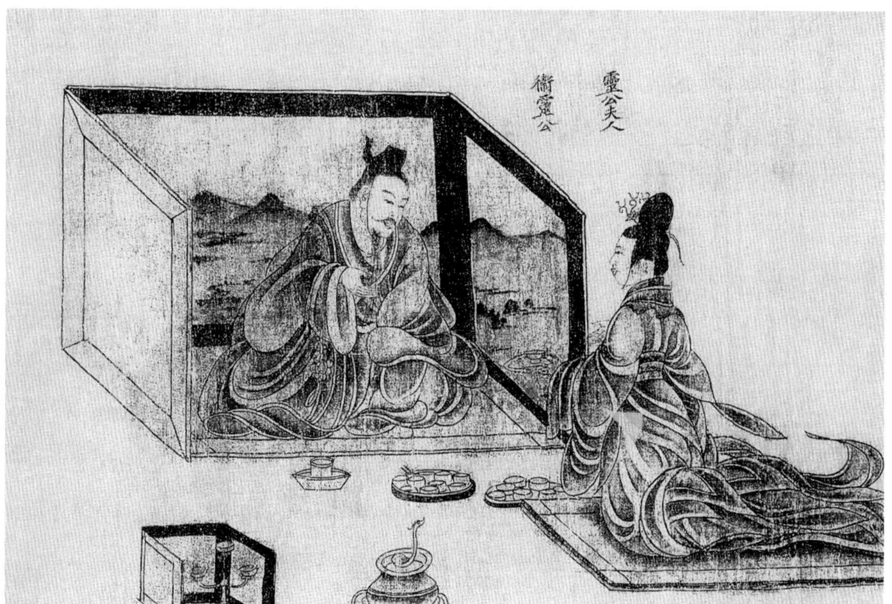

Picture 31 Song dynasty copy of Gu Kaizhi's *Biographies of Outstanding Women* (part)

CHAPTER 18

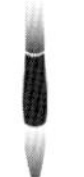

Enlightenment from *The Execution of Chen Shimei* (*Zha Mei An*)

When I was a child, I watched the opera *The Execution of Chen Shimei* (*Zha Mei An*). I felt so strange when I saw the judge writing on the paper in his hand. I wondered how he could write stably with paper in his hand. But the scene was quite common in many traditional operas.

Obviously, this is the continuation of the ancient writing method of "*chǐdú* (尺牍, a model of epistolary art)." The question was, since the advent of paper, would writing in this way still work or was it just for dramatic effect?

I had buried the question in my mind for many years. Then I had a vague idea that there was something to learn about.

According to historical records, due to the limitations of paper-making technology, paper in and before the Jin dynasty was generally not of large size. The extant Wang Xizhi's *Kuai Xue Shi Qing Tie* (*Note on Timely Clearing After Snowfall*) stands 7.1 inches high; *Note on Mid-Autumn* stands 8.4 inches high; the various versions of *Lanting Xu* (*Preface to the Collection of Poems Composed at the Orchid Pavilion*) all stand at 7.5 inches high. The Jin paper is just a foot and a half long. Only jiānbó (缣帛, silk) is long and narrow. For example, *Biographies of Outstanding Women* (Picture 31) was drawn on long and narrow jiānbó.

By the Tang dynasty, paper still followed the size of the Jin dynasty, but the length of paper was elongated thanks to the new technique. The paper then turned into something like a long and narrow scroll-shaped silk. From the late Tang dynasty to the Song dynasty, in addition to the long narrow paper, small pieces of "jiānzhǐ (笺纸, letter paper)" were in fashion, which was associated with the large volume of book printing. In the Song dynasty, people started binding paper together into book form. The famous "*Xue Tao jian*" and "*Chengxintang-zhi* (a high-end Xuan Paper)" were jiānzhǐ made respectively by Xue Tao, a poetess in the end of the Tang dynasty, and Lǐ Hòuzhǔ (Li Yu, 李后主, literally "Last Ruler Li") in the Song dynasty. It was not until the Yuan dynasty that large sized paper was produced.

At the end of the Eastern Jin dynasty, the imperial court ordered: "In ancient times, people used jiǎn (简, bamboo slip or wooden slip) since there was no paper. Now, those who used jiǎn should use yellow paper instead."

What is the "yellow paper"? Historical records show that in the Jin dynasty, Ge Hong dyed hemp paper with the juice of amur cork tree, effectively preventing moth damage. In the Tang dynasty, there was a kind of precious "yìnghuáng (硬黄, hard yellow)" paper. It was thick and looked "bright and transparent" when it was waxed. "Cover the paper over other items; all of the items could be seen clearly. Therefore, people copied the writing of Zhong Yao, Suo Jing, and Wang Xizhi on the paper." The paper was also specifically used for writing sutras. "Hard yellow," as the name implies, "hard" refers to the texture, and "yellow" refers to the color. The paper is thick, strong and tenacious. According to the ancients, the hard yellow paper was "two feet and 1.7 inches long, 7.6 inches wide, and weighed 6.5 *qian* (a *qian* is a unit of weight that is equal to five grams)," indicating its thickness and heaviness. All the facsimiles of Wang Xizhi's characters during the Tang dynasty were copied on hard yellow paper, and people in the Song dynasty continued to do so.

Hard yellow paper was made of hemp, which was the earliest and most common material for paper-making in China. During the Jin dynasty there were generally cocoon paper, sphagnum moss paper, cèlǐ zhǐpaper (侧理纸, made of hemp and bast, and then mixed with a small amount of sphagnum moss and hairlike seaweeds), etc. Cocoon paper was named so because its texture was similar to the cocoon shell; its thickness was similar to today's "Korea paper (a kind of white tissue paper)."Celi paper was named so because of its vertical and horizontal oblique lines. Both of them are hemp paper. Sphagnum moss paper is another name for hemp paper.

In 1997, I saw two scrolls of sutras from the Song dynasty unearthed from a tomb in Yixing. They were about one foot high, two feet long, and the words were the size of a fingernail. The paper was thick and heavy with an ochre color. The recto of the paper is smooth and slippery and was apparently waxed; the reverso is coarse; the texture is inclined and made of hemp. This is probably the so-called hard yellow paper. Because of its early age, the paper had been dampened underground for too long. Even so, when I saw it, the paper was still tenacious and not easily crumpled, let alone in its day of production. I was deeply impressed by its heavy weight in my hand.

In addition, the Jin dynasty also produced paper made of mulberry, or rattan bark, both of which were tough, thick, and not easy to break. Was the paper of such quality made just to avoid fragility during transportation or for the convenience of writing?

CHAPTER 19

Calligraphy Grew from the Posture of Writing

The second year of the reign of Yongning was the end of the Western Jin dynasty (266–316). Wang Xizhi, the master of calligraphy, was born in the Eastern Jin dynasty (317–420). The porcelain figurines and calligraphy treatise of the Western Jin completely proved the writing posture of the people before and during the Western Jin. What about writing posture in the Eastern Jin dynasty? Did Wang Xizhi, whom we have admired from generation to generation, also write like the porcelain figurines of the Western Jin dynasty?

It was not mentioned in the calligraphy treatise of Wang Xizhi, nor was it mentioned by his contemporaries, because it was unnecessary.

There is only one possibility, that things were self-evident. Or the posture he adopted was known to all and considered a norm. To me, the universal "norm" was of significant importance.

Paintings of the same age might unconsciously reflect the writing posture. However, only a few paintings before the Tang dynasty are preserved to this day. I had faith that there will be such paintings. And there are.

Here is the Song-dynasty copy of *Emendating Books* in the Northern Qi dynasty (550–577) (Picture 32):

In the painting, four people are sitting on the couch (Picture 32-1). These men of literature were emendating (making corrections) a book. Books then were not bound in a volume but were in the form of a scroll.

The emendators had different postures: one man took paper in his left hand and wrote with a brush in his right hand, just like the porcelain figurines in the Western Jin; one man held a brush in his right hand for a rest, holding a paper in his left hand at a long distance, as if appreciating his own work.

Another man sitting in the chair on the right (Picture 32-2) held the brush in his right hand, with his left hand pushing down on the bottom of the paper while the top of the paper was stretched by the servant with both hands.

If we take a look at the furniture of the same period, the jī'àn (几案, table-like but shorter) were short, almost the same height as bed or couch. If one wrote on the jī'àn with both arms and elbows in the air, and his vision and hand should be two or three feet apart, it would be impossible to write the delicate small characters as ancients did then. If his entire arms were placed on the table, it would be like having one man's head approaching the feet. I'm afraid the talented Wang Xizhi or

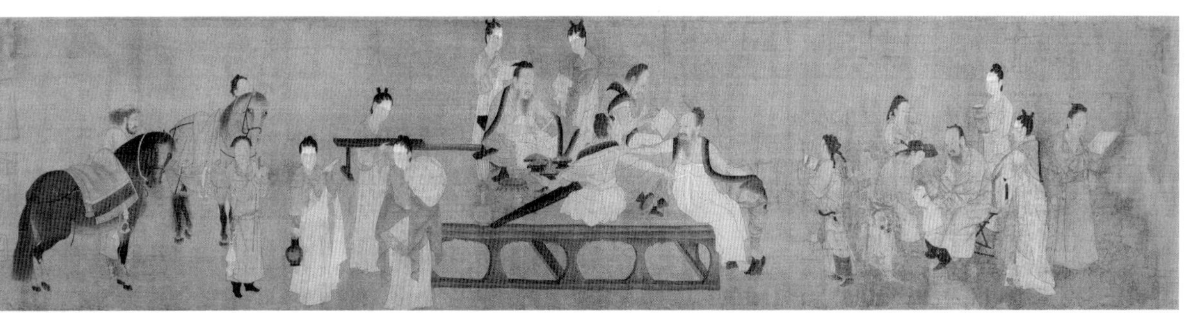

Picture 32 Song-dynasty copy of *Emendating Books* in the Northern Qi dynasty

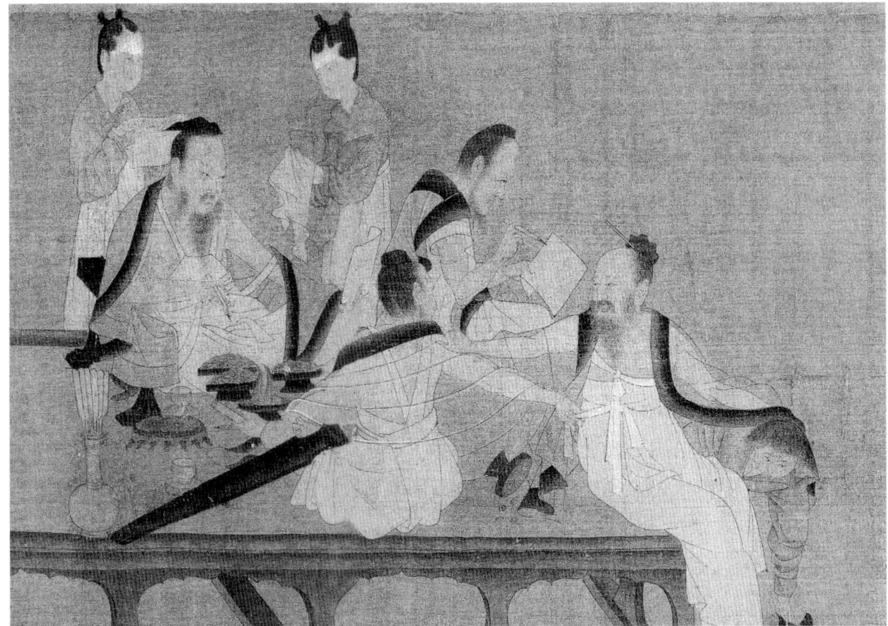

Picture 32-1 Song-dynasty copy of *Emendating Books* in the Northern Qi dynasty (part)

Wang Xianzhi would not embarrass themselves with such an acrobatic trick. That would be incompatible with people's physiological nature, nor could one turn the fingers when doing so.

Wouldn't it be convenient if the man sitting in the chair put the one-chi high and two-chi long paper on the jī'àn to write on? Why did he bother the boy servant to stretch the paper? It proved that scholars of that time normally didn't write on the jī'àn. The ancients always required the company of a boy servant to "grind ink and pull/stretch the paper." "Stretching paper chēnzhǐ (抻纸)" was probably like that in early days.

Emendating Books in the Northern Qi dynasty is the same as the porcelain figurines in the Western Jin dynasty in terms of the writing method.

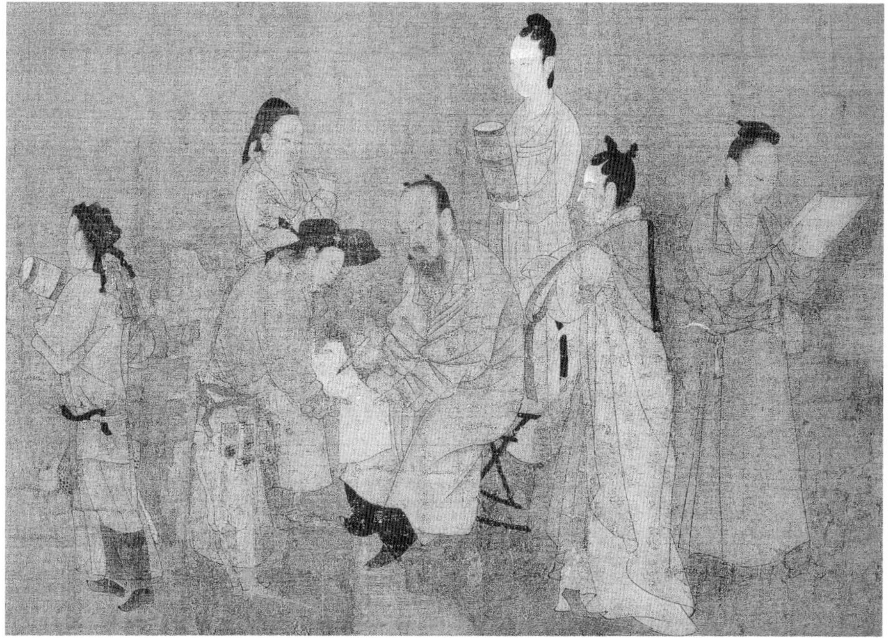

Picture 32-2 Song-dynasty copy of *Emendating Books* in the Northern Qi dynasty (part)

The 300 years between the Western Jin and the Northern Qi dynasties was the peak of Chinese calligraphy, and also a period when the calligraphy of the Wang family was fashionable nationwide. For example, the famous *Seven Sages of the Bamboo Grove* (Picture 33) and *Biographies of Outstanding Women* truthfully reflected the living conditions of "sitting on the ground" at that time.

In *Admonitions of the Instructress to Court Ladies* (Picture 34), a standing court instructress held paper in her left hand and wrote with a brush in her right hand. Looking closely, one would find she was using the "classic" method of holding a brush. That is probably what the ancients quoted "leaning on the horse and writing at once." It is safe to say that Wang Xizhi of the same era definitely did not write on a desk or a table.

The bǐfǎ (笔法, brushwork; literally means the law of brush) thus described is derived from this posture and developed from this posture.

The meaning of "fǎ (法, law)" in shūfǎ (书法, calligraphy) should be first defined on the premise of this posture. And then we can discuss turning brush and fingers.

One of the most key points I observed is, in *Emendating Books*, a man bent the paper backwards while holding it in his left hand, while another man unfolded the entire sheet of paper, which clearly had been bent before for writing. The size of paper was similar to that of its own time, no higher than one foot, and no longer than two feet.

Only when the paper is thick, hard, and flexiblecould one hold it in this way.

Imagine that if one wrote on paper instead of a hard bamboo slip in his hand, without the support of a desk or table, the paper must be stiff, hard, and not easy to break. Therefore, the paper at that time, be it hemp paper, cocoon paper, cèlǐpaper (侧理纸, made of hemp and bast, and then mixed with a small amount of sphagnum and hairlike seaweeds)

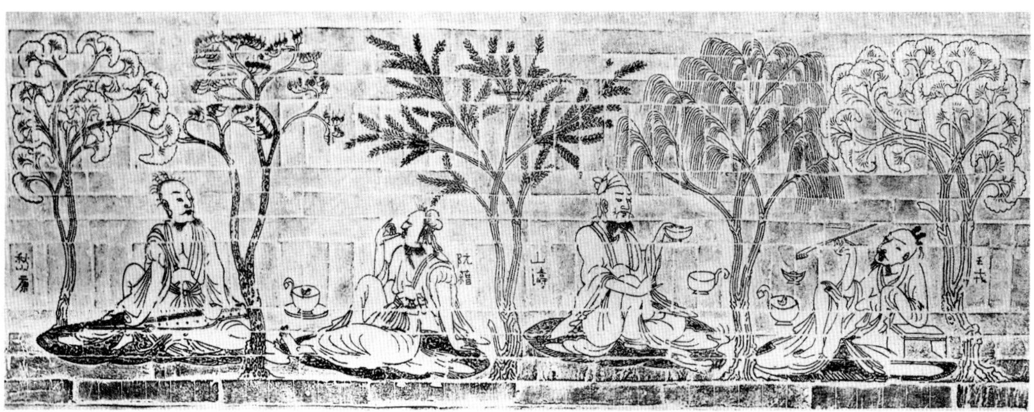

Picture 33 Brick painting of *Seven Sages of the Bamboo* Grove (part), Jin dynasty

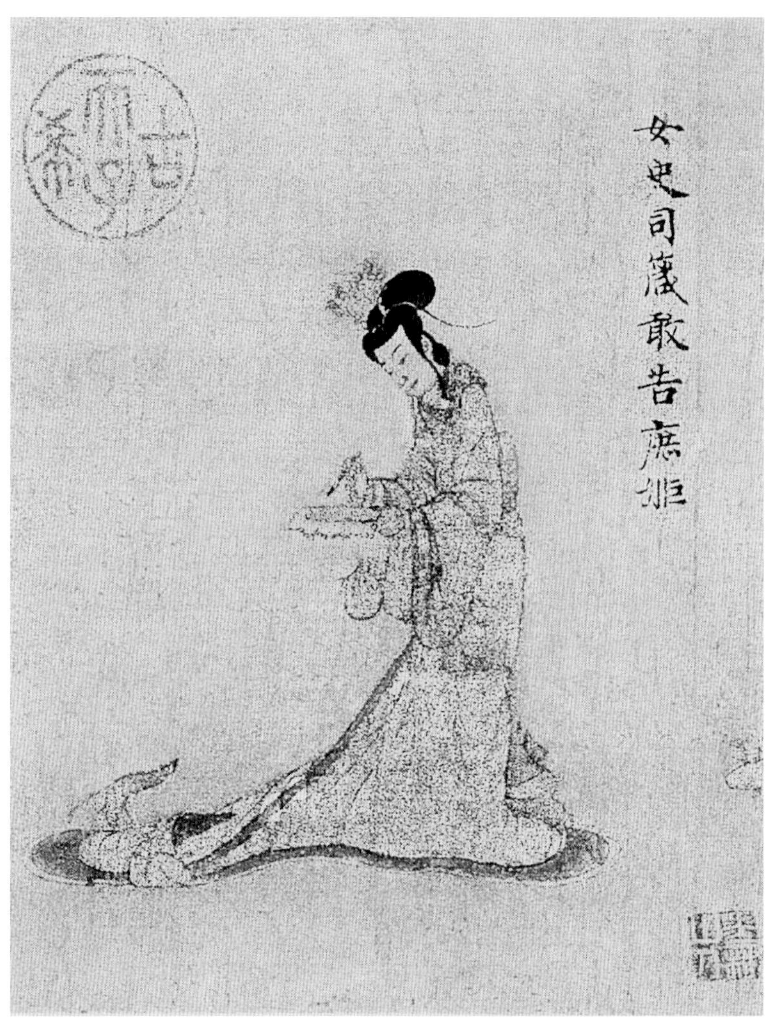

Picture 34 *Admonitions of the Instructress to Court Ladies* (part), Jin dynasty

or rattan paper, all met this requirement. It is convincing that historical books recorded Wang Xizhi's writing on hemp paper or cocoon paper.

After the advent of the table, paper was spread over the table. The calligrapher had the table as support and a chair to sit on, with appropriate visual distance, so the thick, hard, and stiff paper was no longer needed. The xuan paper we use today is so thin and soft that one can't hold it in one's hand to write on anyway.

I was too lazy to go to the library, so I visited the nearest bookstore selling old books to look for *Emendating Books* and *Admonitions of the Instructress to Court Ladies*. I rummaged through the contents of the shelves for three hours, drenched in sweat, having little intention to buy any book. All of the shop assistants looked at me with hatred and profound resignation.

CHAPTER 20

The Farewell Masterpiece of the "Ancient Method"

Paper-making industry in the Sui, Tang, and Five dynasties displayed no innovative spirit and just inherited the legacy of the Six dynasties. I searched and found that in addition to royal and noble painting and calligraphy that still adopted silk, the papers that people used were mainly hard yellow paper, hemp paper, etc.

Good! Another piece of evidence—they still used tough and thick paper. It showed that paper of the Sui, Tang, and Five dynasties is still suitable for holding in the hand and writing without support.

In China, tall tables appeared after chairs and stools. Tables originated from jī'àn. It was not until chairs and stools existed for six or seven hundred years that they began to match high tables. Ji and an were still useful. I couldn't help thinking that in the six or seven hundred years when people sat with their feet on the ground, how did they manage to write with no table to rely upon? Luckily, there are paintings to tell us the real history.

There were already tables in the Tang and Five dynasties, but they were often used for catering and carrying sacrificial utensils. The higher tables in *Ladies in the Palace Indulging in Pleasure* (Picture 35), *Six*

Venerable Arhats (Picture 36), and Zhou Fang's *Listening to a Qin Performance* of the Tang dynasty seemed not to be used for writing.

In the Five dynasties, Gu Hongzhong painted *The Night Revels of Han Xizai* (Picture 37). In this painting, there are several tables beside the bed, as high as today's jī. While in Wang Qihan's *Emendating the Book* (Picture 38) of the same age, behind the man in chair, there is also a high table, whose height just matches the chair in the painting. However, brushes, paper, and inkstones are placed on a square table knee-high in front of him. The painting tells us that this knee-high square table is used for writing.

Again, I want to stress the word "knee-high."

Just imagine, in the Sui and Tang dynasties, people were still writing small characters. When they sat on the chair, whether they wrote with arms in the air or wrote by lying on the knee-high jī, they had to bend their head and upper body to the knee. Who would make fun of

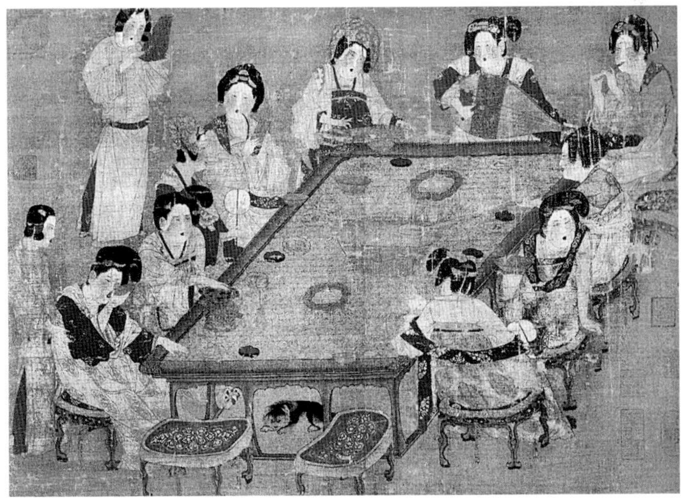

Picture 35 *Ladies in the Palace Indulging in Pleasure* (part), Tang dynasty

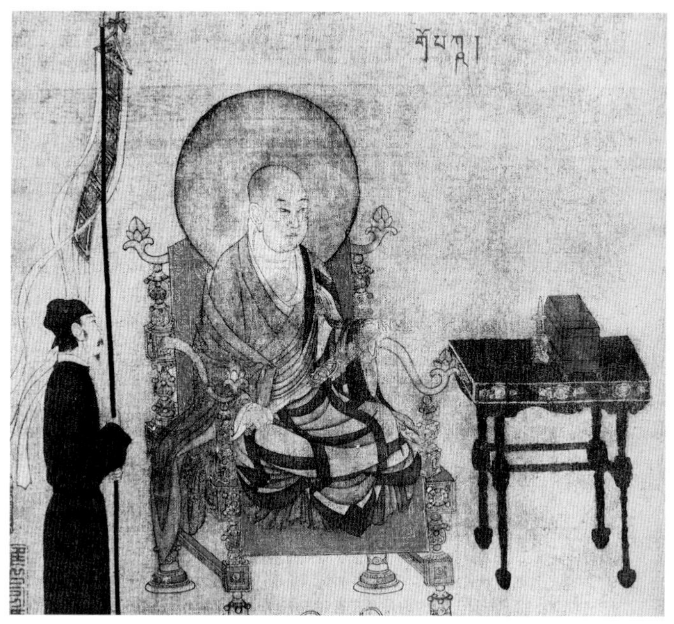

Picture 36 *Six Venerable Arhats* (part), Tang dynasty

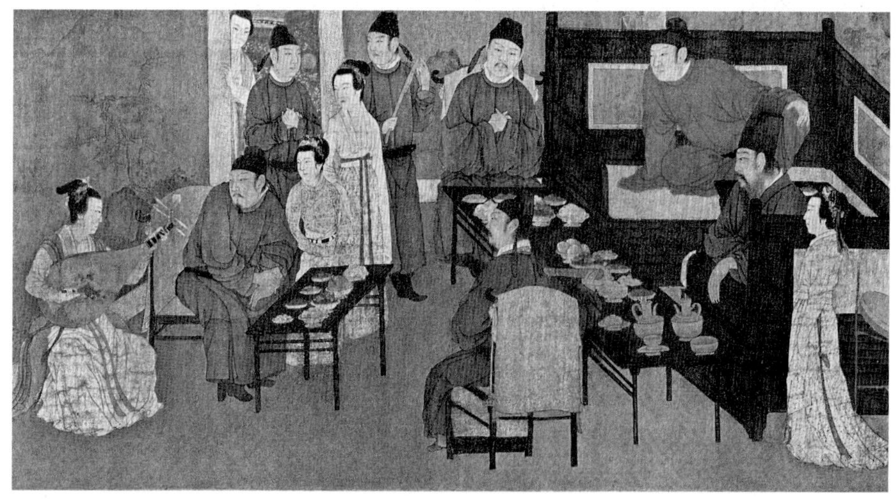

Picture 37 *The Night Revels of Han Xizai* (part) Gu Hongzhong, Five dynasties

themselves in that way? Therefore, I am sure that in the Sui, Tang, and Five dynasties, paper was a legacy of the Six dynasties, as was writing posture. The difference is that in the Wei and Jin dynasties, people were not yet sitting with their feet on the ground. But in the Sui, Tang, and Five dynasties people sat the way we do today.

Píngjǐ (凭几) in the Shang and Zhou dynasties and quānjǐ (圈几) that appeared in the Jin dynasty could well become the support of the elbow when writing. Though I've not yet found exact documents, it's physiologically appropriate. The support to the elbow is sporadic. But that's not critical. As long as you have a try, you'll find out that resting the elbow on the waist is as stable as relying on the armrest.

In *A Garden for Scholars* (Picture 39) by Zhou Wenju in the Five dynasties, we can see a man on the right holding rolled paper in his left hand and writing with his right hand. And the man sitting on the left

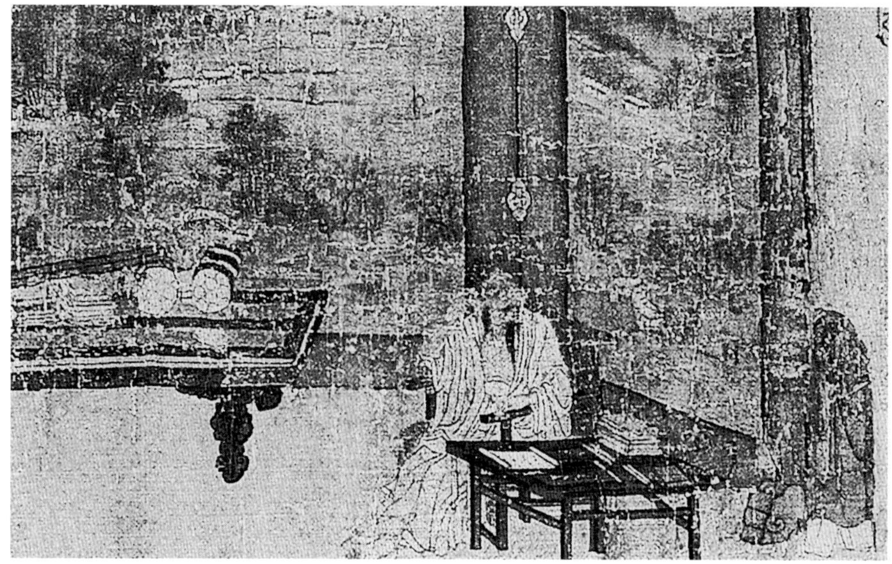

Picture 38 *Emendating the Book* (part), Wang Qihan, Five dynasties

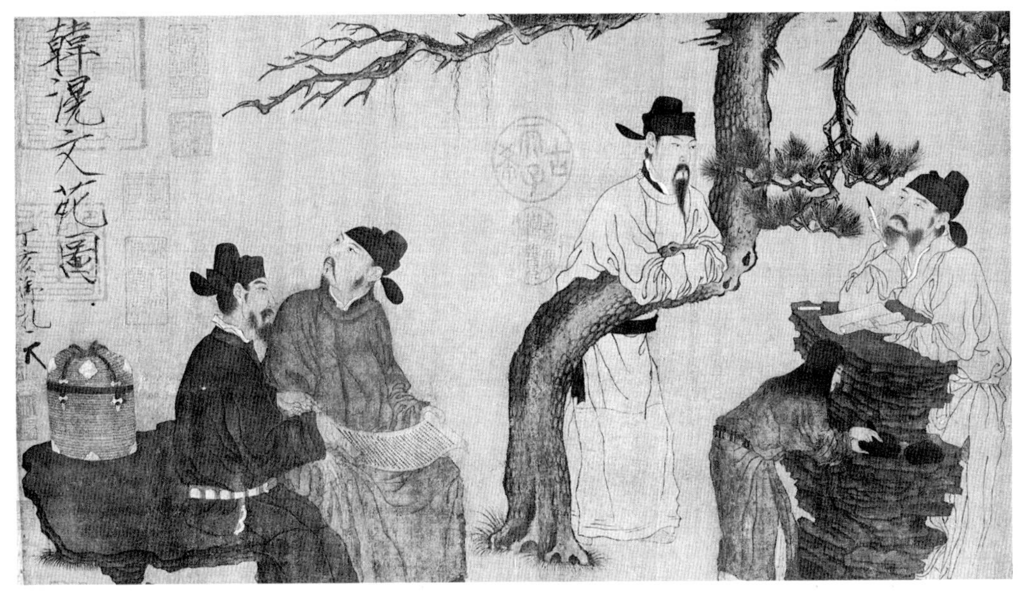

Picture 39 *A Garden for Scholars* (part), Zhou Wenju, Five dynasties

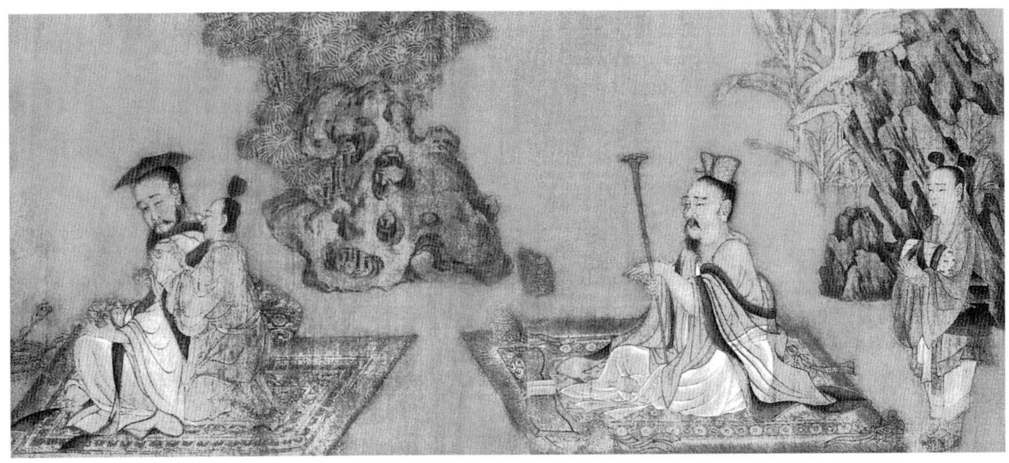

Picture 40 *Unrestrained Spirit of the Seven Sages of the Bamboo Grove* (part), Sun Wei, Tang dynasty

is looking at paper covered with densely written small characters. It's another example of a man holding paper in his hand to write.

I previously gave an example of *Monk Kukai Holding the Brush* when he studied calligraphy in China. The most interesting thing is that the hand in the painting is "raised" and the Chinese words "zhuǎndòng (转动 rotating)" were written clearly on the painting, just as Chenggong Sui in the Western Jin dynasty said, "move the slim fingers," and "lift the weak wrist." Only when one is writing on the paper in hand will it be possible for him to "raise" the brush.

Mr. Sha Menghai called this posture "xiéshì (斜势 sidelong posture)" in his *Preliminary Study on the Brush Holding of Ancient Calligraphy*. He said: "Mr. Qi Gong provided me with a piece of material. It was a fragment of a Tang dynasty painting collected by the Japanese artist Nakamura Fusetsu. The fragment was unearthed from Turpan in Xinjiang Autonomous Region. A man facing the scroll is writing in the painting. Mr. Wang Bomin also, at my request, entrusted Mr. Duan Wenjie to copy the Tang dynasty mural in Cave 25 of the Yulin Grottoes in Anxi, Gansu Province. In the mural a man was writing sutras under a tree." Although I have not seen the aforementioned paintings, I've got authentic evidence from Mr. Sha.

Whether ancients wrote on the ground or by leaning against the war-horse (an idiom which refers to writing while leaning against a warhorse before going to battle), they all wrote on the paper they held in their hands. So, to what extent the angles of "raising" and "sidelong posture" are appropriate varies personally and depends on the reading of individuals.

Unrestrained Spirit of the Seven Sages of the Bamboo Grove (Picture 40) by Sun Wei in the Tang dynasty is the remains of *The Seven Sages of the Bamboo Grove*. In the painting, four men sat on the ground, one of whom spread an open scroll on the ground. In addition to depicting the life style of the learned men in the Jin dynasty, the painting provides important information to study the life style of the literati in the late Tang dynasty.

It is absolutely true that "Tang people attached importance to the ancient law or rule of calligraphy."

People in the Sui and Tang dynasties began to write on jī or table. But it was just a start. It was not popularized, nor was it "regular." Despite a few people who "started" using jī or table, the vast majority of "ordinary folks" chose to "advocate the ancient method."

Calligraphers of later generations always said "The ancient method saw its decline" after the Tang dynasty. I think the "ancient method" refers to the brushwork of holding paper in hand. "The method declined" due to the use of tables, and of course the method without support was on the wane.

The ancient method of the Tang dynasty signaled the prelude to the last masterpiece.

CHAPTER 21

Unconscious Loss

It's time we turned to paintings in the Song dynasty.

In the famous *Riverside Scene on the Pure Brightness Festival* (Picture 41) by Zhang Zeduan in the Northern Song dynasty, high tables and matching stools can be seen everywhere.

The Eighteen Scholars (Picture 42) in the Song dynasty clearly shows us the writing posture of people at that time: a man sits on the couch with a high table in front. A piece of paper is spread on the table. The paper is still one foot across by two feet long, and the man tries to write on the paper. Two sticks are placed at each end of the paper to smooth it out. This is the paperweight we use to this day. A paperweight is made of metal, jade, hardwood, and other heavy objects. Paperweights are produced to make paper flat on the desk so that the paper won't easily roll or move. It plays a similar role to stretching paper.

In *Elegant Gathering at West Garden* (Picture 43) by Ma Yuan in the Southern Song dynasty, we could see a man standing by the side of a table, with a long and narrow scroll lying flat on the table. The man writes on the paper with his elbow and arm in the air. There is also something similar to a paperweight on the paper.

In the Song dynasty, Liu Songnian's painting *Grinding Tea and Scholarly Gathering* (Picture 44) depicted the state of writing comprehensively. A monk sits on a round stool, leaning his elbow on a long àn (案) to write scrolls; the left and right corners at the top of the paper are pressed with pebble-like paperweights. I notice that the tip of the brush in the monk's hand is only a little black. It can be observed in many ancient paintings. There are several possibilities: first, two kinds of hairs were combined in the brush hair; second, the ancients only dipped the nib of brush in the ink when writing; third, ancients did not soak the entire brush in the ink, only one-third of the brush hair. All of the three possibilities accorded with the requirements of the ancient brush using.

This reminds me of the painting *The Night Revels of Han Xizai* (Picture 45-1) by Gu Hongzhong in the Five dynasties, copied by Tang Yin in the Ming dynasty. Tang Yin took liberty to add a long, high table

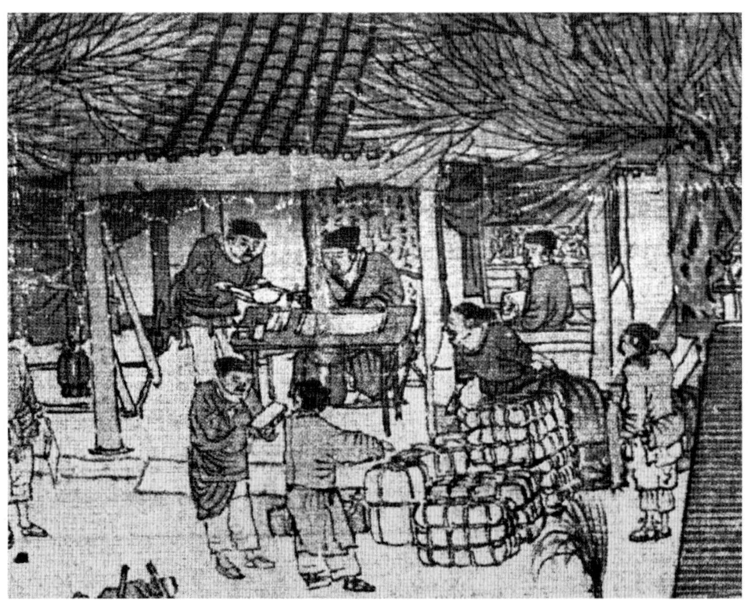

Picture 41 *Riverside Scene on the Pure Brightness Festival* (part), Zhang Zeduan, Northern Song dynasty

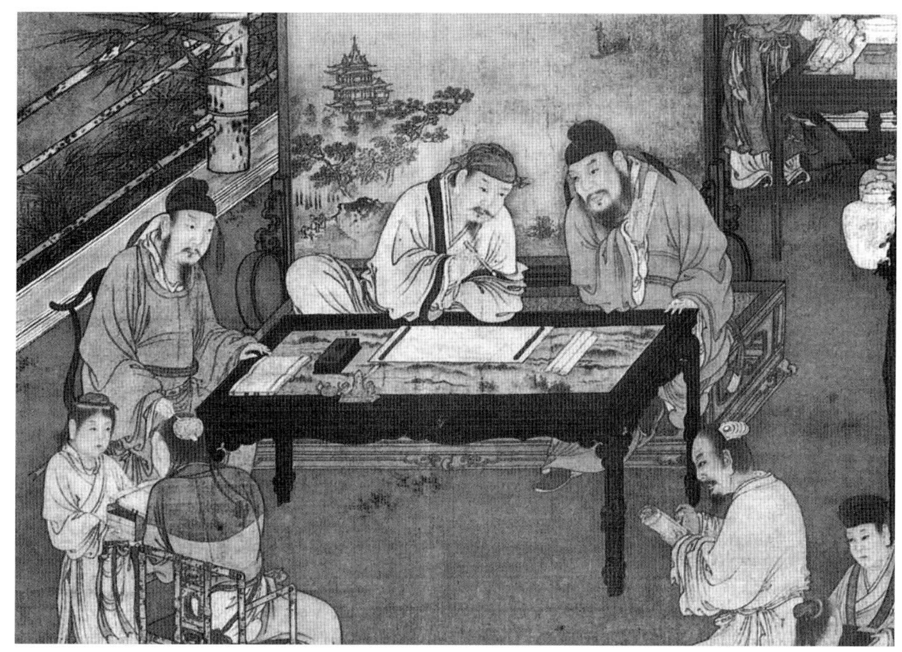

Picture 42 *The Eighteen Scholars* (part), Song dynasty

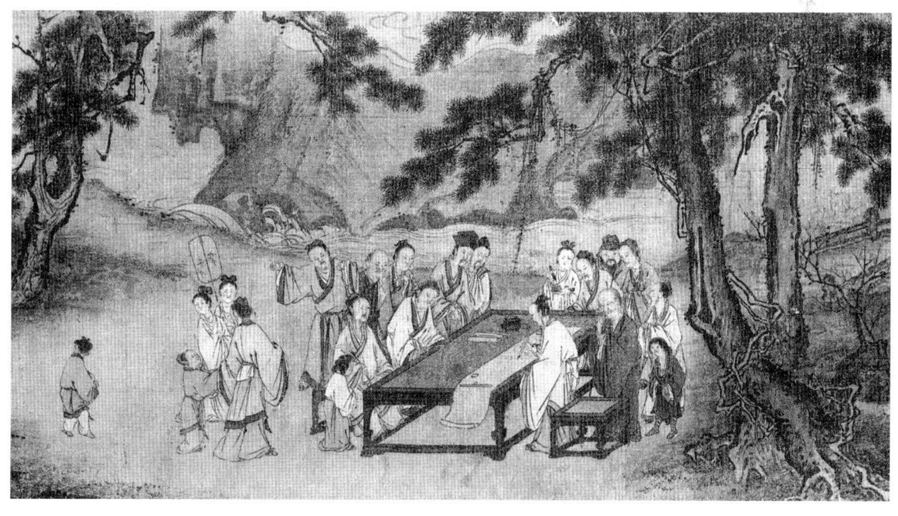

Picture 43 *Elegant Gathering at West Garden* (part), Ma Yuan, Song dynasty

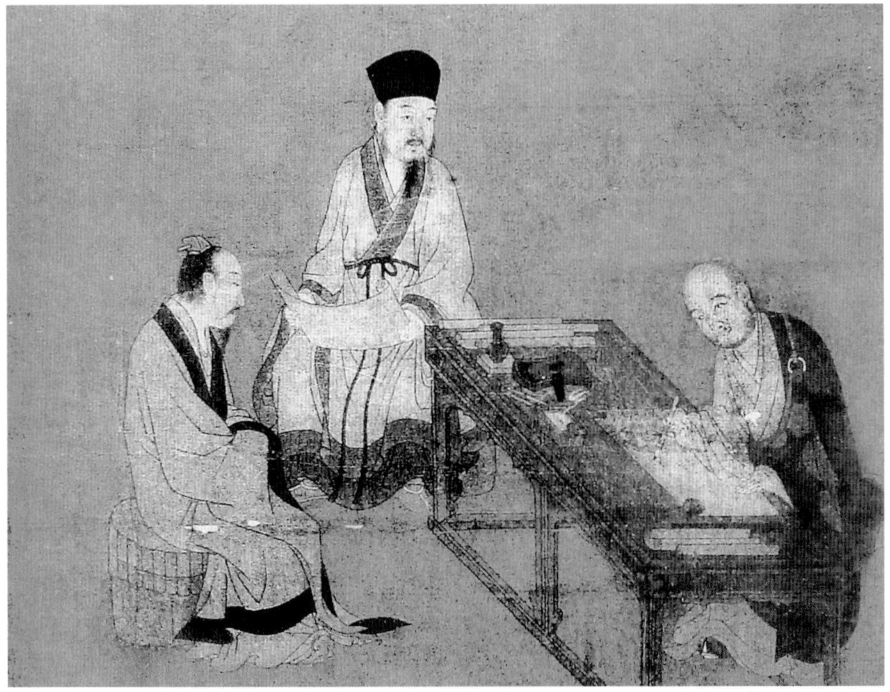

Picture 44 *Grinding Tea and Scholarly Gathering* (part), Liu Songnian, Song dynasty

behind a seated guest surrounded by two women at the end. The table is covered with ink, brush, and a roll of paper. There is even a "paperweight" on the paper. In the original work by Gu Hongzhong in the Five dynasties (Picture 45-2), however, there are only chairs, jǐ, and a knee-high square table. No tall table can be found in the painting. At most in the Tang or the post-Tang Five dynasties, people placed a jǐ on a couch for writing, as is clearly reflected in Wang Wei's *Fu Sheng Expounding The Book of Documents* (Picture 46) and Wei Xian's *A Noble Scholar* (Picture 47) from this period. This is entirely consistent with the development of furniture during the Tang and Five dynasties.

Tang Yin was so romantic that he imposed the scene of the Ming dynasty "bending over the àn" writing in the Five dynasties, reflecting the fact that people in the Ming dynasty were not well acquainted with the way of writing before the Five dynasties. This phenomenon was ridiculed by Mr. Qian Zhongshu in *Qīzhuìjí* (七缀集, literally means *Seven Stitched-Together Collection*): "Du Mu in his *Yùyìbiān* (寓意编, *Compilation of Famous Paintings and Calligraphic Works*) said that when Wang Wei painted the image of Fu Sheng, Fu Sheng was not drawing on a bamboo slip with both knees on the ground, but was sitting on the ground with legs casually spread out and stretched the roll of paper on the jǐ. As Tang Yin didn't care whether Fu Sheng's sitting posture was similar to that of the Western Han dynasty, Tang's drawing can be compared to Musa basjoo (a species of flowering plant in the banana family) in winter."

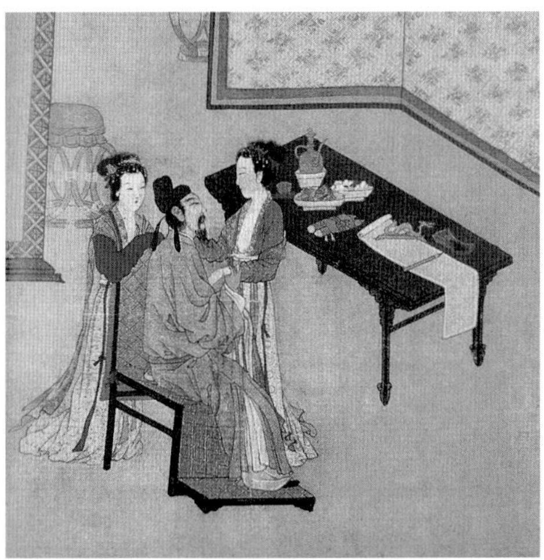

Picture 45-1 *The Night Revels of Han Xizai* by Gu Hongzhong in the Five dynasties, copied by Tang Yin in the Ming dynasty (part)

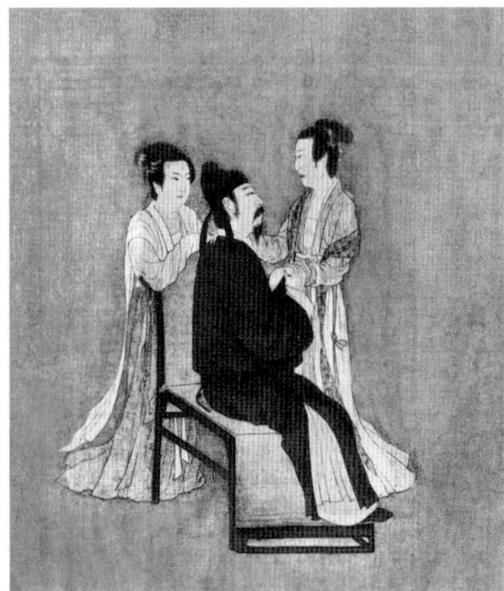

Picture 45-2 *The Night Revels of Han Xizai* by Gu Hongzhong in the Five dynasties (part)

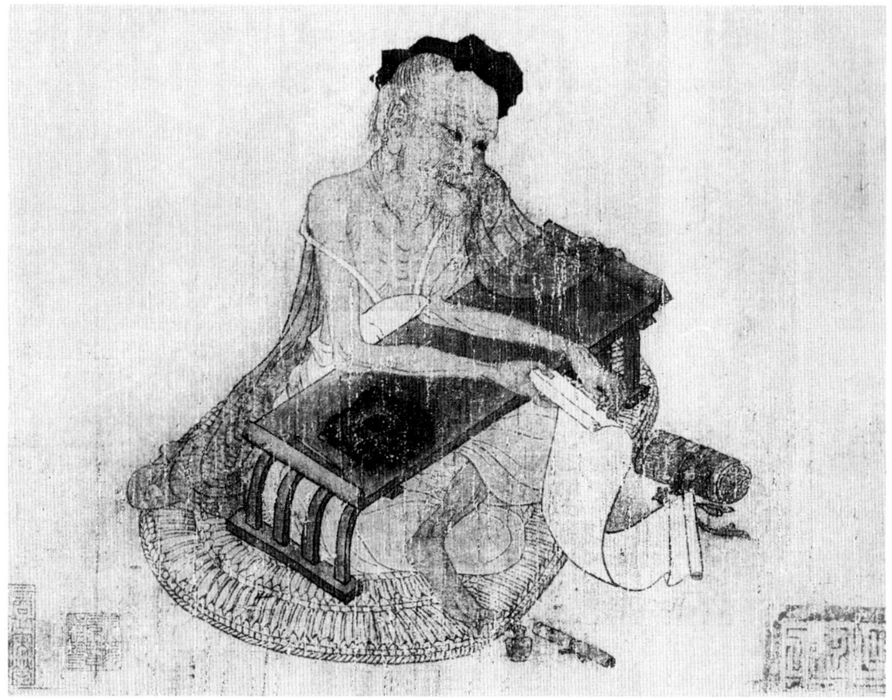

Picture 46 *Fu Sheng Expounding The Book of Documents* (part), Wang Wei, Tang dynasty

Obviously, Wang Wei also imposed the customs of the Tang dynasty on Fu Sheng in the Western Han dynasty, which is like trying to grow Musa basjoo in the snow of severe winter. It seems that the "Guan Gong battles Qin Qiong (two senior generals from two different dynasties)" has been around since olden days. Despite the romantic nature of Tang and Wang, they truly mirrored the objective background of the author's time.

Therefore, Song painting explicitly reveals the real writing style of that era. When we read the calligraphy treatises and theories of the Song dynasty, we found the Song people still paid attention to turning the brush and moving fingers. However, what differed from the past was that the paper was no longer held in the hand but was spread flat on the

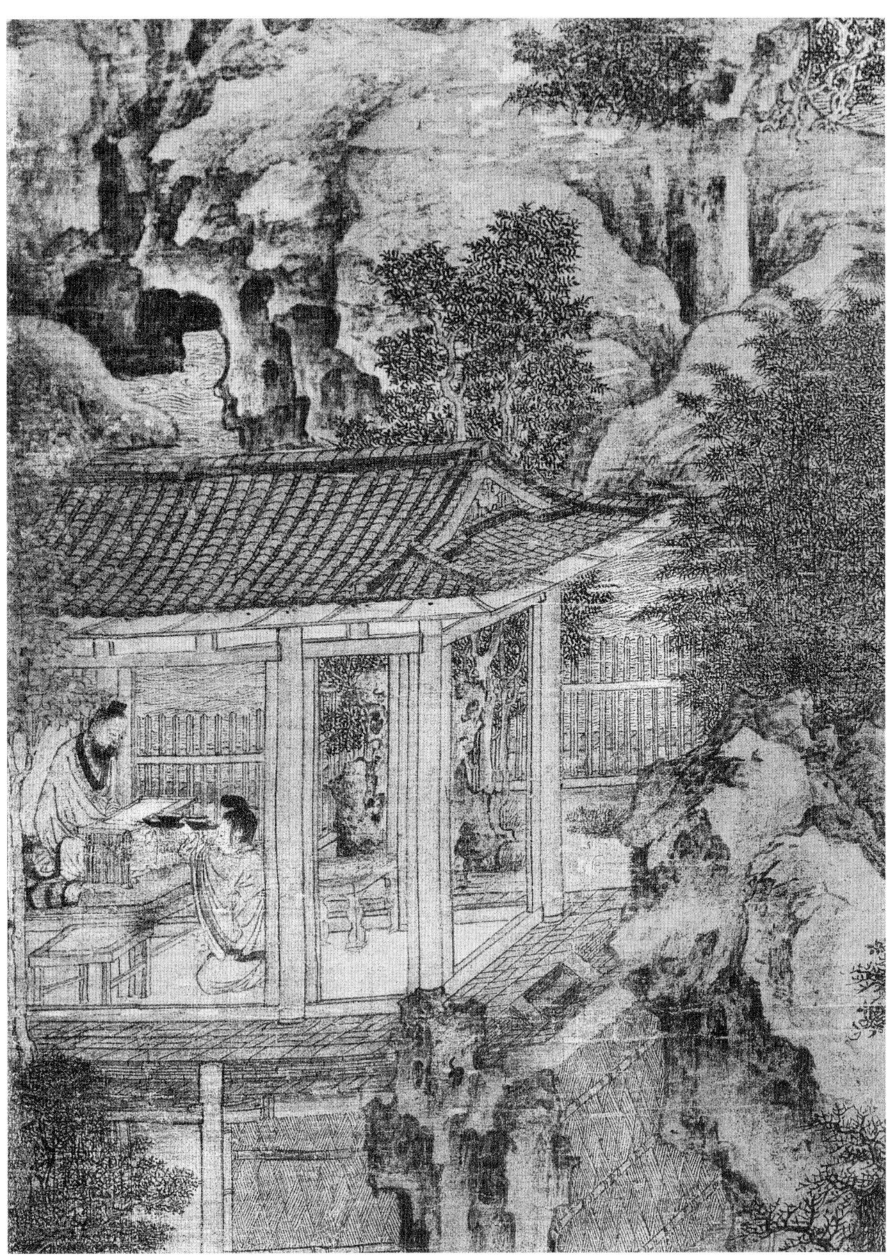

Picture 47 *A Noble Scholar* (part), Wei Xian, Five dynasties

desk; the hand holding the brush changed from "raising wrist" to a "flat wrist"; the brush touching the paper evolved from being vertical to the reading surface to being vertical to the table.

The change may seem insignificant, but is a crucial one.

When the hand holds the brush without support and is perpendicular to the reading surface, due to the physiological limitations of the hand, the flexible moving of fingers and the raising of wrist are restrained within a small range, so it is unsuitable for writing large characters. Moreover, as the left hand holds bamboo slip or paper, it could not remain absolutely stable. Once the table surface has replaced left hand as support, it becomes absolutely stable. After the brush is perpendicular to the desk, not only are fingers able to move around more flexibly, but another huge change is brought unconsciously.

CHAPTER 22

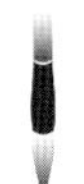

Merits and Demerits of the Table

After the table was used as support, people found that without the "ancient method" of turning the brush, one could still write words steadily and freely. Therefore, the ancients said, "If the ancient writing method was not passed on, people would grow accustomed to what they were familiar with (their elbows relying on the surface). As they grew used to writing with support, the ancient writing method was no longer passed down."

The so-called "growing accustomed to what they're familiar with" refers to relying on the desktop with the wrist at will, without mastering the brush turning technique. It is not only us modern day people; from the Song dynasty, Chinese people have been using desks and chairs since birth, and gotten used to resting their arms, elbows, and wrists naturally on a table. Over time, we have omitted a crucial point: there are two totally different writing postures, namely, not using a desk or chair and using a desk or chair. Different writing postures inevitably involve different brush use. If we ignore this historical fact, there will be a series of misunderstandings and confusion.

Calligraphers after the Song dynasty reiterated the need to standardize the writing style, and to hang the elbow and wrist in the air to maintain a non-support posture, so as to facilitate the ancient method of using fingers to move the brush and retain the authenticity of calligraphy. Zhu Lüzhen, a calligrapher of the Qing dynasty, said: "Writing with the arm in the air was the method that ancients did not change. In the even remoter age, when ancients sat on the ground by the jǐ, there was no àn for them to write upon. All calligraphers of later generations wrote with their arms in the air. However, normal folks since their childhood wrote words with the support of the *àn*. They escaped difficulty and embraced the comfortable and easy posture, and feared the ancient method. To them the ancient writing posture was not a custom but an unusual thing."

This is what happened 200 years ago. The ancient method was declining then and only a few calligraphers knew the archaic method. Two hundred years later, those few calligraphers have long passed away. Pen, ballpoint pen, pencil, and watercolor brushdominate the world. Children born in the new century type words with computers and may not even need the pen. Who else would ask for the authentic brush technique? And what is the point of emphasizing the so-called correct writing, with elbow and wrist hanging in the air?

Our wise ancestors invented convenient writing techniques and completed the beautiful and unique shapes of Chinese characters under the primitive condition where their arms were not supported. Calligraphy has since become a mysterious and profound art in the hands of scholars and poets of all dynasties for more than two thousand years and has been the pride of Chinese descendants. Just because our wise ancestors made people comfortable by bringing the support of desks and chairs for the arms and wrists to rely upon when writing, people from generation to generation gradually made light of the brushwork, and finally lost it.

Should we celebrate for it or should we grieve over it? Should we be happy or sad about it?

Nevertheless, it reminds me of Xin Qiji's *Lyrics to the Bodhisattva Melody:*

Blue mountains cannot hinder
The waters that must eastwards flow.

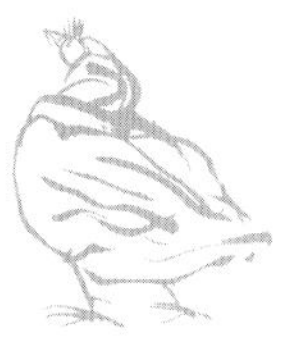

CHAPTER 23

Introduction of the Broad Chancery Style (Bāfēn Clerical Script)

After giving a long sigh about the past, I still have to turn back to the distant history.

As I concluded in Chapter 15, if the diameter of the hard-hair brush or hair-combining brush is 0.6 cm or 0.7 cm, when you write with gliding force, the strokes tend to be a squarezhé (折, break) in straight regular script. In the history of calligraphy, bāfēn (八分, a new type of clerical script first appeared in the mid-Eastern Han dynasty) and kaize (楷则, model) are always correlated; therefore, they are termed as bāfēn kǎizé (八分楷则).

Do you remember "the bāfēn script" created by Wang Cizhong in the Eastern Han dynasty? And the three explanations about "the bāfēn script"? It's time to go back to it.

The first is that "The style is a fusion between approximately two-tenths of the clerical script and eight-tenths of the small seal script." These are the words of Cai Yong, passed down by his daughter Cai Wenji. Literally speaking, it means two-tenths of the bāfēnscript looks like the clerical script, and eight-tenths of the bāfēnscript resembles the small seal script.

The contemporary concept of the clerical script is a chirography. From the perspective of character development, the clerical script is created for convenience. It is much like a stenography for the official characters.

I temporarily refer to this concept as lì huà (隶化, transformation from seal script into clerical script)

The official characters developed all the way from small seal, regular script, lǎosòng (regular), and guǎngé (scholar) to block style and artistic calligraphy. Lìhuà continues the form of simplicity and forms rules to develop towards cursive script and running script. The practicality and art of Chinese characters sometimes are like on a double-track and sometimes overlap. And they have both been developing synchronously.

In ancient times, the appellation of fonts varied from time to time, which easily caused confusion. Therefore, when we read or try to understand an ancient treatise, make sure to verify the dynasty of the scholar. The Tang scholars referred the regular script as the clerical script, and when they said bāfēn, what they meant was official script. Zhang Huaiguan said, "Bāfēn reflects the swiftness of seal script and the lì (隶, literally means clerical script) contains the swiftness of bāfēn." Here lì (隶) undoubtedly refers to the regular script; but the lì (隶) mentioned by Cai Yong must refer to bāfēn kǎizé.

In the Eastern Han dynasty, the text of tablet inscriptions was generally written in official script, while the head of tablets was written in seal script. Different from qínzhuàn (seal script in the Qin dynasty), they were written with the method of lì (or termed as kǎizé). Starting from the Eastern Han dynasty, it was customary to write tablet inscriptions with seal characters.

It then occurs to me that during the transition from the Eastern Han dynasty to the Western Jin dynasty, in the famous tablet of the

Three Kingdoms—*Recording the Merits during Tianxi Reign of the Kingdom of Wu* (Picture 48), the shape of words basically resembles the seal character, but the brush writing method is shaped like a "dangling needle," which is the kǎizé brushwork of lì.

About twenty years before *Recording the Merits during Reign Tianxi in the Kingdom of Wu*, a tablet appeared in the reign of Zhengshi Period of the Wei Kingdom: *Stone Inscriptions in Three Scripts* (Picture 49). In the tablet, almost all the ancient seal script was written with "dangling needles," enough for us to imagine the original form of the words. Zhu Lüzhen in the Qing dynasty described "bāfēn clerical script" as "powerful,

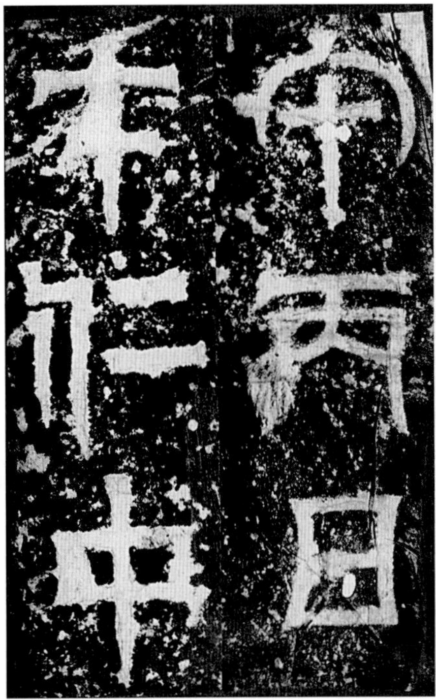

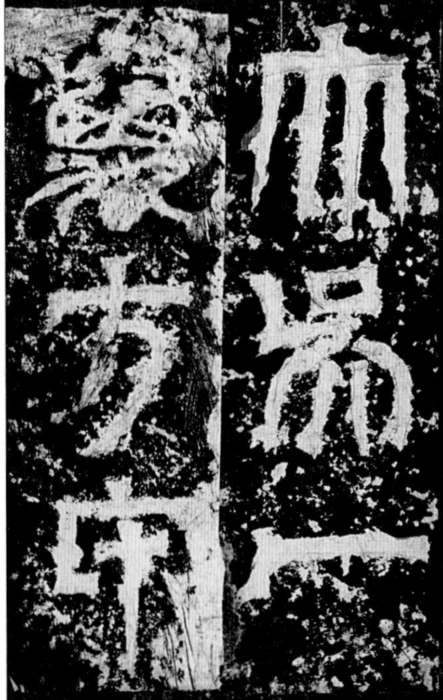

Picture 48 *Recording the Merits during Tianxi Reign of the Kingdom of Wu* (part), Kingdom of Wu

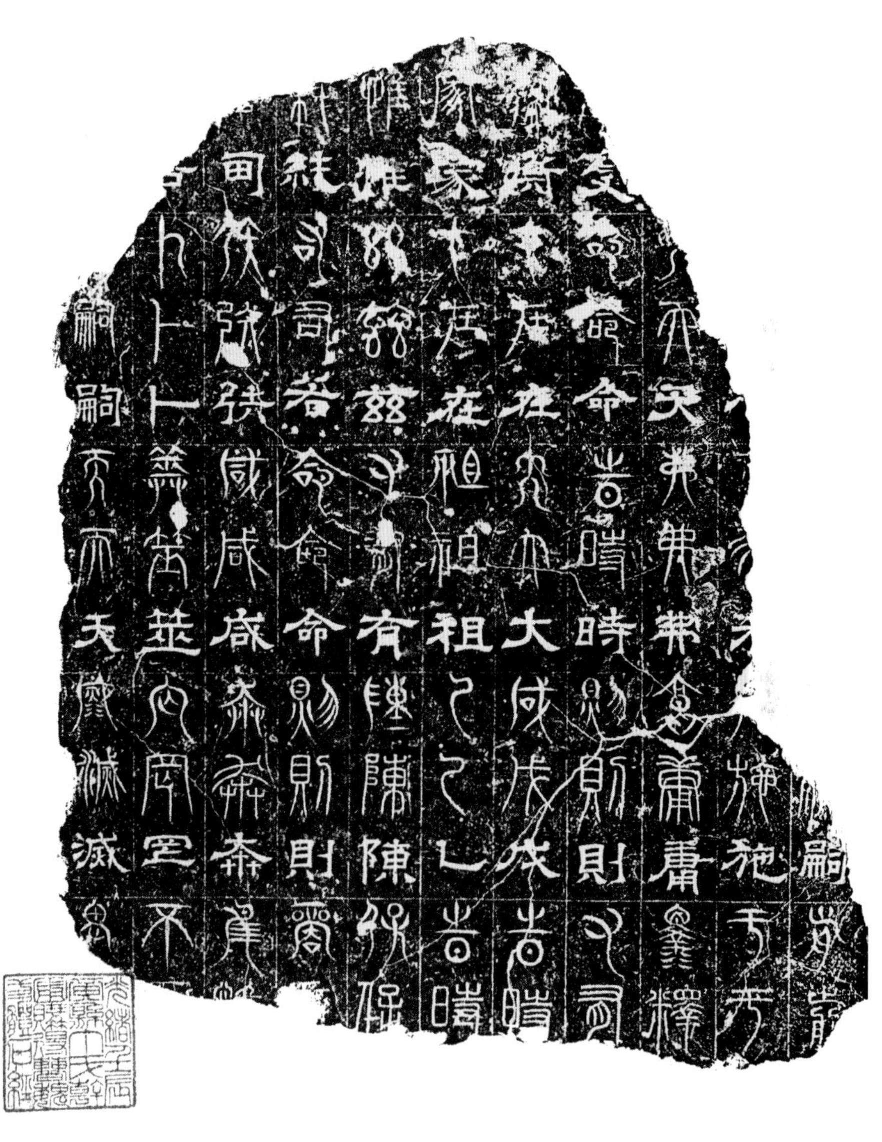

Picture 49 *Stone Inscriptions in Three Scripts* (part), Kingdom of Wei

classic, resolute and decisive." His words were more than appropriate to describe the brushwork of the two tablets.

Cai Yong's explanation probably refers to seal characters written with the brush holding method of regular script.

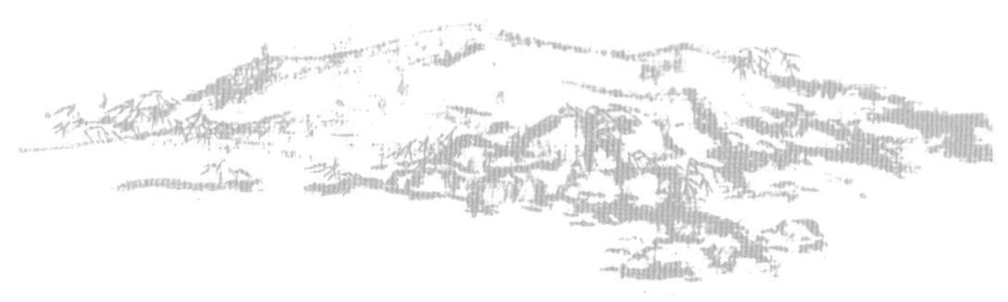

CHAPTER 24

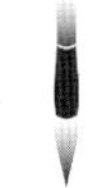

The Forms of *Xiang* and *Bei*

The second explanation is that there is a clear distinction of all the parts of a character in terms of the brushstrokes just like the shape of character "八" (bā, eight): the right and the left. Chen Yizeng in the Yuan dynasty explained it this way:

"Xiàng (向) the head part is quickly written on the left-up-right, then right-up-left; the tail part is quickly written on the left-up-left, right-up-right; stay slanted and write quickly when it is sideways slanted.

Bèi (背) is the opposite of xiàng.

Xiàng (向) looks like two men facing each other; bèi resembles them turning their backs to each other. Ouyang Xun illustrated several examples that belonged to "xiàng-type": 非, 卯, 好, 知, 和, etc.; Words that belonged to "bèi-type": 北, 兆, 肥, 根. The examples seem quite obvious. If one learnt some ancient brush turning methods, it would not be hard to conclude that:

"Xiàng (向)" means first turning brush to the left, and then turning brush to the right. "Qiǎng (抢)" means the brush touches and writes on the paper rapidly.

"Bèi," contrary to "xiàng," means first turning brush to the right and then to the left.

The core of brushwork is no more than turning brush to the right and left. "Xiàng" and "bèi" are two rounds of moving left and right. It's returning to the original position. The character "八" (bā) can be written in the direction of either "xiàng" or "bèi," which means that while writing an character we can first turn left and then turn right, or first turn right and then turn left. The so-called "fen" means clearly discerning the brushstrokes of "xiàng" and "bèi" to return the brush back to the original position.

It can be seen as a reasonable method. By turning the brush back and forth and creating a force of inertia, a word is written. By extension, and continuously creating inertia, one could write a line of words, or a full text without stop. This is what the ancients called "one-stroke writing." This reasonable method of brush use is in line with the "convenient" trend of the development of characters.

This kind of inertia is fast and smooth. When the force is generated, the momentum is unstoppable. Therefore, *Jiǔ Shì* (九势, *Nine Types of Force*) by Cai Yong (蔡邕 cài yōng) was timely: "When I wrote by conforming to nature, Yin and Yang were therefore born; so did form and force," "when a force comes, it cannot be stopped, and when it goes, it cannot be repressed." The "nature" of the left and right brush turning establishes "Yin and Yang," while "Yin and Yang" refers to the "xiang" and "bei" which give birth to "form-force (形势 xíngshì)." And the "shi (势, force)" in calligraphy must be like this.

The ancients said "qǔ shì (取势, taking the force)," that is, to design different "stroke force" according to different strokes. The "stroke force" is based on the favorable direction of brush hair formed by inertia of turning the brush to the left or right. "Taking" refers to selecting, deciding and using. "xiàng bèi (向背)" couldn't happen without brush turning; the "force" couldn't be "taken" if the favorable direction is not chosen.

Wang Xizhi said, "Ten times late and five times urgent, ten times curved and five times straight." His words indicated the state of using the brush during qǔ shì (taking the force). This kind of brush turning to take force is subtle and crafty; a little mistake can turn the characters into "shì bèi (势背)." As Wang Sengqian, a calligrapher of the Southern dynasties, said: "A tiny difference in xiàng bèi will cause the life-death distance like a tiny thread of hair that causes life and death." People who don't understand the trick can't observe it. Huang Tingjian said, "There is a brush in a character, as there is an eye in Buddhist. One needs to have such an eye to know the meaning in the craft."

Ancients racked their brains to explain and record these scientific writing methods.

The method that Cai Yong adopted to create the "fēibái shū script (飞白书, also termed cursive seal, which features white parts exposed in strokes as if they are written with a dry brush)" is a brilliant idea. Heavy ink easily covers up many methods of brush using. However, through the "fēibái script" of the brush and ink, the turning direction, points of force and dexterity of the brush hair are exposed clearly, which can be used to show and teach people. Later generations interpreted that "fēibái is a script lighter than bāfēn." I'm convinced by this point of view.

I have been trying to find the valued pieces of fēibái script, but it is hard. In Mǐ Fú's *Chi Du* (Picture 50), the brush turning strategy at the stroke joints can be observed in the white parts of the strokes.

Eight Principles of yǒng, or the aforementioned yǒng (永) with eight strokes, with a character of "永 (yǒng)," explained all the brush strokes and "taking force" method in the most general, accurate and intuitive way. The Eight Principles has thus won people's favor, so has been inherited for the longest time, and also spread the most widely.

The "convenience" of regular script lies originally in the "convenience" of brushwork, and in the "convenience" of the scientific cooperation between hand and brush.

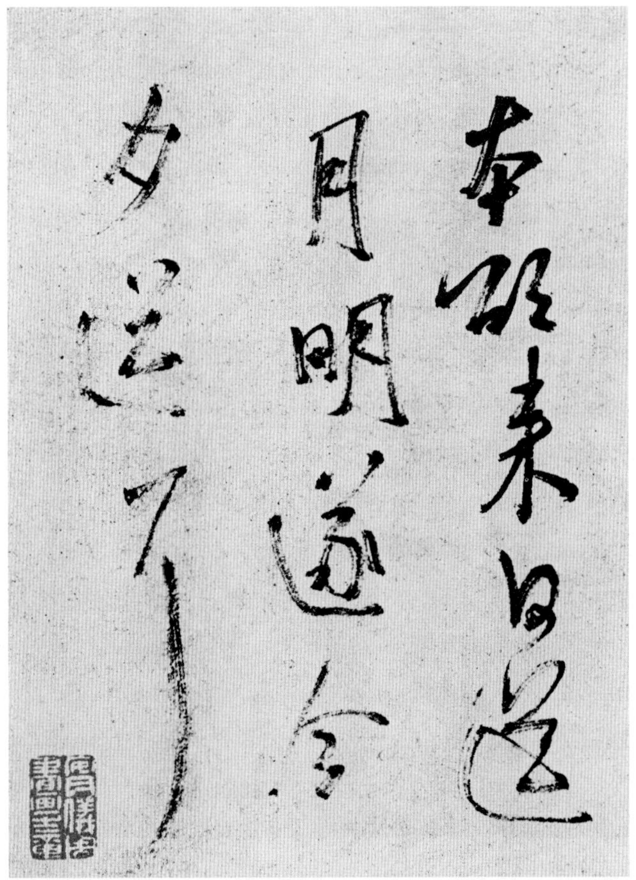

Picture 50 *Chi Du* (a model of epistolary art) (part), MǐFú (米芾), Song dynasty

CHAPTER 25

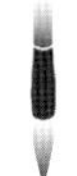

What a Giant Elephant!

The third explanation is that a character should be eight *fens* (a unit in length, and one *fen* is one-third of a centimeter) in size.

If the diameter of the hard-hair brush or hair-combining brush is 0.6 cm or 0.7 cm, with the brush hair within 2.5 cm, you can adopt the classic writing style of the porcelain figurines of the Western Jin dynasty by hanging your elbow and wrist in the air, and turning the brush from side to side and reverting through "xiàng bèi." The characters written will be exactly eight *fens* large, which is less than one inch. It confirmed what Zheng Biao in the Yuan dynasty said: "The character is within an inch; the law lies in the palm and finger," "the copybook for calligraphy in the Wei and Jin dynasties all show characters written with the strokes of palm and fingers."

I pondered the three interpretations one by one and put them together, and I am suddenly enlightened that the three did form an elephant, as in the famous image of the blind men and the elephant, each trying to understand an elephant solely by touching it.

CHAPTER 26

"Zhāngcǎo" Ends the Evolution of Calligraphy

During the reign of Emperor Yuan of the Han dynasty, an intermediate official (titled Huangmen Ling) named Shi You wrote *Jíjiù Zhāng* (*Children's Reading Primer*). His handwriting was called "zhāngcǎo (章草, a type of cursive script)," and also known as "zhāngcǎo shū (Picture 51)."

As is known to all, this early form of cursive script is *zhāngcǎo* (章草) which was created by Shi You to quickly record words or to facilitate one's handwriting. "Zhāng (章)" literally means "orderliness," "law," "explicitness," etc. As Wang Yin was quoted in *Shū Duàn* (书断, *Judgments on Calligraphers*), "*Jíjiù Zhāng Children's Reading Primer*)" "freed the official script by adopting a rough style; the tradition of writing in the Han dynasty was thus simplified and the new writing method was gradually followed."

Many words in zhāngcǎo are completely unrelated to regular script and indecipherable. Therefore, "*Jíjiù Zhāng*" is a comparison of regular script and zhāngcǎo. It is composed of rhyming words by daily classification, such as zhāngcǎo dictionary, which was popularized among schoolchildren. It's named jíjiù because the first sentence contains the two words "急就 jíjiù." Chao Gongwu in the Song dynasty, in his book

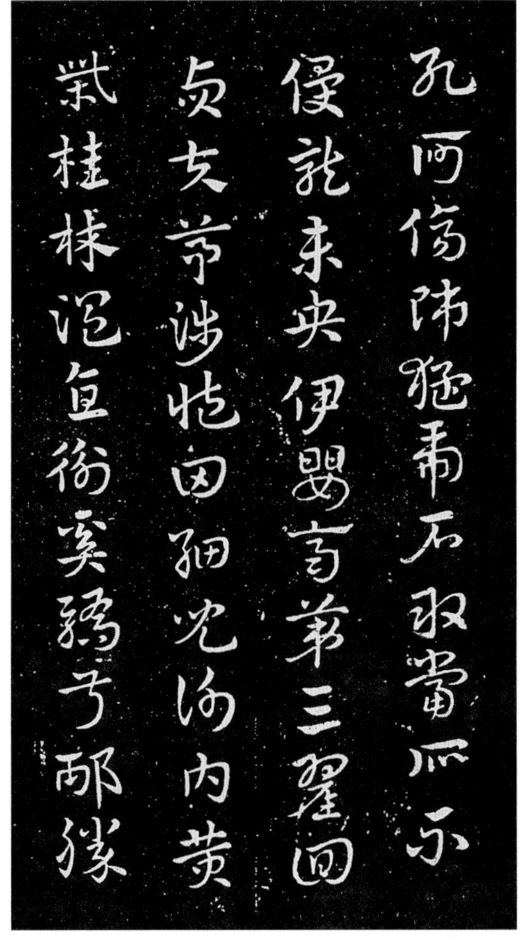

Picture 51 *Children's Reading Primer* (part), Huang Xiang, Kingdom of Wu

Picture 52 Hu (a flat long ruler-like board used at court for the taking of notes, usually made of bamboo or wood)

Reading Annals in the Administrator's Residence (郡斋读书志 jùnzhāi dúshū zhì), said, "Those who are in a hurry are those who find it difficult to know words. The meaning of *jíjiù zhāng* is that one can look up the book for indecipherable words in case of urgent need."

Later, "jíjiù zhāng" evolved and referred to an article of hasty completion. Literally, "jíjiù (急就) means dealing with emergency; "zhāngchéng (章程)" also falls under the category of official duties. To my knowledge, the original "jíjiù zhāng" has another meaning, that is, urgent writing, which is simplified, rule-based, and standardized cursive script and adopted when an official is formally submitting a written statement. It's quite like a modern book teaching shorthand skills. The nature of "jíjiù" is the same; only the methods are different.

In ancient times, when the emperor and officials had no paper to write on, the officials usually held a long and narrow board recording items to be reported, or to record the emperor's orders at any time. This board is "hu (a flat long ruler-like board used at court for the taking of notes, usually made of bamboo or wood)" (Picture 52), also known as "hand board." "Jíjiù zhāng" is written on the "hu," often used along with the hairpin brush inserted in the men's hair. Since there was a table, people had gradually accustomed to writing by bending over the desk, so "hu" later became an ornament for officials when they went to the court.

"Zhāngcǎo" originated from the clerical script and "freed clerical script." At first sight, there were many eye-catching strokes of "nà (捺, dismemberment)."

Before the dot stroke in regular script was standardized, "nà" was also called "wave (波挑 bōtiāo)." "Nà" originated from very early days. Strokes similar to "nà" are abundant in the inscriptions on the bronzeware (Picture 53) of the Zhou dynasty. These are undoubtedly the traces left by brush writing; the brushwork of the rest of the strokes are most invisible after carving, burning and casting. The characteristics of "nà" are so remarkable that after several rounds of damages it still retains the old tracing.

I've always dreamed of seeing the original brushwork of inscriptions on ancient bronze objects, and the *State Covenant Unearthed at Houma* is probably the best reference. The words were written in cinnabar on top of the black jade; the strokes are neat, orderly, resolute, and decisive. And there were many "nà" in the strokes. We could see that large seal script

Picture 53 Great Yu Tripod (大盂鼎 dà yú dǐng) (part), Western Zhou dynasty

(大篆 dàzhuàn), including inscriptions on tortoise shells, were all written in this way. Of course, small seal script (小篆 xiǎozhuàn) is no exception. We can also observe that brush work in Kang Likui's *Volume of Poems by Li Bai* (Picture 54) in the Yuan dynasty is very close to that in *State Covenant Unearthed at Houma*—though both works were separated by nearly two thousand years!

The use of "nà (捺)" was halted in small seal script (小篆 xiǎozhuàn). Evidently, it is because of the evolution into artistic calligraphy. This was totally not the case in the bamboo slips of the Qin dynasty.

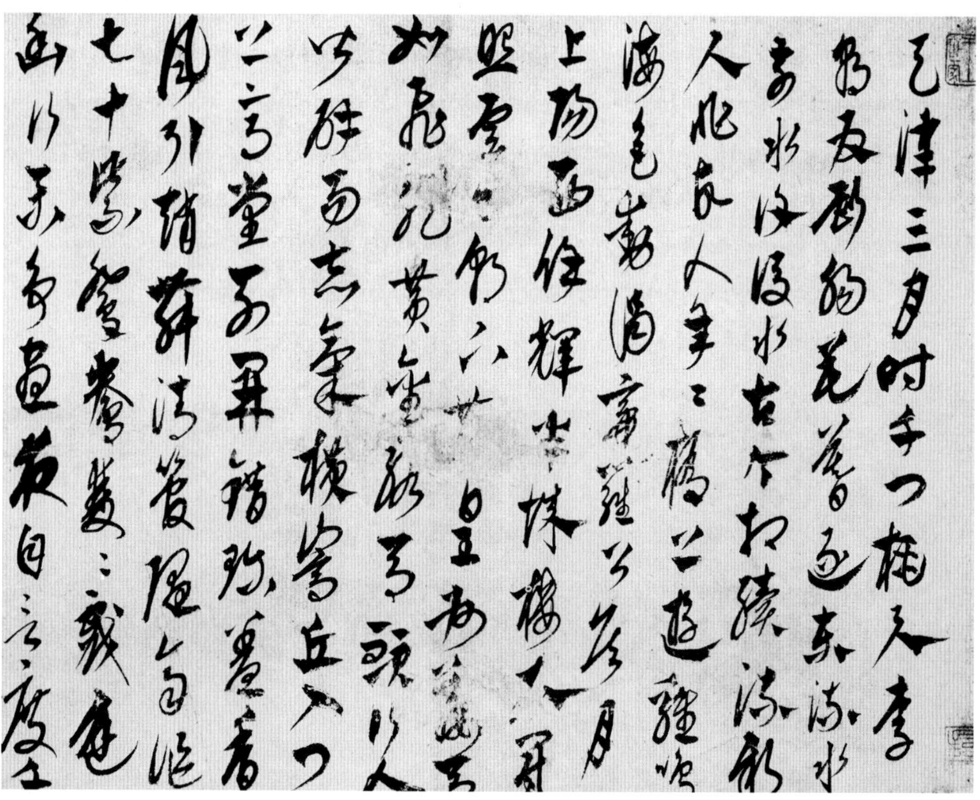

Picture 54 *Volume of Poems by Li Bai* (part), Kang Likui, Yuan dynasty

Please refer to the concept of "lìhuà (transformation from seal script into clerical script)" in Chapter 23. I will name the phenomenon of temporary halt of "nà" as "měihuà (美化, the transformation into artistic calligraphy)."

"Nà (捺)" has always been a mystery to me.

When I was practicing calligraphy as a kid, I spent most of the effort in "nà," but still found it hard to write it well. I often thought "What was the beauty in nà"? It was so strange that ancients took trouble to create such a stroke. By the time I had figured out the ancient brushwork and a series of issues, the mystery was solved.

The left-right brush-turning began when the writing brush was invented. As the ancients said, "it originated from nature." In the process of turning the brush, it was impossible to evenly turn the brush from head to tail, because we had joints in the fingers. In writing one stroke it usually took two or three times of pressing forcefully, as the ancients said, "one wave and three twists (一波三折 yībōsānzhé)."

"Nà (捺)" with the common downward trend in inscriptions on ancient bronzeware occasionally resembles "Piē (撇, a slant)," a "dangling needle," which results from two times of force-generation. The angle of "nà" is the product of the third time force-generation of brush turning.

According to common sense, if the writing speed is calculated according to the number of brush turning, the fewer times, the faster. Therefore, writing speed is the fastest when the number of brush turning is minimized. This is the principle of bāfēn, upon which zhāngcǎo was created. Often a word is best controlled within one round of left and right turning. If a word according to its structure cannot be written so conveniently, the ancients would create a smooth word according to the rule of turning left and right only once. Therefore, we can find that in cursive script, the writing styles of certain words are completely unrelated to the structure of the regular script, such as Chinese characters "cáo (曹)," "děng (等)," "yí (疑)," "ài (爱)," and "yù (欲)" (Picture 55).

While writing zhāngcǎo, we try to reduce the number of force-generation, so we often adopt brushwork in the same direction continuously. When there is more than enough strength, the strength could be "sent out" without reservation. Therefore, the"nà" in zhāngcǎo is not in accordance with the normal rule.

There are two kinds of"nà" in zhāngcǎo: one is in the upward shape, and the other is in the downward shape. The former clearly represents the last force-generation of the left-turning, and the latter represents the last force-generation of the right-turning.

Zhāngcǎo was written on the paper held in hand, and the support was unstable. One character cannot be linked with another character. One character was written after a finish of one brush turning. Gradually, the skills of brush turning were enriched. One could form the technique himself. The force was not subject to the restriction of one-word for one finishing of brush turning."nà" as a symbol of returning was cancelled. The brush returning at the end of a character was disrupted. People dexterously put "returning" in the next word to form a state of word-connection. "Jīncǎo (今草, contemporary cursive script)" was thus formed (Picture 56).

Undoubtedly, whether it's zhāngcǎo or bāfēn, the core of their original creation is due to the rapid and smooth brush turning. Smoothness is "convenience."

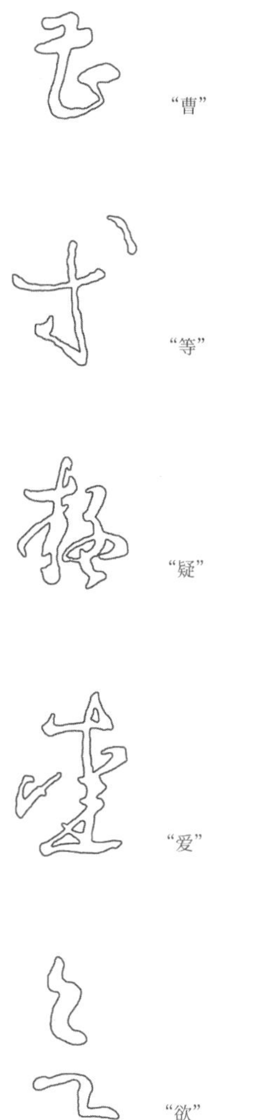

Picture 55 Chinese characters "cáo," "děng," "yí," "ài," "yù"

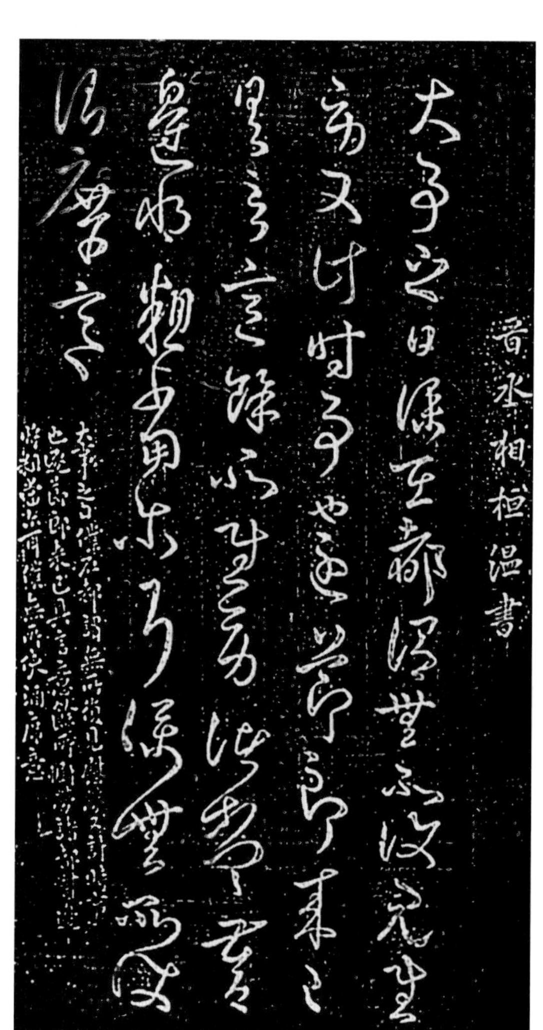

Picture 56 The cursive script in Huánwēn Dàshì Tiè (桓温大事帖, *Great Events of Huan Wen*), Jin dynasty

CHAPTER 27

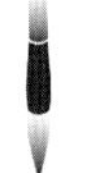

The Physiological Limits of "Lìhuà" and "Měihuà"

I've sorted out a lot of clues. Please allow me to summarize them first.

Please note that in the last few chapters I mentioned the concepts of "lìhuà" and "měihuà."

The skills and methods of brush turning began when the writing brush was born. At the beginning, there perhaps was no legal regularity. It is not difficult to see from the hieroglyphics that there are many repeated rounds of brush turning in each character. Up until the oracle bone script, the structure of Chinese characters had been basically formed, still there were lots of brush turning. To sum up, multiple brush turnings affected speed, and people were constantly trying to improve it. This process of improvement was the process of "lìhuà," and also the process of "convenience." Obviously, "lìhuà" aimed at manipulating the brush manually.

Undoubtedly, the process of "lìhuà" is always accompanied by "měihuà" which is a visual requirement. One typical example is small seal script, whose extremely symmetrical font, straight and smooth lines show its preciseness as the official text.

To put it bluntly, "lìhuà" and "měihuà" refer to the hand and the eye, which is the most important distinction between "calligraphy" and "artistic lettering."

The original creation of "the bāfēn script" adopted the principle of taking force of "xiang" and "bei." In the process of "lìhuà," the most convenient and important result of "fǎ (法, doctrine or law)" in shūfǎ (书法, calligraphy) was achieved. Subsequently, the creation of zhāngcǎo pushed the development of convenience to the ultimate limit.

What is the ultimate limit then? The musical note high C is a limit of the human voice. Even with the aid of medicine, men's 100-meter sprinters have not yet run a record time of 9.5 seconds. Men always face biological limits. In calligraphy, for instance, the evolution of the shape of Chinese characters is limited by the brush; the brush is limited by twisting and turning; the twisting and turning are limited by the hand; and the hand is limited by the thumb: the upper part of human thumb is only about three centimeters long. That's how far we can go with the brush.

In other words, all convenient brushwork techniques are restricted within the physiological limit. Zhāngcǎo of "lìhuà" and "bāfēn" of "kǎifǎ (楷法, law or method of regular script)" have performed the skills within the physiology limit to full potential.

As a result, the development of the shape of Chinese characters stopped.

I think I've found out the key to the questions raised in Chapter Four.

CHAPTER 28

Three Thin Ropes Twisted into One Thick Rope—"Wán Fǎ (完法, Completing the Standard/Method)"

When I was young, I had passion for sports. Though I don't feel like working out now, I still enjoy watching games. The winning or losing of any game, the level of players, the mood of audience, and the commentary outside the arena, are actually completely determined by the game rules. Only when the game rules are complete will there be the corresponding level of players, not to mention the comments.

This is a well-known and simple truth. It is the same in calligraphy.

Only when the rules of writing and shape of Chinese characters were completed would there be judgment and theory. That's why not until the Eastern Han dynasty, when the evolution of Chinese characters stopped, that a complete theory of calligraphy appeared.

In the Wei and Jin dynasties, paper-making and brush-making techniques were further matured and refined. Many calligraphers together used and developed brushwork. By gathering talents and pooling wisdom, they integrated the brushwork with the beautiful shape of characters. Following great calligraphers such as Cai Yong, Zhong Yao, Zhang Zhi, Suo Jing and Lu Ji, one man appeared, who is a master of all forms of Chinese calligraphy, whose handwriting was compared to "a dragon jumping over the gate of heaven and a tiger crouching in the residence of phoenix," and whose work "rose above all others" and "had no equal in the world." This man is Wang Xizhi.

Wang Xizhi had seven sons, the youngest of whom was named Wang Xianzhi. He was said to have changed his father's writing style. Contrary to Wang Xizhi's calligraphy, one of Xianzhi's accomplishments is the extensive use of the "one-stroke writing" (Picture 57) technique for cursive script, which is widely admired as "no trace of brush turning could be found," "otherworldly, liberating and serene demeanors," and "most romantic and unconventional." Though several of his siblings were notable calligraphers, only Xianzhi was able to eventually equal his father in status, with the pair later attaining the appellation, "The Two Wangs (二王)."

Wang Xizhi apparently wrote one character with one cycle of turning the brush from left to right, so that each character was broken off from the other, and the traces of each turn of the stroke could be observed (Picture 58). Xiao Wang (小王, Junior Wang, referring to Wang Xianzhi) had "changed his father's writing style" and created the "one-stroke writing," which laced together several characters (typically three to four) into a single stroke, which was not limited to one cycle of turning the brush to form a single character. He cleverly packed "momentum" so that the brush turns "had no trace of being detected."

Please notice that this, as I've mentioned earlier, is the essence of "jīncǎo (今草, contemporary cursive script)."

The emergence of Wang Xizhi and the calligraphic style of "The Two Wangs (二王)" marked the full maturity of Chinese calligraphy as "fǎ (法, standard or method)" and the perfect unification of "lìhuà" and "měihuà," and of brushwork and vision. It symbolized an unparalleled peak in the history of calligraphy. It was the era that nurtured numerous opportunities that produced heroes and geniuses.

First let's take time to appreciate Wang Xizhi's *Sāng Luàn Tiè* (Picture 59), *Èr Xiè Tiè* and *Dé Shì Tiè* (Picture 60).

If we were to draw a curve of a mountain peak, with the crest being the Wei and Jin dynasties, the uphill side on the left would range from the origin to the maturity of Chinese characters and the brushwork.

This continuous writing history is like a thick rope twisted with three strings, i.e.:

I. The physiological characteristics of the right hand when writing without support.

II. Relatively suitable tools (including brush, bamboo and wooden slips, paper, etc.).

III. The human tendency towards convenience and simplicity in reporting things.

These three strings are conventionally twisted together with mutual control, and pushing forward, forming common rules.

It can be compared to sporting games which are based on man's physiological nature, coupled with appropriate equipment and rules. The evolving sports equipment has also upped the performance of players. When I ran the 100-meter race as a child, I wore spiked shoes to avoid slipping on the cinder track. After artificial surfaces came into use in the 1970s, athletes no longer needed to wear spiked shoes, because the track was flexible. After that, players immediately broke the 10-second world record in the 100-meter race.

With calligraphy, however, this process seems a bit too long. Starting from the inauguration of writing brush, this thick rope has been twisted and rubbed for six or seven thousand years. During that time, although

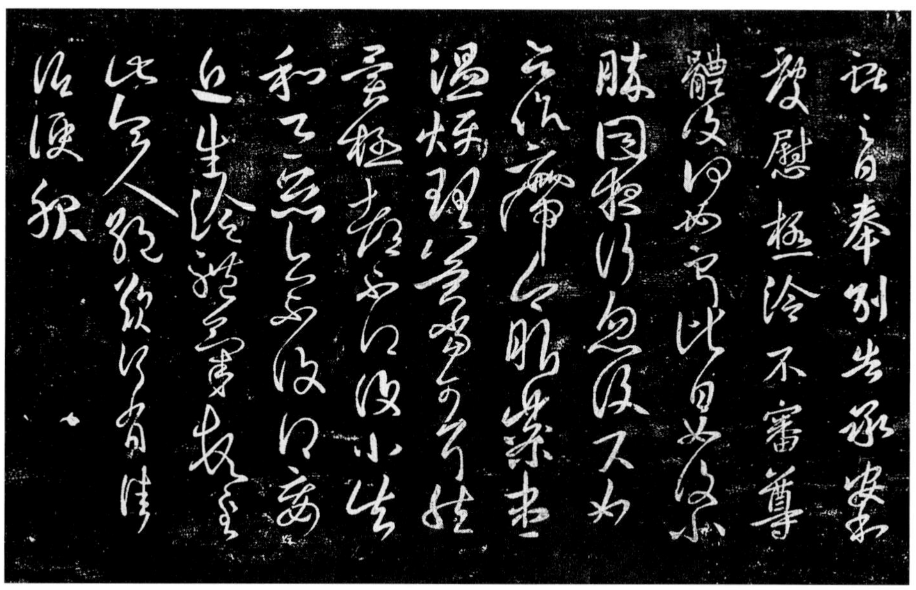

Picture 57 *Fèng Bié Tiè* (a letter that informed Wang Xianzhi's friend of his physical state and asked the friend to keep away from coldness and drink good wine). Wang Xianzhi, Jin dynasty

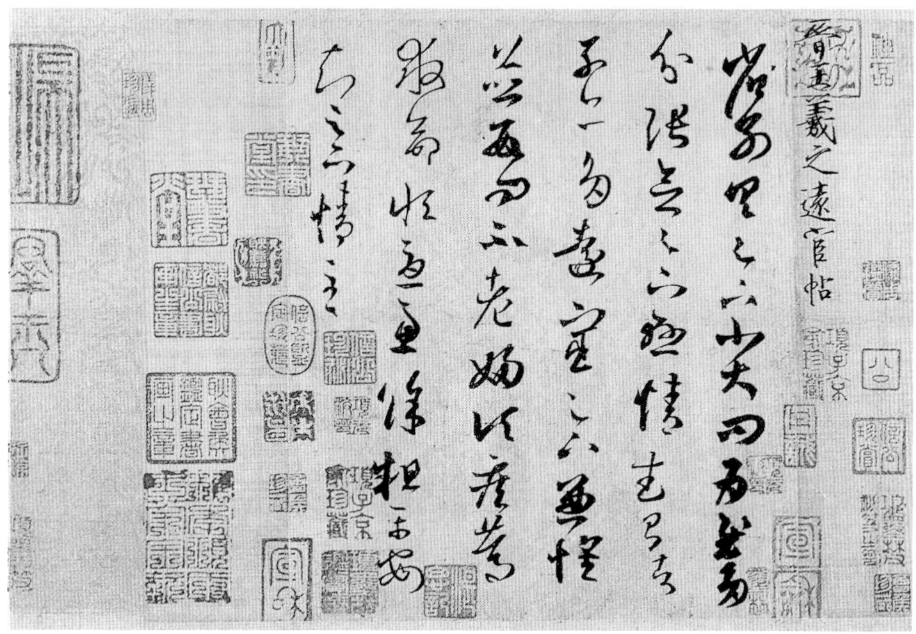

Picture 58 *Xǐng Bié Tiè* (a letter of reply that informed Wang Xizhi's friend of the seriously ill state of Wang's wife). Wang Xizhi, Jin dynasty

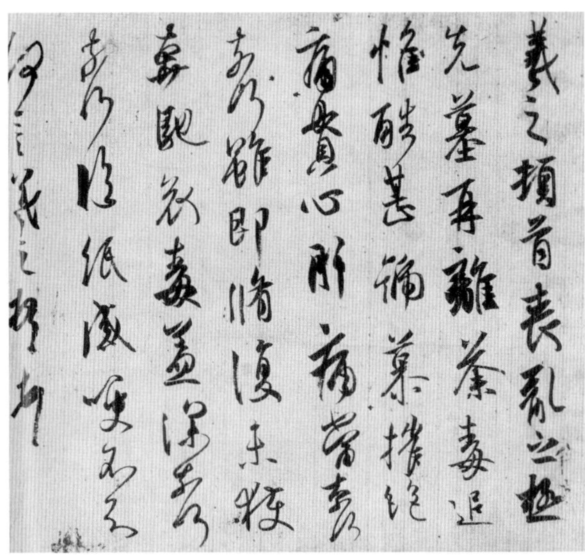

Picture 59 *Sāng Luàn Tiè* (a letter of grief and indignation to Wang's friend informing him that the tombs of Wang Xizhi's ancestors were destroyed by the army). Wang Xizhi, Jin dynasty

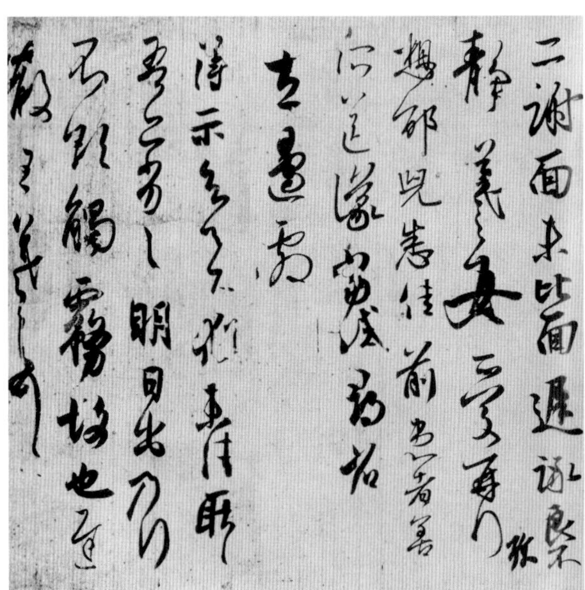

Picture 60 *Èr Xiè Tiè* (a letter that informed a friend of not having met Xie An and Xie Wan recently) and Dé Shì Tiè (a letter of reply that showed Wang's concern for his friend's health). Wang Xizhi, Jin dynasty

the brush maintained both the control and aesthetics required by human vision, the main focus of humans must have tended toward the "convenience" of manipulating the brush by hand, and creating and perfecting "fǎ."

Vision then depended on "fǎ" and was subject to the constraints of "fǎ."

In view of this, I generalize it as the process of "wánfǎ (完法, completing the standard/method)."

CHAPTER 29

Engraving Wang Xizhi's Calligraphy in Their Minds—"Shàng Fǎ (尚法, Upholding the Method)"

Unfortunately, so few authentic works were left for future generations at the pinnacle of the Wei and Jin dynasties. There are two main reasons for this.

First, in the Wei and Jin dynasties, the erection of monuments was forbidden, so only a few stone carvings remained; even if there were, they were only a handful.

Second, the only thing used by calligraphers to write on was jiān (缣, thin silk) and paper, and the life span of jiān and paper was only a thousand years. How could they survive until today? The only authentic Jin-dynasty calligraphy we can see is jìn jiǎn (晋简, bamboo or wooden slips of the Jin dynasty) or a few remnants of ancient paper.

The Southern dynasties advocated writing on tiè (帖, a book containing models of handwriting or painting for learners to copy). Therefore, the era remained the time of Wang Xizhi and Wang Xianzhi. Their writing styles were popular throughout the Eastern Jin as well as Southern dynasties. In the Northern dynasty, kǎi fǎ (楷法, law of regular script) prevailed, leaving numerous stone carvings to be appreciated. About a decade ago, a friend of mine said to me: "Between the stone tablets in the Han dynasty and those in the Northern Wei dynasty, there seemed a emptiness in the period of transition, with no stone tablets but cursive script or running hand. What was the missing part"? This question inspired me.

The lineage of inheritance has been clear and identifiable from the bamboo or wooden slips in the Han dynasty to the cursive and semi-cursive script in the Wei and Jin dynasties, up until the writing style of the Sui and Tang dynasties. I firmly believe that the lineage of inheritance is coherent, and the missing part is due to the "ban on the erection of monuments in the Wei and Jin dynasties." To put it in another way, the ancient people paid close attention to the neatness and solemnity of characters when carving monuments; therefore, it would be most appropriate to inscribe regular script on monuments. Zheng Biao in the Yuan dynasty said in yǎn jí (衍极, *On the Evolution of Chinese Calligraphy*): "Since the Wei and Jin dynasties the cursive and semi-cursive script had been written only on simple thin pieces of wood or bamboo slips. Regular script alone was adopted in stone carvings." We have the impression that only regular script was written in the "stone tablets of the Wei" period, that was because cursive and semi-cursive script were not suitable for stone tablets. As long as we refer to the difference between the solemnity of Han stele and casualty of Hanjiān (wooden and bamboo slips), we would find that it's been a long tradition for ancients to inscribe regular script alone into steles.

Or we can take a look at the paper remnants of the Jin-dynasty calligraphy (Picture 61) unearthed from Loulan (楼兰, an ancient kingdom from the second century BC, in today's Xinjiang Autonomous Region). Although it's not written by any well-known calligrapher or scholar, it immediately brings to mind the famous *Píngfù Tiè* (a letter that extended Lu's regards to a heavily ill friend) by Lu Ji (Picture 62). And then compare them with the copy by the Tang people, we could believe that the calligraphy style of the Jin people is truly so.

One surprising thing is the epitaph and inscription on the memorial tablet within a tomb unearthed in Xinjiang Autonomous Region from Gāochāng (a city in northwest Xinjiang near the city of Turpan today) Period. Thanks to many tombstones where the words were written in ink but not engraved, they provide us with the "authentic writing" and the original features of the "stele" at that time. Since Gāochāng was located in the far northwest of China; though the imperial court of the Jin dynasty had moved south, it still intactly retained the legacy of the Wei and Jin dynasties, which was similar to the style of calligraphy in the Southern dynasties (Picture 63).

The Tang dynasty was the golden age of calligraphy, and the Tang emperors enjoyed the reputation of being adept at calligraphy. Along with political, economic, and cultural advancement, it was commonly known as the "The glorious Tang dynasty." As Emperor Taizong (Táng tàizōng 唐太宗, 598–649) worshipped Wang Xizhi's calligraphy, the imperial government spent heavily on searching for the authentic works of Wang Xizhi. They "obtained and purchased 290 pieces of Wang's genuine work of semi-cursive script which were collected in seventy volumes; 200 pieces of cursive script collected in 80 volumes," including the "peerless" *Preface to the Collection of Poems Composed at the Orchid Pavilion* (兰亭序, commonly known as *Lántíng Xù*). Emperor Taizong then ordered Wei Zheng, Yu Shinan, Chu Suiliang, Feng Chengsu, Zhao Mo among others to identify the authenticity and to copy Wang's handwriting with shuānggōu kuò tián (双钩廓填, a method of tracing or outline and fill-in: the calligraphers outlined the silhouettes of each character and filled

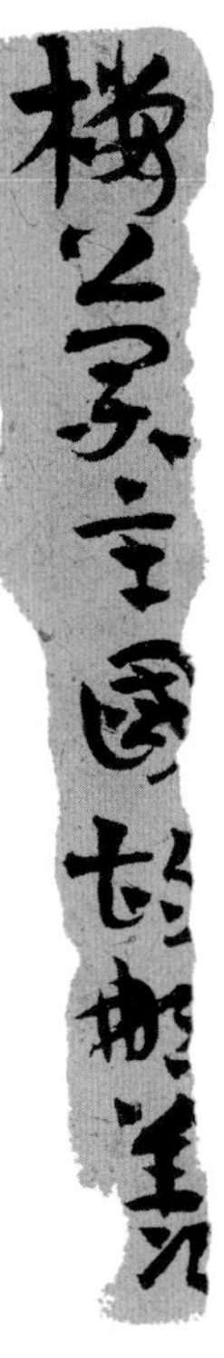

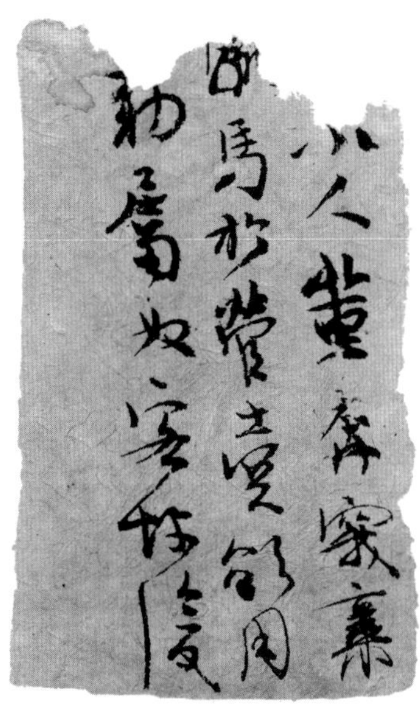

Picture 61 Relics of calligraphic works, Jin dynasty

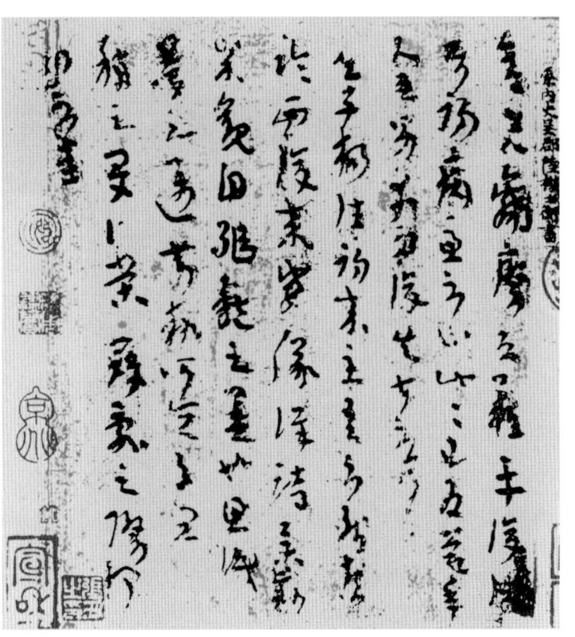

Picture 62 *Píngfù Tiē*, Lu Ji, Jin dynasty

in the outlines with ink). Emperor Taizong admired Wang's work so much that the original *Preface to the Collection of Poems Composed at the Orchid Pavilion* (or *Lántíng Xù*) was said to be buried with the emperor in his Zhao Mausoleum (昭陵 Zhāo Líng). The rest of the original works could not be well preserved to this day even if they did exist. The earliest copies of Wang's writing that we now see were copied by the Tang people, who deserve a lot of credit for the inheritance of calligraphy.

Opinions varied concerning the authenticity of Wang's calligraphy among later generations. I believe that if it is a copy by a Tang calligrapher,

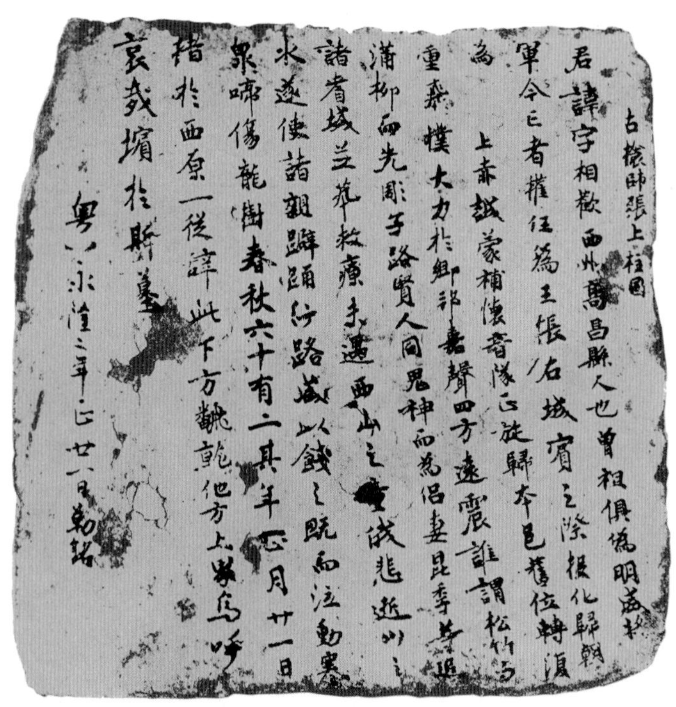

Picture 63 *Epitaph of Zhang Xianghuan* (Zhāng Xiānghuān Mù biǎo), unearthed at Gāochāng, Northern and Southern dynasties

even if it were not a copy of Wang's authentic work, it would be the writing of a first-class master. Just take a look at the work of Emperor Taizong himself (Picture 64), the rigorous regular script of Tang-dynasty calligraphers Ōuyáng Xún 欧阳询 (Picture 65) and Liǔ Gōngquán 柳公权 (Picture 66), the copy works of Wang Xizhi's authentic *Preface to the Collection of Poems Composed at the Orchid Pavilion* (or *Lanting Xu*) by Yú Shìnán 虞世南 (Picture 67), Chǔ Suìliáng 褚遂良 (Picture 68) and Féng Chéngsù 冯承素 (Picture 69), the sophisticated semi-cursive of Yán

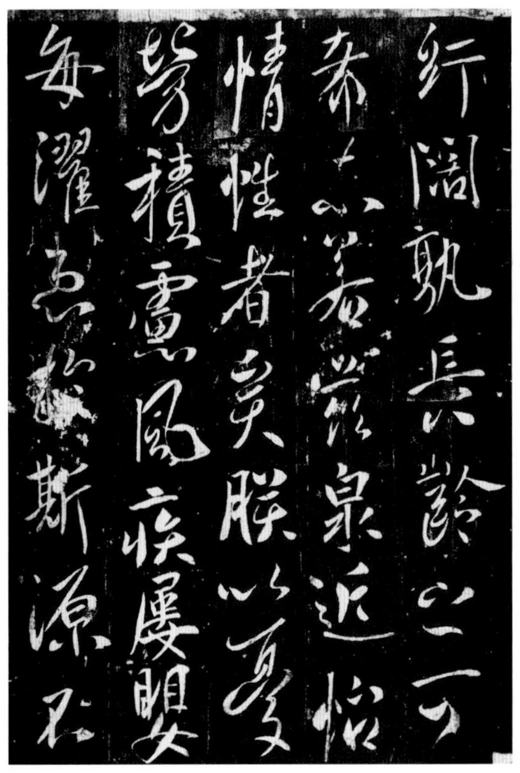

Picture 64 Wēnquán Míng (温泉铭, semi-cursive tablet inscriptions that extolled the hot springs in Lishan Mountain) (part), Li Shimin (Emperor Taizong), Tang dynasty

Zhēnqīng 颜真卿 (Picture 70), the incisive and wild cursive of Zhāng Xù 张旭 (Picture 71) and Huái Sù 怀素 (Picture 72), and also the treatise of handwriting at that time. You would find that calligraphers of the Tang dynasty imitated Wang's characters and followed him carefully. It is evident that the Tang calligraphers knew Wang's characters by heart and Wang's calligraphy was engraved in their mind.

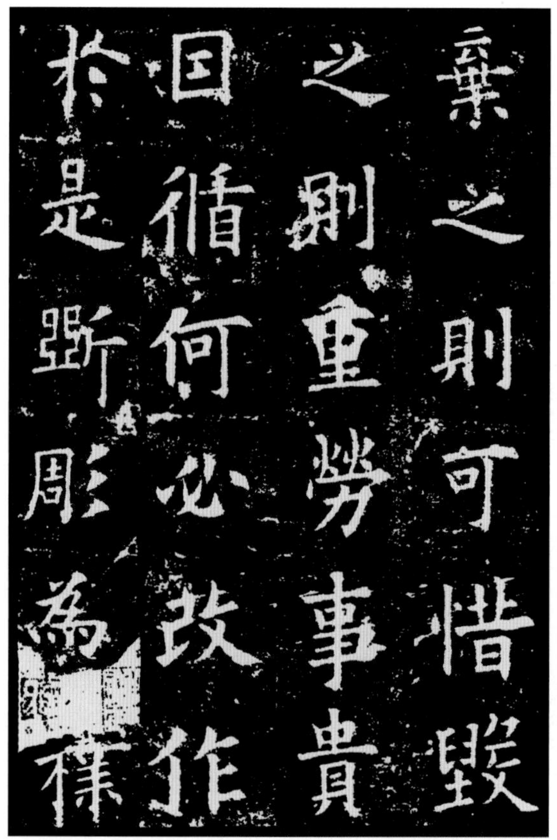

Picture 65 *Stele of the Jiucheng Palace Regular script* (inscriptions that introduced the history of Jiucheng Palace and extolled its magnificence) (part), Ouyang Xun, Tang dynasty

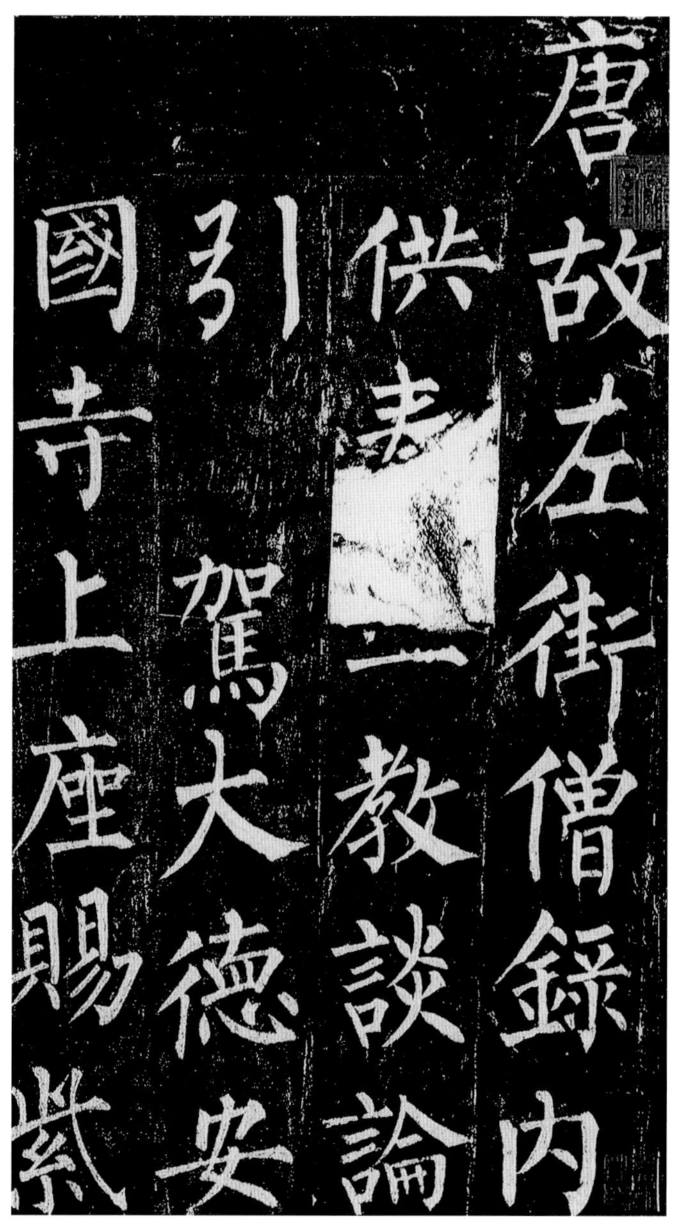

Picture 66 *Stele of the Xuanmi Pagoda* in Regular script (inscriptions that commemorated the courteous reception of the great Buddhist monk Duan Fu during the reign of Emperors Dezong, Shunzong and Xianzong, and celebrated Duan Fu's accomplishments) (part), Liu Gongquan,

After wánfǎ (completing the standard/method) in the Wei and Jin dynasties, the next step was undoubtedly the popularization and application of the standard.

In the Tang dynasty, fǎ (法, standard or method) was pushed forward to the forefront of the world's attention. For example, calligraphy was the main subject of focus in the establishment of the imperial examination system; when selecting officials, the candidates were required to be "calligraphic talents" who "can write beautiful regular style." The world-known Sun Guoting's Shū Pǔ (书谱, *Treatise on Calligraphy*), Zhang Huaiguan's *Shu Duan* (书断, *Judgments on Calligraphers*), Zhang Yanyuan's *Fashu Yaolu* (法书要录 Fǎshū yàolù, *Compendium of Calligraphy*) and other calligraphy histories and treatises, as well as a group of outstanding calligraphers including Ouyang Xun, Yu Shinan, Zhang Xu, Chu Suiliang, Liu Gongquan and Yan Zhenqing among others, had helped the peak of the "fǎ" of the Wei and Jin dynasties to have sustained five or six hundred years.

This is surely a process of "shàngfǎ (尚法, upholding the method)."

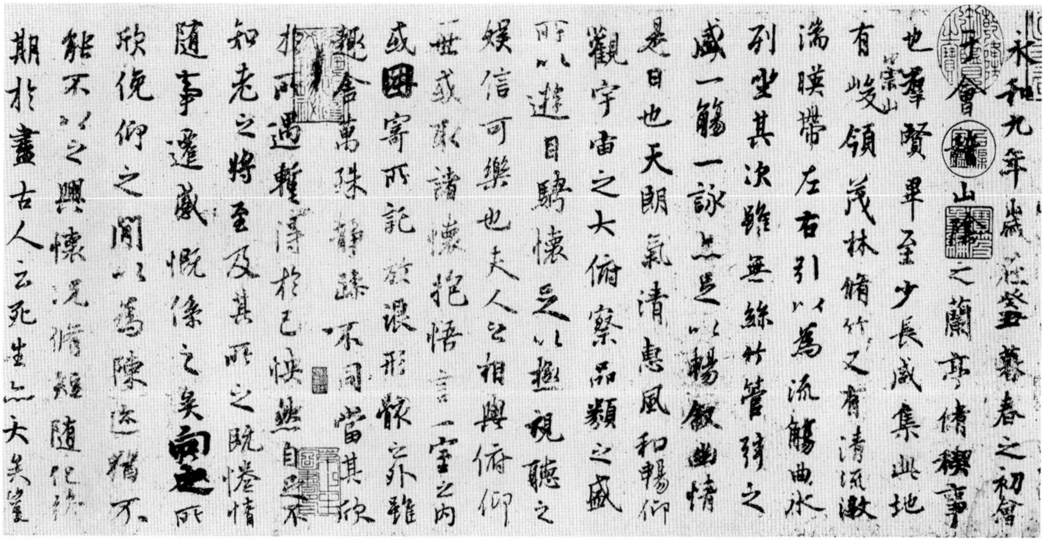

Picture 67 A facsimile edition of Wang Xizhi's *Preface to the Collection of Poems Composed at the Orchid Pavilion* (or *Lanting Xu*) (part), Yu Shinan, Tang dynasty

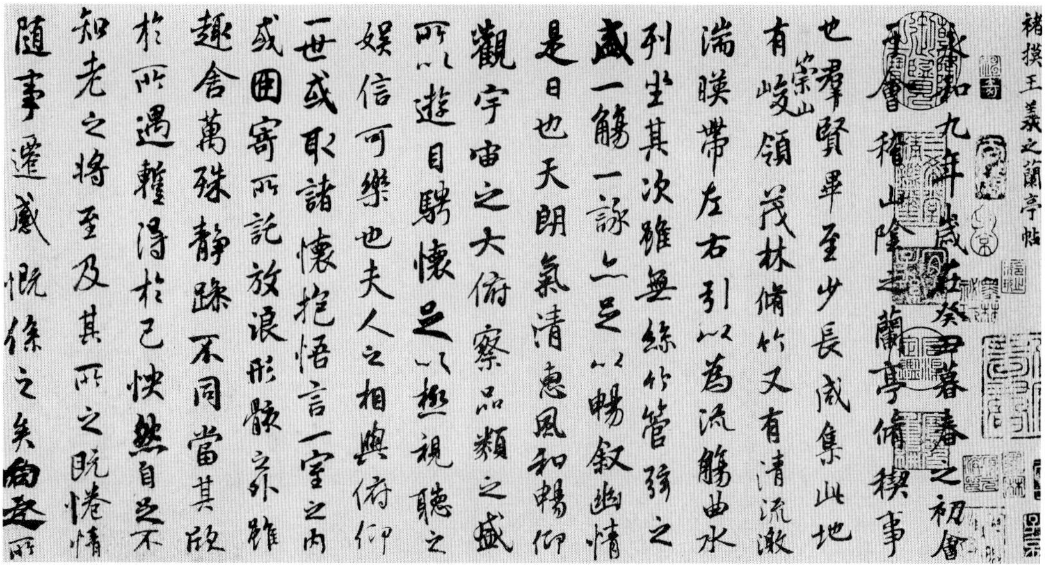

Picture 68 A facsimile edition of Wang Xizhi's *Preface to the Collection of Poems Composed at the Orchid Pavilion* (or *Lanting Xu*) (part), Chu Suiliang, Tang dynasty

Picture 69 A facsimile edition of Wang Xizhi's *Preface to the Collection of Poems Composed at the Orchid Pavilion* (or *Lanting Xu*) (part), Feng Chengsu, Tang dynasty

Picture 70 *Ji Zhi Wen Gao* (*Draft to the Memory of His Heroically Sacrificed Nephew Yan Jiming*) (part), Yan Zhenqing, Tang dynasty

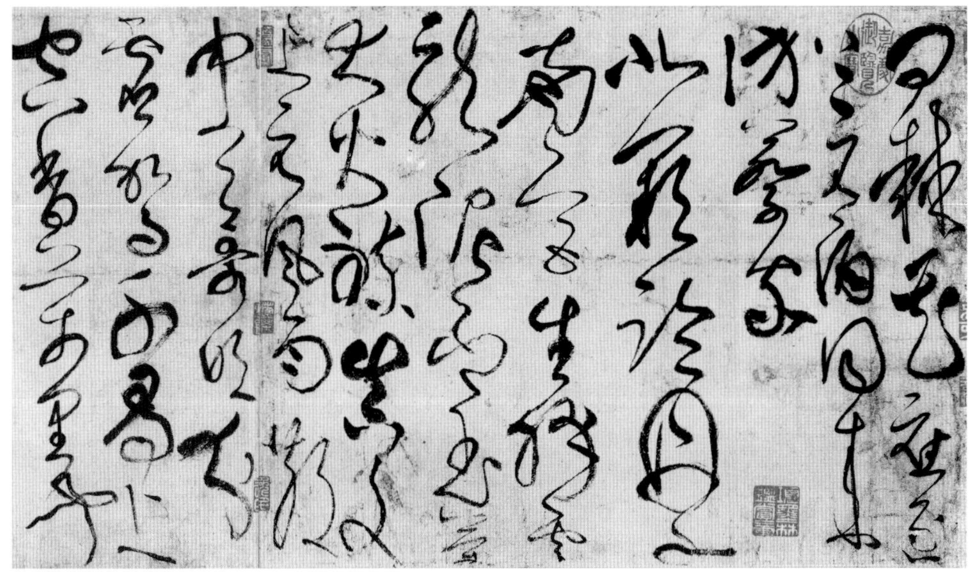

Picture 71 *Gushi Sitie* (*Four Ancient Poems*) (part), Zhang Xu, Tang dynasty

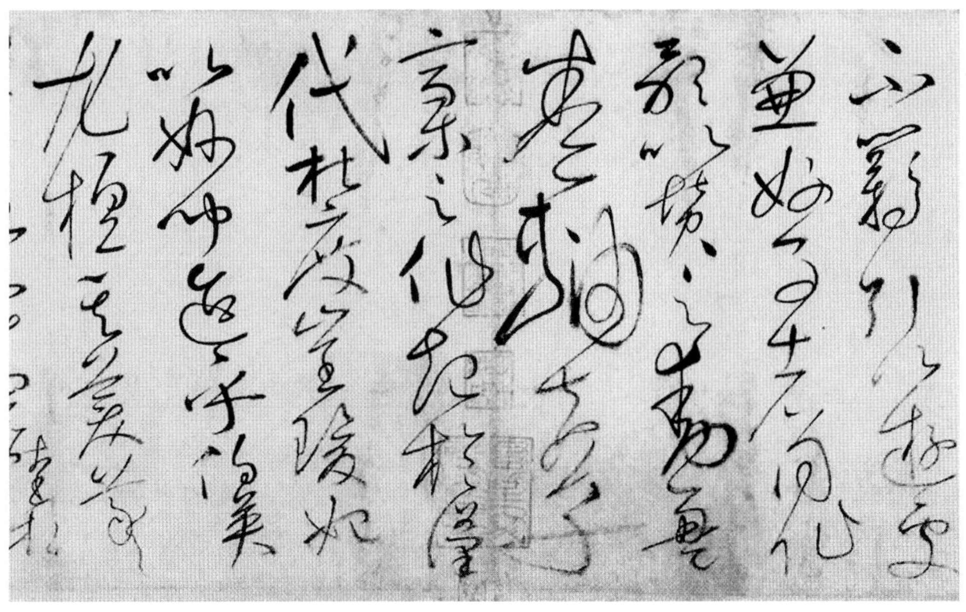

Picture 72 *Zi Xu Tie* (*My Narration*) (part), Huai Su, Tang dynasty

CHAPTER 30

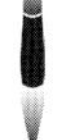

"While the Structure of Calligraphy and the Arrangement of Dots and Strokes Change with the Times, the Use of the Brush Remains the Same for Thousands of Years"—"Biànfǎ (Changing the Method)"

After that, what is the downward sloping surface on the right?

As a result of the use of the "fǎ," the subsequent result is nothing more than the shape and posture of the character.

In the process of "wánfǎ," the shape of the character is, in principle, determined by the convenience of gesture, in which vision does not play a dominant role. Once the rules are formed, the task of creating the shape of the character is over; "fǎ" is no longer the main focus. In contrast, under the premise of applying the standard and obeying the rules, the change in the style and form of the Chinese characters gradually turns into the main focus.

At this point, vision changes from "being subordinate" to the status of "being dominant."

This is a very important concept.

Liang Songzhai in the Qing dynasty said: "The Jin dynasty worshipped poise and charm; Tang worshipped fǎ (standard); Song advocated interest and unruliness; Yuan and Ming advocated posture." Well said.

Once again, I'd like to quote the incisive words by Zheng Biao in the Yuan dynasty in *Yan Ji* (*On the Evolution of Chinese Calligraphy*, 衍极 yǎnjí): In terms of characters, "The fǎ (power generation) lies in the palm and fingers within for characters no larger than one inch; for characters larger than one inch, the fǎ extends to the elbow and wrist. Palm and finger show the normalcy of fǎ; elbow and wrist show the change of fǎ. Tiē (帖, a book containing models of handwriting or painting for learners to copy) in the Wei and Jin dynasties were covered with words created by palm and fingers." The "palm-finger method" in the Wei and Jin dynasties continued for four hundred years, and absorbed the "elbow wrist method."

Before the Song dynasty, there was no such thing as "wànfǎ (wrist technique)." As paper was held in the hand to write, once the "finger-palm method" was operated, the wrist became immovable, without being affected. It was not until the Yuan dynasty that Chen Yizeng's *Crucial Tips for Members of Imperial Academy* mentioned the "wrist method," which was summarized into three types: "Zhěnwàn (wrist pillowing on the hand) refers to the right wrist pillowing on the left hand. Tíwàn (lifting the wrist) refers to the elbow lying on the àn (案) and the wrist half-resting in the air.Xuánwàn (hanging the wrist) is the most powerful when the wrist is hanging in the air."

Chen discusses "wánfǎ" following the posture of "stirring the lamp wick" and "finger method," which refers to the three states of the wrist when the brush is turned and fingers are moved. All of the three states are relative to writing on the table, not referring to moving the wrist without moving fingers.

Zhěnwàn (wrist pillowing on the hand) (Picture 73), which prevents the right wrist from moving, is mainly controlled by the palm, and is limited to writing words in the size of a square cùn (寸). However, an immovable wrist is not conducive to the horizontal use of the brush, but is convenient for the vertical use of the brush. So, the shape of words written with the "wrist pillowing on the hand" method is necessarily narrow and long. Gao Ershi (1903–1977), a contemporary Nanjing calligrapher, applied this method, which is today rarely used among calligraphers.

Tíwàn (lifting the wrist) (Picture 74) refers to turning the brush and moving fingers with the elbow as the fulcrum, which is suitable for writing characters with the size of a duck egg.

Xuánwàn (hanging the wrist) (Picture 75) refers to turning the brush and moving fingers with the arm as the fulcrum, which is suitable for writing larger characters.

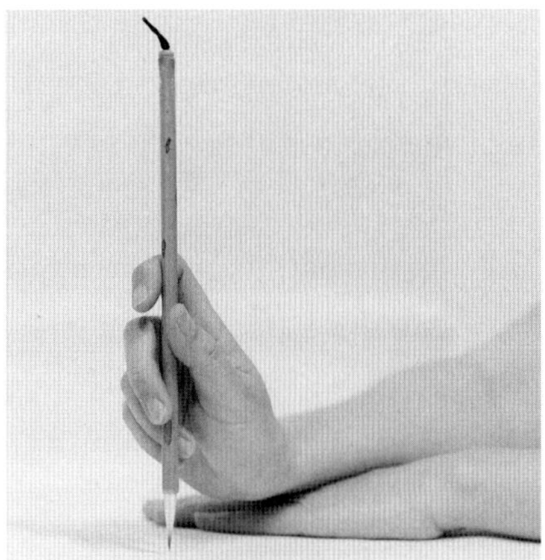

Picture 73 Zhěnwàn (wrist pillowing on the hand)

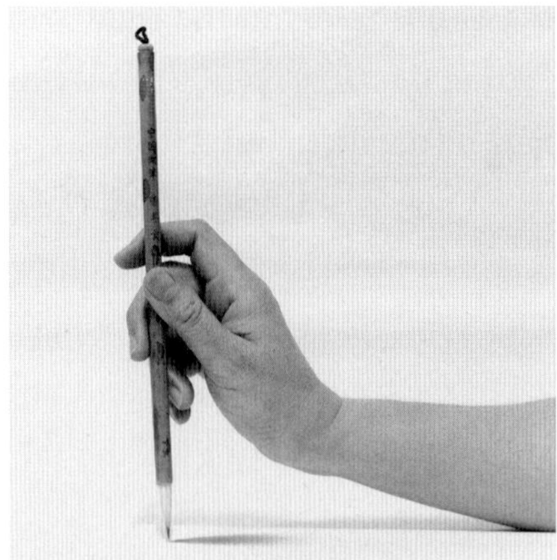

Picture 74 Tíwàn (lifting the wrist)

Wrist assists finger-moving in the latter two "wrist methods," for which the ancient calligraphers often said, "The structure of small characters should be stretched." "Small characters" are all "within a cùn," applying the "palm-finger method"; "large characters" are all "beyond a cùn," applying the "elbow-wrist method." In other words, the method of writing small characters by turning the brush and moving fingers, coupled with the elbow and wrist, contributes to the completion of large characters. Thanks to the table that supports the elbow, Song callighraphers found that even if their fingers did not move enough to write the words, the wrist could make up for it.

Zhu Lüzhen said, "Fǎ comes from fingers." Only when the fingers are moved can it be called fǎ. "Elbow and wrist form the change of fǎ," meaning that both elbow and wrist used are still in the category of "fǎ." If we do not move our fingers, it means we cannot "change fǎ," so it becomes "no fǎ."

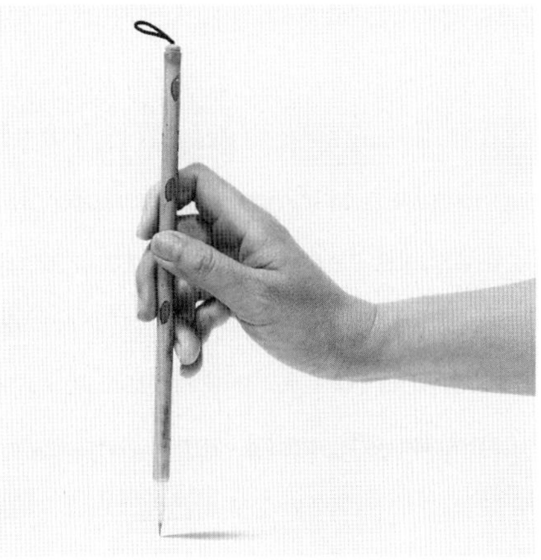

Picture 75 Xuánwàn (hanging the wrist)

This is an important watershed regarding "fă."

Well, so far, let me classify the process: since tables and chairs have been widely applied for writing in the Song dynasty till the beginning of the Qing dynasty (roughly eight hundred years), the brush vertical to the surface turned into being vertical to the desktop; "lifting the wrist" turned into "making wrist flat." This process seemed to be called "change of fă."

Once there is any "change" in "fă," plus the three "wrist methods," the shapes of the characters are also varied. In the era of "bianfa," we can see the different styles of Emperor Huizong of Song, Mi Fu and Huang Tingjian (Picture 76), Su Shi (Picture 77), Xianyu Shu (Picture 78), Zhao Mengfu (Picture 79), Zhu Zhishan, Wen Zhengming and Xu Wei (Picture 80), Song Ke (Picture 81), Xing Tong, Dong Qichang, Huang Daozhou, Zhang Ruitu, Ni Yuanlu, Wang Duo and Fu Shan. They gave full play to their respective visual talents and brush turning habits. Besides, the masters were adept at writing on both raw paper and processed paper, with long fēng (锋, (sharp stroke) or short fēng brushes and with soft hair or hard hair brushes. Their writings covered an endless variety of forms and styles.

Yang Weizhen, a Yuan dynasty calligrapher, is worth mentioning. The characters in his *Alms-Giving for Zhenjing Temple* (真镜庵募缘疏卷 zhēn jìng ān mù yuán shū juàn) (Picture 82) are often taken as an example or precedent for "deformation," "exaggeration," or even "innovation." In fact, he adopted thetíwànmethod to infiltrate zhāngcǎo strokes, and moved his fingers to exert force, which was a fierce and free approach.

In *Portrait of Ni Yunlin* drawn by Zhang Yu (Picture 83) collected in the "Taipei Palace Museum," Ni is seated on a bed with his back by a quanji, holding paper in his left hand and a brush in his right. The

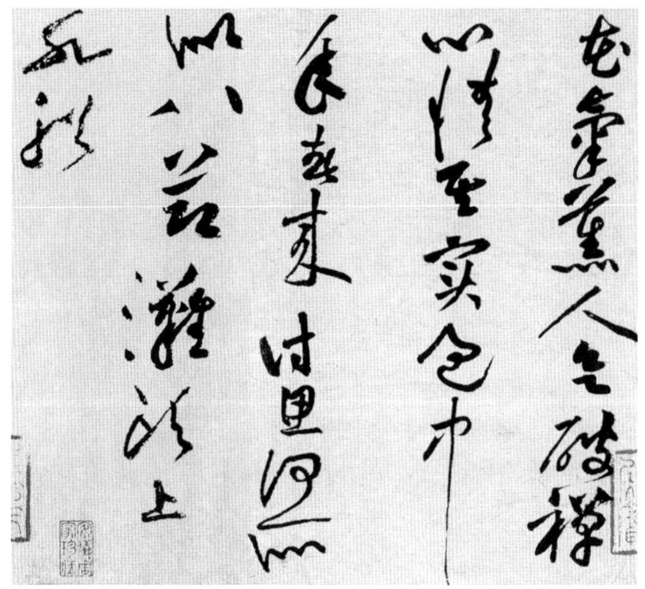

Picture 76 *Seven-Character Poem* (part), Huang Tingjian, Song dynasty

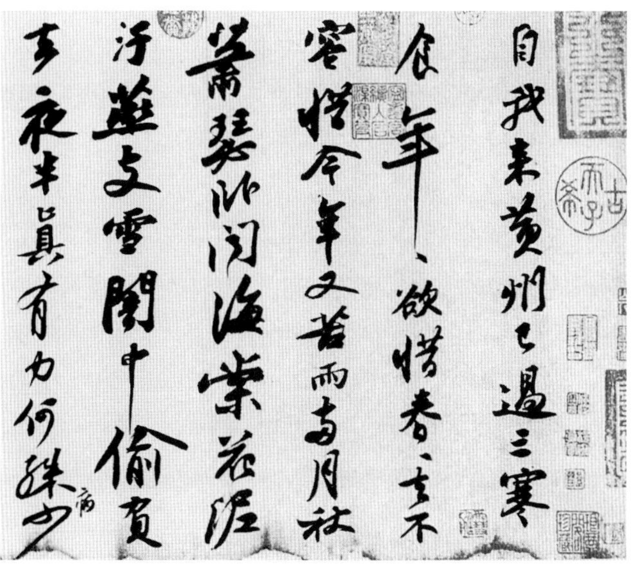

Picture 77 *Poem on the Hanshi Festival* (the day before Pure Brightness when only cold food is served) *in Huangzhou* (part), Su Shi, Song dynasty

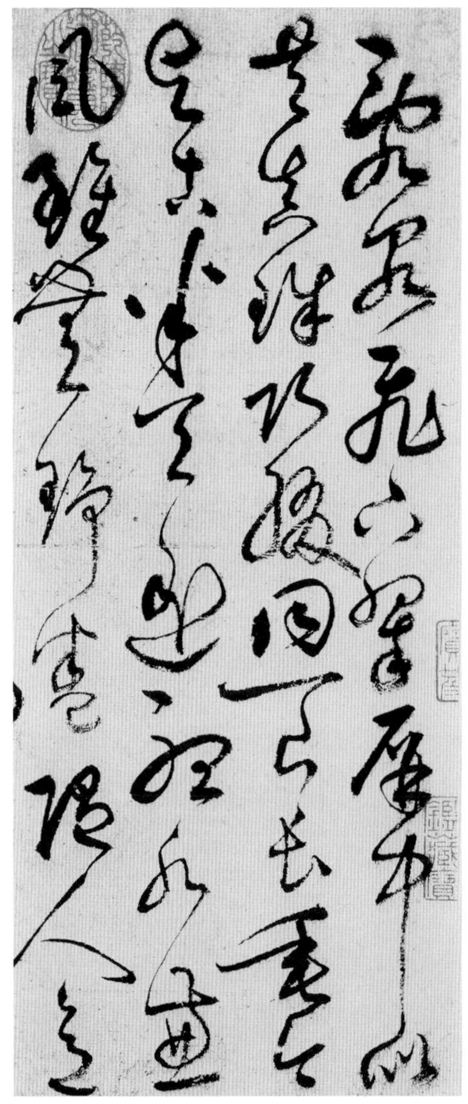

Picture 78 *Han Yu's Explanations for Studies* (*Jinxue jie*) (part), Xianyu Shu, Yuan dynasty

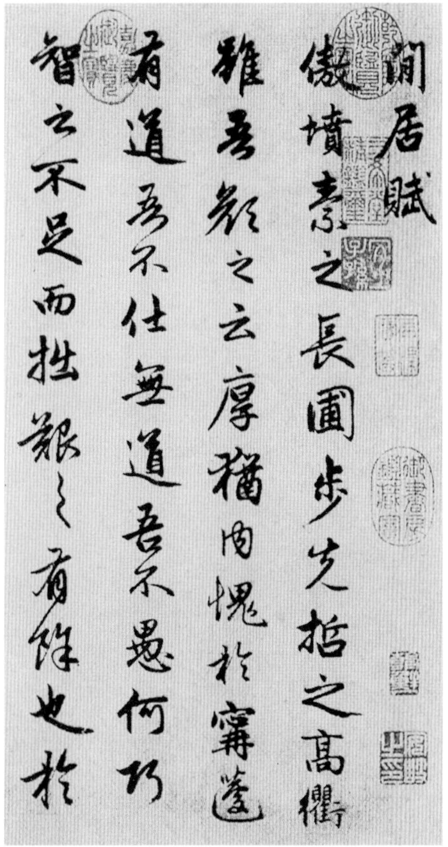

Picture 79 *Ode on Leisurely Living* (part), Zhao Mengfu

Picture 80 *Seven-Character Poem*, Xu Wei, Ming dynasty

Picture 81 *Liu Zhen's Poem on Attending a Banquet*, Song Ke, Ming dynasty

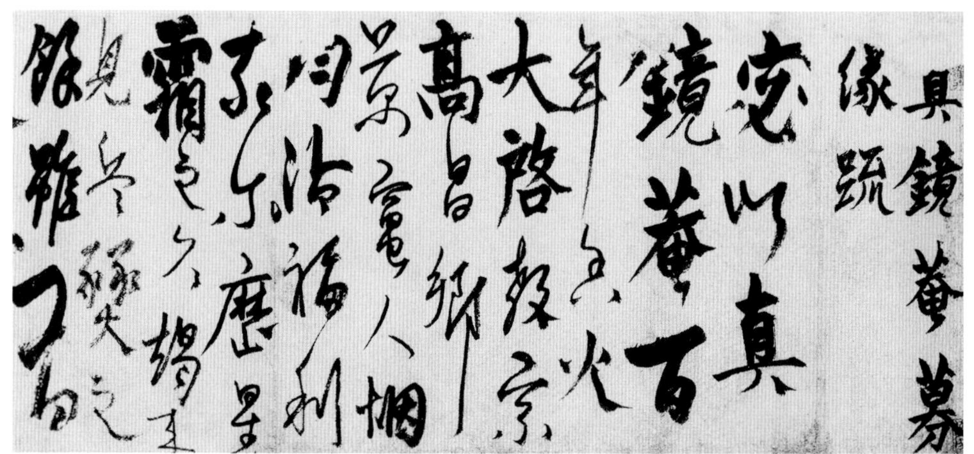

Picture 82 *Alms-Giving for Zhenjing Temple* (part), Yang Weizhen, Yuan dynasty

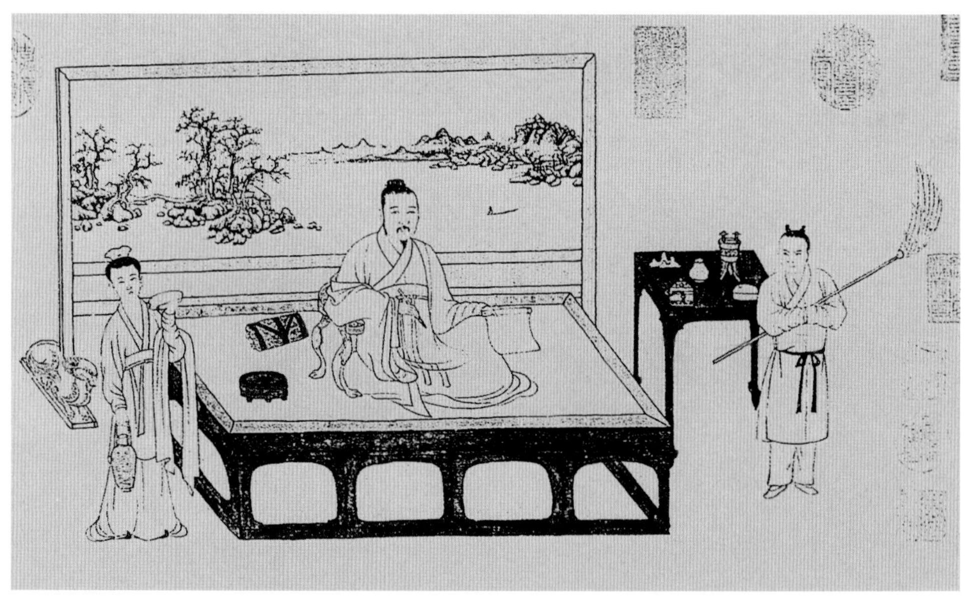

Picture 83 *Portrait of Ni Yunlin* (part), Zhang Yu, Yuan dynasty

painting depicts vividly the Wei-Jin style of writing maintained by the literati of the Yuan dynasty.

Ni Yunlin (Picture 84) has a somewhat peculiar use of brush, with a particularly distinctive feature. The structure of his characters is not smooth, and even not big. The characters are horizontal and vertical as they should be. They might be written in the posture as shown in Picture 83.

These great calligraphers, whether they were called self-conceited men or no matter how unrestrained they seemed, they still adhered to the last tradition of turning the brush and moving fingers and wrist. Let us revisit the earnest instruction of Zhao Mengfu, "While the structure of calligraphy and the arrangement of dots and strokes change with the times, the use of the brush has remained the same for thousands of years."

Picture 84 *Poem on Seclusive Mind*, Ni Yunlin, Yuan dynasty

CHAPTER 31

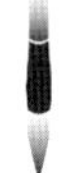

The Fact I Least Want to Admit—Without Fǎ

Since people neither turned brush nor moved fingers, they have begun to control the shape of characters completely based on vision. The change should be considered a process "without fǎ."

On second thought, I really couldn't bear using the word "wúfǎ (无法, no method)." However, it is hard to find the exact word to describe it.

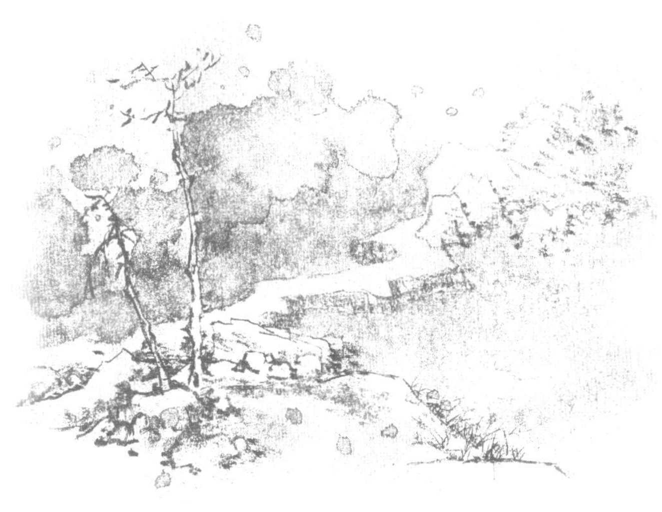

CHAPTER 32

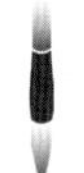

Is Calligraphy a Visual Art?

Calligraphy undoubtedly has been completely classified into "visual art." The judgement seems cut and dried; perhaps no one has doubted it so far. As far as I can see, it is not that simple.

Shall we classify calligraphy in this way?

Characters are made up of "liù shū (六书, six types of forming and using Chinese characters)." Although one of the types is "pictographs," characters belong to the category of words. What calligraphy leaves for future generations, whether in brushwork or spirit, is true record through ink, which is undoubtedly visual perception. In this sense, calligraphy is indeed a "visual art."

However, the process of calligraphy brushwork, that is, the skill of brush turning by hand, is precisely the core of calligraphy. Ancients always view that "heart and hand express emotion," "heart and hand are two in one," and "using the heart instead of the eye," indicating that in the writing, vision is effective but not decisive, because the hand's brush-turning skills virtually control and limit vision. In this sense, could calligraphy be considered a complete "visual art"?

I therefore doubt it.

In fact, ancients have described the cooperation between calligraphic vision and hand clearly and thoroughly. We just failed to delve into it.

I remember having talked to a friend who was then engaged in science. He was puzzled and insisted that I explained it "clearly" before leaving. I had to obey. We talked from when the sun was above in the sky till the sunset. Finally, we straightened it out. I even talked myself hoarse.

I know well that it is really difficult to explain it clearly.

That's why I mentioned the example of Nine Linked Rings Puzzle (jiǔ liánhuán, 九连环) before just to inform you of the many other important issues concerned.

Now, I will come to them one by one.

CHAPTER 33

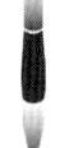

Decrypting "Water Stains on the Wall," "Crack in the Wall," "Twirling the Hairpin," "Painting with an Awl on the Sand," and "The Seal Stamping into the Clay"

Having clarified the origin and development of calligraphy, and after repeated trials and experiments, let's turn back to the ancient treatise on calligraphy. Those famous sayings and descriptions are precise and clear, which are totally different from what people comment as "shrouded in mystery."

I'd like to give some examples, hoping to correct them.

The most frequently told ones are "water stains on the wall," "crack in the wall," "twirling the hairpin," "painting with an awl on the sand," and "the seal stamping into the clay."

"Water stains on the wall" and "crack in the wall" were quoted by Huai Su and Yan Zhenqing when they commented on cursive script. "Huai Su said, 'I see many strange peaks in the summer clouds, and I should always learn from them. The delighted part is like birds coming out of woods and the frightened snake sneaking into the grass. Then I see the crack in the wall, which is natural.' Zhenqing said, 'How about comparing it to water stains on the wall?'"

Literally, "crack in the wall" refers to the trace of wall crack. "Water stains on the wall" refers to the traces of rain flowing down from top to bottom. They both mean the natural trajectory left by an object after being stressed. From the perspective of brushwork, it means that once you exert your strength, the strokes will follow the trend. The "force generated" by "water stains on the wall" obviously stands for the natural trend formed by turning the brush. However, "crack in the wall" sets no certain trend for the strokes. You can generate force by either turning left or right; it depends on how you "generate the force."

The "hairpin (钗股 chāi gǔ)" is an ancient metal tool in the shape of a semicircle. "Twirling the hairpin" is the brush style of Zhang Xu (also known as Zhang Changshi for his official post), and it mainly refers to the mellow and full brush turning in cursive script. After turning the brush for a circle or more, the brush is halted powerfully, leading to a "curb (勒 lēi)" or "bundle (束 shù)." And the end of the brush after a sudden halt often looks like a broken hairpin with uneven fracture.

The theory of "painting with an awl on the sand" and "the seal stamping into the clay" can be found in Yan Zhenqing's account of Zhang Xu's words: "I once asked Chu Suiliang (the Duke of Henan), he replied that 'Writing with the brush as if you are stamping seal in the clay.' I couldn't understand his words, until later I visited Jiangdao Island and saw the flat sand and serene ground. The scene did arouse my desire to write. So, I used the sharp edge to draw and write. Its precipitous appeal was bright, radiant and enchanting. Then I realized that using the brush was like painting with an awl on the sand. You must hide its spearhead to render the painting composed and calm. When using the brush, try to make the stroke powerful and profound as if the force penetrated through the paper, then we could call it ultimate success."

People of later generations continued to say that his words described the "hidden edge or hidden spearhead (藏锋 cángfēng)," but this was only one side of the story. In the past, the brush hair was made of hard hair or jiānháo (兼毫, brush that was made by combining hair from two different types of animals) such as rabbit hair. As the brush core was hard, the tip of the brush was always wrapped when turning the brush, especially in the state of dry brush (枯笔 kū bǐ). "The ink is gradually drying from both sides till the center hair is as thin as silk, the ink is crystal clear, and on the other side of the paper the stroke is so thin as if it were painted with needle." The sharp and hard "awl (锥 zhuī)" refers to the hard core. When painted on the sand, the sand goes towards both sides and the line painted by the awl is centered, deep and thin. "Painting with an awl on the sand" also refers to the typical stroke that often occurs when a hard-hair brush is turned, namely, a thin line in the center. As early as in *Jiǔ Shì* (九势, *Nine Types of Force*), Cai Yong clearly stated that "Let the tip of the brush always move within the middle of the stroke." The "fēibái shū script (飞白书, also termed cursive seal which features white parts exposed in strokes as if they are written with a dry brush)" created by Cai confirms that "fēibái" is the dry brush, and often when the brush is dry, a thin line can be seen in the middle of the stroke. This is the other side that has long been neglected.

So is "yìnyìnní (印印泥, the seal stamping into the clay)." The seal is made of stone or copper and the lines of characters engraved are hard, while the ink pad is soft. When the seal is pressed upon the ink pad, the ink pad will overflow to both sides along the center of the lines, just like "zhuī huà shā (锥画沙, literally means an awl on the sand; when the tip of the awl is drawn into the sand, there forms a concave middle line)." Therefore, the ancients always talked about yìnyìnní (印印泥, the seal stamping into the clay) and (zhuīhuàshā, painting with an awl on the sand) together.

The famous saying of Cai Yong, however, has been repeatedly misunderstood by later generations. Since the late Qing dynasty, calligraphers have emphasized zhōngfēng (中锋, centered tip) and thought that if the brush were held perpendicular to the paper, "the tip of the brush would always be within the middle of the stroke," which is a big mistake.

Only "lì fēng (利锋, sharp tip)" could bring out "precipitous appeal." Similar to "yìnyìnní (印印泥, the seal stamping into the clay)," "zhuīhuàshā (锥画沙, painting with an awl on the sand)" attempts to penetrate the force "through the paper." This kind of force arises from "qǔ shì (取势, taking force)" when one turns the brush, rather than from making one's "effort (力lì)." In the Tang dynasty, Lin Yun described Lu Zhao's words: "I learn calligraphy in seeking the lì (力, force), but I didn't know that the lìof using the brush doesn't lie in exerting the strength; if we made too much effort in exerting strength, the brush would be dead."

As mentioned in the previous chapter, the force generated by "qǔshì" is undoubtedly violent, bold, swift and handy. No matter in which chapter the ancients discussed calligraphy, you could find everywhere metaphors describing the swift writing and the exaggerated force when using brush, such as "Warrior stretching a hook," "drawing a hundredweight-bow," "a stone falling from a perilous peak," "lightning accompanied by peals of thunder," and the character "八" (bā) explained in the *Eight Principles of Yong*. In the Southern Song dynasty, Jiang Kui said, "Speed makes strength," indicating that the precipitous "qǔshì" came from speed. The rapid brush using in "qǔshì" can be observed from Huai Su's poem: "There are dozens of pink-walled corridors, which relieve my stressful and unhappy state. Suddenly, I shout out three or five times, and the wall is covered with thousands of words." The ancients enjoyed writing on the wall, because no paper could be as large. The posture of writing on the wall is most suitable for generating force when turning the brush; and the space is large enough for the arm to move up and down, which is most conducive to fully express the temperament. But how could there be so many walls to write on? Calligraphers could only do so occasionally.

The ancients always commented that "calligraphy isqiú (遒, vigorous and sturdy) and mèi (媚, charming)," and this word "qiú (遒)" was accurately interpreted by Mr. Zhou Ruchang, the well-known scholar andhóngxué jiā (红学家, a scholar studying the novel *Dream of the Red Chamber* (*Hónglóumèng* 红楼梦) by Cao Xueqin). "Qiú (遒)" incorporates swiftness, vigor, tightness, control and crispness. It is a perfect "realm" that accurately controls the rapid force-generation. In fact, the metaphor about brushwork that ancients realized by "watching Gongsun Daniang's sword dancing" is authentic and incisive, just as the ancients described brushwork as "stirring the lamp wick," "water stains on the wall" and "the seal stamping into the clay" from other different angles of "lì."

People today refer to "lì" as tí'àn (提按, lifting and pressing)," which along with the brushwork of "centered tip" came from the late Qing dynasty. If one didn't move fingers nor turn the brush, would the only thing left to generate force be "lifting and pressing"? I deeply understand it because I have been "lifting and pressing" for twenty years, since I was a child.

People create the thickness of strokes by the force of "tí'àn," while the ancients did so by generating force through "qǔshì (取势)" of brush turning. People today don't turn their brushes but take the shape with eyesight; ancients turned their brushes and took the shape with shì (势).

These are totally two different things, and cannot be mentioned in the same breath.

There is no "tí'àn (提按, lifting and pressing)" in the ancient calligraphy dictionary.

CHAPTER 34

Q&A for "Wú chuí bù suō, wú wǎng bù shōu (无垂不缩, 无往不收) A Return Stroke is Necessary at the End of the Writing, So That the Closing Stroke is Round; Whatever Direction the Strokes Go in, There Must Be a Closing Stroke"

When people around talk about brushwork in calligraphy, "无垂不缩, 无往不收" (wú chuí bù suō, wú wǎng bù shōu, a return stroke is necessary at the end of the writing, so that the closing stroke is round; whatever direction the strokes go, there must be a closing stroke)" has become a pet phrase. This is a famous saying of Mi Fu. Later generations continued his instructions by adding, "If you want to go down, go up first; if you want to go up, go down first; if you want to go left, go right first; if you want to go right, go left first." These mysterious words have overwhelmed beginners. I was also "trained" in this way as a child.

Why should we "make" strokes in this way? It sounds laborious and unnatural. I was confused, but found no answer.

After I later figured out the principle of "brushwork," I naturally understood the meaning behind it.

Jiang Kui of the Southern Song dynasty reasonably explained: "If you have expressed your feeling to the utmost, then you should use "xuánzhēn

(悬针, dangling needle)"; if you haven't fully expressed your feeling, you need to regenerate the intention of brushwork, then you don't need to use chuí lù (垂露, dropping dew)." Mi Fu's "*wuchui busuo*" obviously refers to "dropping dew." "Wú wǎng bù shōu" (无往不收) means that whatever direction the strokes go, there must be a closing stroke. It holds a similar meaning to "wú chuí bù suō." The so-called "regenerating the intention of brushwork" means "regenerating the momentum of brush turning."

Mi Fu was explaining his own brushwork. He "regenerated the intention of brush turning" before "the momentum of the brush" was exhausted. That is to say, before the momentum is exhausted, he turns the brush once again to write the next character. Therefore, there are often traces of "link" between strokes.

In his 1982 booklet entitled *Q&A: The Art of Calligraphy*, Mr. Zhou Ruchang referred to it as "mángjiǎo (芒角, an edge formed between two strokes when turning the brush)." The term "mángjiǎo" originated from

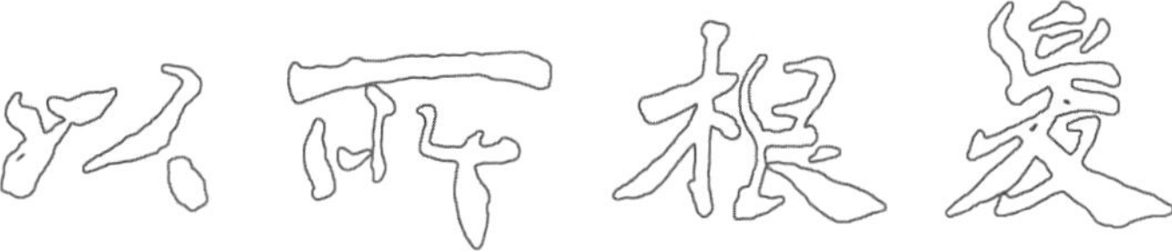

Selected characters from *Large Script of Yin Fu Jing or Natural Laws*, Chu Suiliang, Tang dynasty

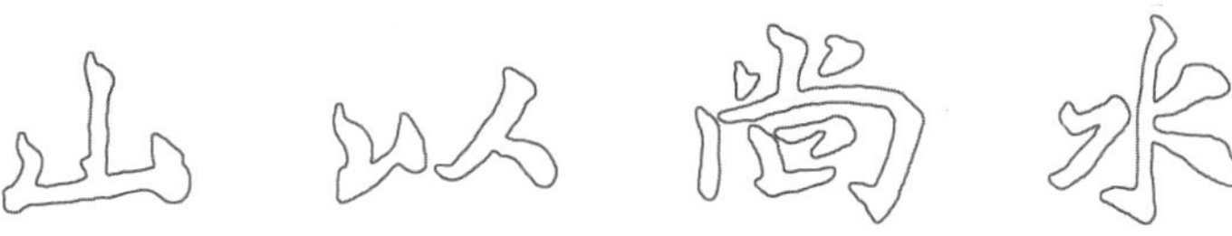

Picture 85 Selected characters from *Epigraph of Minister and Deputy Minister of Rites* (礼部侍郎, *LǐbùShìláng*), Mi Fu, Song dynasty

Emperor Wu of Liang's treatise on calligraphy: "If you hold the brush in the right manner, there will be no mángjiǎo; if you hold the brush in a loose manner, the handwriting will be weak and soft ..." Mr. Zhou pertinently added that the history of calligraphy was a "history of the gains and losses of mángjiǎo."

There is no "link" in regular script. The articulation between one stroke and another is vividly described by Huang Tingjian as "a fast horse entering a formation of a team." Wang Xizhi in *Inscription after Lady Wei's Picture of Ink Brush* said: "Paper is zhèn (阵 formation)." The metaphor of "fast horse" by Huang Tingjian must have come from the posture of "stirring the lamp wick." The "lamp wick" refers to the five fingers and the brush is the "horse," so "fast horse" must refer to the fast turning of brush. "A fast horse entering a formation of a team" means that the horse's hooves gallop outside the "formation" and "enters the formation" from the air. As for brushwork, it means that before the brush touches the paper, it has already been turned quickly and has generated force. The "link" that "regenerates the intention of brush turning" when one stroke is connected to the next stroke is often formed in the air, and the handwriting left on the paper has "expressed the feeling to the utmost" and is not "regenerated."

The "articulation" between strokes can be observed in the regular script, such as in Chu Suiliang's *Wild Goose Pagoda Saint Teaching Sequence* and *Large Script of Yin Fu Jing or Natural Laws* (Picture 85), among others. The typical slight curve on the tip of erect (竖 shù, downward stroke) and slant (撇 piě, falling leftwards) is the left bend of the previous stroke, which symbolizes the right turn next.

The reason why Sun Guoting's *Treatise on Calligraphy* (Shū Pǔ 书谱) is so "wretchedly dotted" is because "mángjiǎo" and "articulation" are everywhere. To put it bluntly, it means leaving the key and technique of brush turning on the paper as much as possible, so as to fully expose the brushwork.

As for the aforementioned "if you want to go down, go up first; if you want to go up, go down first; if you want to go left, go right first; if you want to go right, go left first," the answer could be found in the previous explanation of the brushwork of "xiàngbèi (向背)." It is about "qǔ shì (取势)" of the turn of the brush, specifically the force generated when turning the brush at the start of the stroke. The result is inevitable as long as it is based on the power of turning the brush.

For example, if a person wants to turn right, he must exert the whole body quickly to the left before the force can be generated; to throw something upward, he must first generate force downward; to throw a punch, one must first make a proper fist. This is the simplest common sense of generating power, but is too often ignored.

Nowadays, in the copybook for regular script printed for beginners, most have a "illustration chart" to explain the "standardized" strokes. The strokes are hollow and only the silhouettes of each character are outlined. According to the current understanding of "if you want to go down, go up first; if you want to go up, go down first; if you want to go left, go right first; if you want to go right, go left first," learners need to gradually fill in the outlines with ink. How absurd!

CHAPTER 35

Explanation of the Terms "Nèiyè (内擫, Internally Pressing Down" and "Wàituò (外拓, External Expansion)"

In the treatise of calligraphy, the ancients often used the terms "nèiyè (内擫, internally pressing down" and "wàituò (外拓, external expansion)" to describe brushwork.

"Yè (擫, pressing down)," as previously mentioned, is in the shape of "yèdí (擫笛, pressing down the flute when playing the musical instrument)" and "yèmài (擫脉, a doctor pressing the patient's wrist exactly on artery or veins when taking his pulse)." When turning the brush to the right, the palm turns inward and the tips of the index, middle and ring fingers exert force respectively, that is "nèiyè (内擫, internally pressing down"). "wàituò (外拓, external expansion)" is quite the opposite. "Tuò (拓, expansion)" refers to the thumb pressing the brush handle in the shape of "yā (押, support)," denoting the left turn of the brush. The terms "nèiyè" and "wàituò" do not describe the specific state of the strokes in characters, but the continuous state of hand movements, which indirectly and naturally reflects the state of the strokes.

For example, the stroke of "héng, (横, horizontal, rightward stroke)" (Picture 86-1) that is tilted upward, is a "wàituò" stroke with a left turn; quite the contrary, the "héng" (Picture 86-2), which is tilted downward, is a "nèiyè" stroke with a right turn. The same is true for the stroke of "nà, (捺, pressing forcefully and falling rightwards)."

For example, "花" (huā) in cursive script (Picture 86-3) is "external expansion (wàituò)," with a left turn of the brush, but it forms a right turn at one point to restore the move; "王" (wáng) in cursive script (Picture 86-4) is "internally pressing down (内擫 nèiyè)," with a right turn of the brush. Wang Xizhi used to turn left at the last stroke to restore "external expansion."

For example, for the character 地 (dì), the radical "土 (tǔ, earth, on the left side)" can be written by "external expansion" (Picture 86-5)" with a left turn of the brush, in a left-wrapped shape, or by "internally pressing down" (Picture 86-6) with a right turn of the brush, in a right-wrapped shape.

Another example is the character "也" (yě) in Sun Guoting's *Treatise on Calligraphy*, which is written in two ways: "internally pressing down"

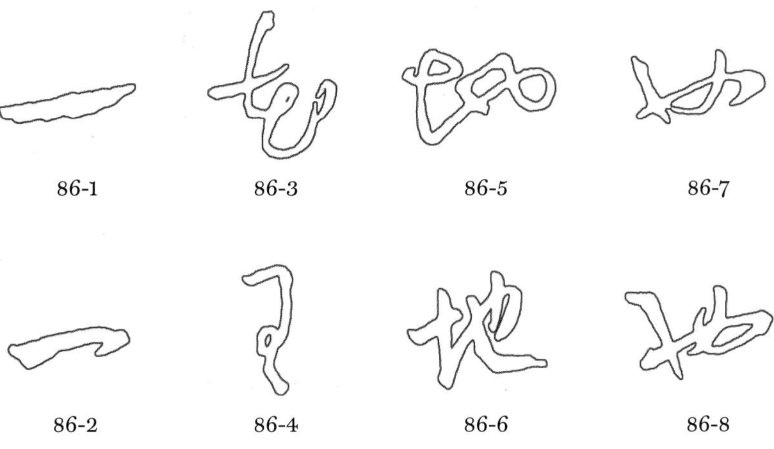

Picture 86

and "external expansion." In the former case (Picture 86-7), it starts with a right turn of the brush, and the last stroke immediately turns to "external expansion" in the left (Picture 86-8)." In the latter case, it starts with a left turn of the brush and immediately turns to "internally pressing down" in the right till the end.

Ouyang Xun's characters usually starts with a right turn, i.e. "nèiyè," but ends with "wàituò," which is a "bei" powered stroke. Therefore, the shape of the character is tightened (Picture 87). On the contrary, Yan Zhenqing's character starts mostly with a left turn, i.e. "wàituò," and closes with a "nèiyè," which is a "xiang" powered stroke. Therefore, the shape of the character is wide and thick (Picture 88).

In a word, calligraphy starts from "nèiyè" and must stop at "wàituò"; if it starts from "wàituò," it must stop at "nèiyè"; when it begins with the left turn, it stops at the right turn; when it begins with the right turn, it stops at the left turn.

The so-called ancient calligraphy masters are adept at both "wàituò" and "nèiyè." They freely put comprehensive techniques to full play. When I have immersed in the sea of calligraphy for a long time and seen the "brush" in "characters" and the "eye" in the "zen," I couldn't help exclaiming that the great calligraphers that have been famous since ancient times are all flexible and versatile in technique. Their dotting and painting skills are impeccably all-around.

Whether they adopt more "wàituò" or "nèiyè," whether they use more left turns or more right turns, it entirely depends on personal habits and individual differences, so there is a saying known as "the penmanship should not be rigid or fixed 法无定法 (fǎ wú dìng fǎ)."

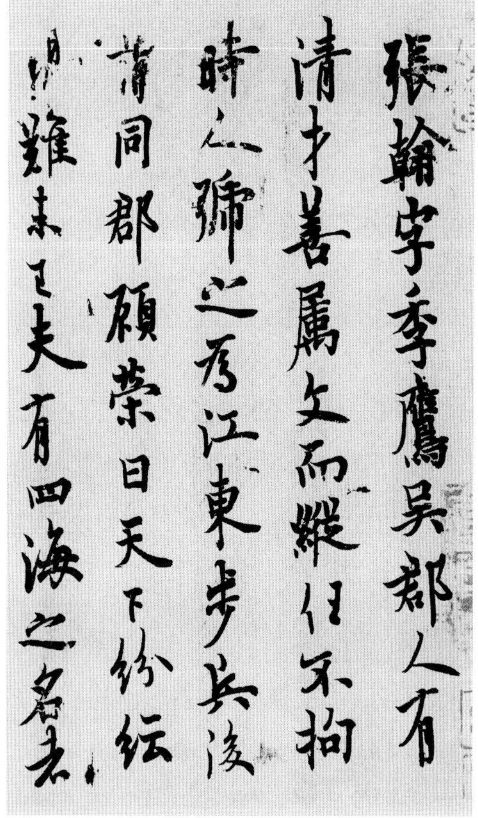

Picture 87 *Zhāng Hàn Tiè* (张翰帖 a note describing how Zhang Han in the Jin dynasty missed his hometown when he found the autumn wind blew) (part), Ouyang Xun, Tang dynasty

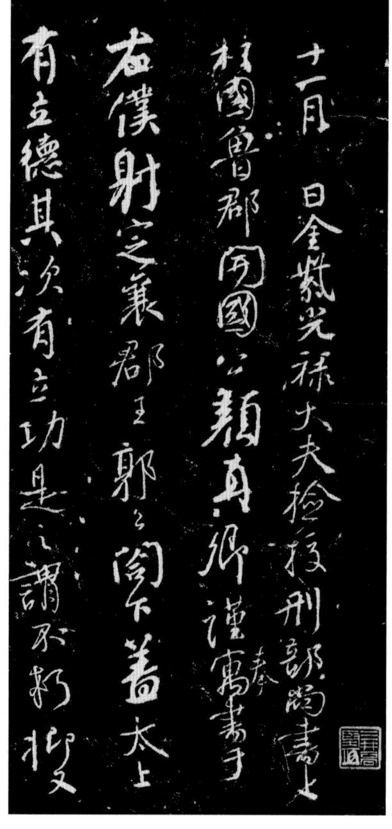

Picture 88 *Zhēng Zuòwèi Tiè* (争座位帖 a letter to Guo Yingyi in which Yan reprimanded the barefaced Guo who arranged the seat of the powerful eunuch Yu Chao'en before other higher-ranking officials during a ceremony) (part), Yan Zhenqing, Tang dynasty

CHAPTER 36

Semi-cursive Script, the Last to Take the Stage

Of all the scripts, semi-cursive was the last to take form. Zhuang Huaiguan in his *Shū Duàn* (书断, *Judgments on Calligraphers*) said that "Semi-cursive is the small pseudonym of the regular script. It features simpler shape, and is therefore popular liúxíng (流行). That's why it is called semi-cursive xíng shū (行书)."

According to the history of calligraphy, semi-cursive started to take form in the Eastern Han dynasty. In the Song dynasty (Southern dynasties), a scholar called Wang Yin said, "Since the Jin dynasty, calligraphers have been famous for their semi-cursive script. In the past, Zhong Yao, courtesy name Yuanchang, excelled in semi-cursive script. Later Wang Xizhi and Wang Xianzhi's semi-cursive script attained a level that their predecessors never reached before."

In terms of calligraphic style, semi-cursive script is between regular and cursive. When it is close to regular script, it is called xíngkǎi (行楷); when it is close to cursive, it is called xíngcǎo (行草). The ancients had "kǎifǎ (楷法, the method of turning the brush to first to the left, then to the right and finally restoring to the original place)" and "cǎofǎ (草法, a simplified method of brush turning compared to kǎifǎ)." But why was there no "xíngfǎ (行法, method of writing semi-cursive script)"?

The original meaning of the aforementioned "kǎifǎ (楷法)" is that a character is completed with a single round of left and right strokes. To determine if the handwriting meets the standard of the bāfēn clerical script is to see if a character has its "force separated" like bāfēn, which is the root of the regular script. The term "kǎifǎ (楷法)" does not refer to the method of the regular script, but to the method of the left and right stroke restoration, which is not limited to the regular script. To be more precise, "kǎifǎ (楷法)" should be understood as "the method of the regular model."

When I was young and read the ancient small regular script, or xiǎokǎi (小楷), I found the ancients always wrote with one stroke broken off after another stroke. Though people today appraise their writing as "of antique beauty," they don't know how the writing came into being. Actually, the characters were like "a fast horse entering a formation of a team." The calligrapher often turned the brush in the air and left one part of the stroke on the paper. As the strokes were incorporated with the action of turning the brush in the air, the break between the strokes happened.

This can be seen in the slip in the Eastern Han dynasty (Picture 89) and Zhong Yao's *Jiànjìzhí Biǎo* (荐季直表, *Recommending the Old Official Ji Zhi*) (Picture 90), where the strokes are also broken with breaks in between, making each stroke clear. The calligrapher used the force of gliding which broke the strokes to minimize the pressure of the brush hair touching the slip or paper, so as to render the writing swifter and more stable.

"Zhāngcǎo" (章草, a specific kind of cursive script) is based on the "bāfēn kǎifǎ (model of regular script in Broad Chancery Style)." "Jīncǎo (今草, contemporary cursive)" is not limited to one round for a single

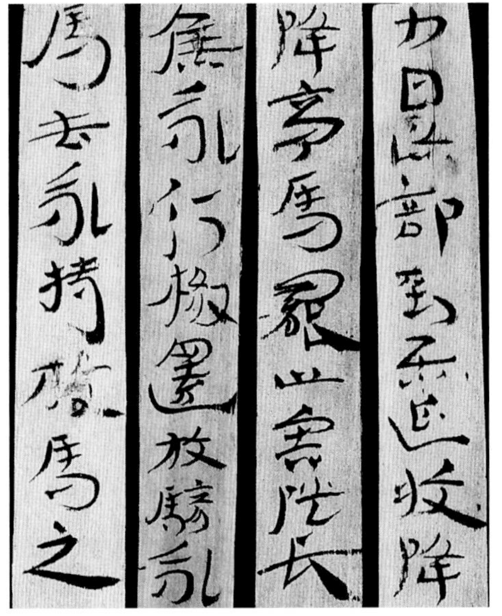

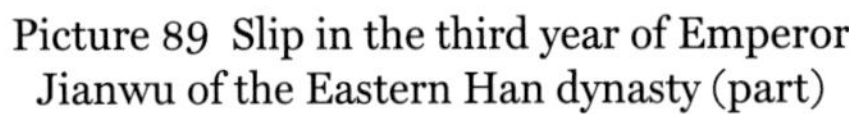

Picture 89 Slip in the third year of Emperor Jianwu of the Eastern Han dynasty (part)

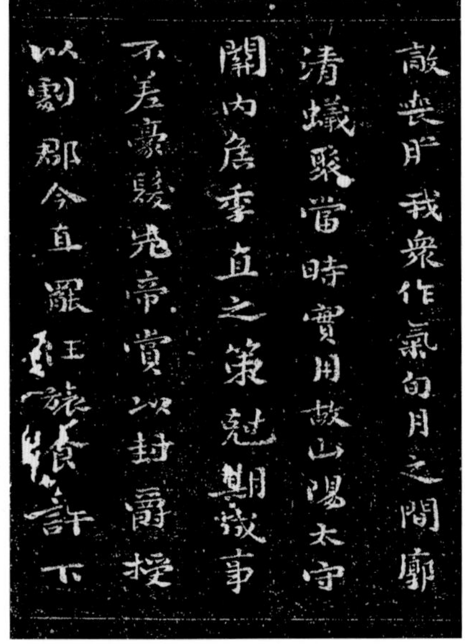

Picture 90 Jiànjìzhí Biǎo (荐季直表, *Recommending the Old Official Ji Zhi*) (part), Zhong Yao, Kingdom of Wei

character; rather, it incorporates the power of turning left and right in the entire process of the continuous use of the brush. I have explained this earlier.

However, just because the strokes of the brush are broken in the regular script, which is time-consuming and troublesome, if the strokes are continuous like grass (cursive), it will not be easy for most people to recognize it. As a result, the semi-cursive script which is time-saving and easy to comprehend is widely promoted.

If the turning of brush in the air is less reflected on the paper, then it is xíngkǎi; if the turning of brush in the air is reflected more on the paper, it is xíngcǎo. Semi-cursive script has no specific standards because it is dependent on kǎifǎ (楷法, the method of turning the brush to first to the left, then to the right and finally restoring to the original place) or cǎofǎ (草法, a simplified method of brush turning compared to kǎifǎ).

The reason why the Tang Regular Script was so beloved by later generations is because the details of the left and right power generation of the brush are clearly reflected on the paper and on each stroke, so that they could be appreciated, taught, and learned.

When the ancients talked about kǎifǎ or cǎofǎ, they were not referring to the shape of the characters in regular script and cursive script, but to their different methods of brush turning. Just as the ancients used to say, when one learnt certain calligraphers' characters or certain styles, he was learning the brushwork of the calligraphers, not simply the shape of characters.

I have to emphasize a point which might easily cause confusion. If the brushwork of different people is similar, the shape of the characters they write will naturally be similar. Since no one has pointed it out to them, later generations often mistakenly think that they are just learning the shape of the characters. This misunderstanding should not be underestimated, as it can lead to a thorough misunderstanding of the ancients.

CHAPTER 37

How "Unique Styles" in Calligraphy Are Formed

If you understand "xiàngbèi (向背)," then you can interpret the brushwork of the ancients in detail. Let's try some examples.

In the Song dynasty, Mi Fu's handwriting had been all the rage for many years. The "vertical hook," which is slightly slanted outwardnǔ (努) at the lower end, has been considered a symbol for the "Mi's characters." This is a feature that people today emphasize and carry forward in order to prove that they have learned "Mi's characters." Have they ever wondered why Mi Fu handled the stroke in this way?

Generally, the ancients often turned right when dealing with the "horizontal hook héng zhé gōu (横折钩)" or "vertical hook shù gōu (竖钩)," and used the ring finger to "prop up jù (拒)" and then form the "hook." However, Mi Fu's strategy was to first turn right to the bottom of the vertical stroke and then turn a bit left (external expansion) and at last the hook went up, borrowing the "xiàng (向)" momentum of the left turn, so that the characteristics of the "Mi's characters" were naturally born (Picture 91).

There are also many people who learn from Zhang Ruitu. But they don't know that Zhang Ruitu was used to turning left (when expanding externally). In dealing with "héng (横, horizontal stroke)" or "héngzhé

(横折, horizontal stroke with a vertical turn)," he used to turn left for a horizontal curb, and then at the "zhé (折, vertical turn)" he suddenly turned right. So whenever encountering such an occasion, he always had his strokes carried upward in a supine posture, with a concave center and a sharp and square turn, forming a unique "shoulder-like shape" (Picture 92)."

Ni Yuanlu was accustomed to adopting a right turn, often switching to a left turn at the close of the character, in order to continue the right turn in the next. As multiple right turns were often used in one character, when the brush handle reached the root of the thumb by the time the turn was near completion, the extension of strokes was limited. Therefore, Ni's characters were always long and comforting on the left but narrow and cramped on the right (Picture 93). Du Mu's *Poem of Zhang Haohao* (Picture 94) in the Tang dynasty also demonstrated that Du was good at the right turn as well (Picture 94).

In his later years, Wang Duo's calligraphy was so tangled and unrestrained that people called it "disheveled and unkempt," which is now known as the "the Zhongyuan Calligraphy Style zhōngyuán shūfēng (中原书风)." This is because people know some parts of it, but they don't know all of it. Anyone who has seen the calligraphy that Wang Duo created before he was 40 years old (Picture 95) cannot miss the fact that he followed in the footsteps of Wang Xizhi and Wang Xianzhi. His later years coincided with the introduction of the long-tipped brush chángfēng bǐ (长锋笔) and the use of raw Xuan paper, both of which were the material basis for Wang Duo's "biànfǎ (变法, change of method)." With the long-tipped goat hair, he held the brush at a high position, and when he turned the brush, the tip of the stroke formed an inertial winding that was difficult to stop, thus creating his unique calligraphic

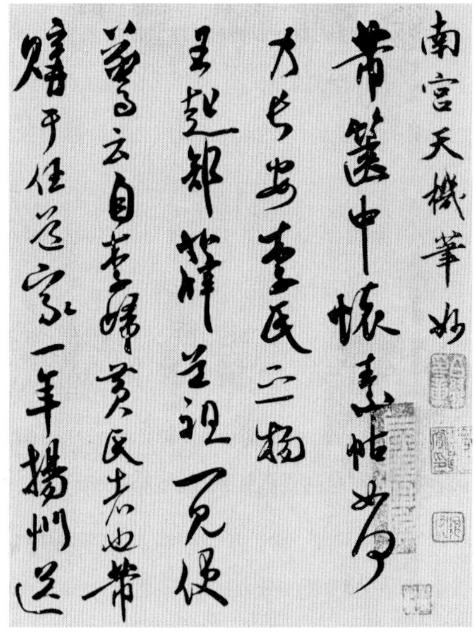

Picture 91 *Letter to His Excellency Jing Wenxi* (part), Mi Fu, Song dynasty

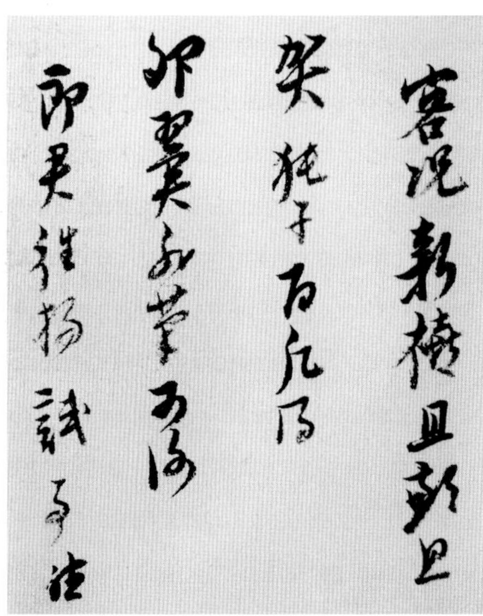

Picture 93 *New Year Letter to the House Butler* (part), Ni Yuanlu, Ming dynasty

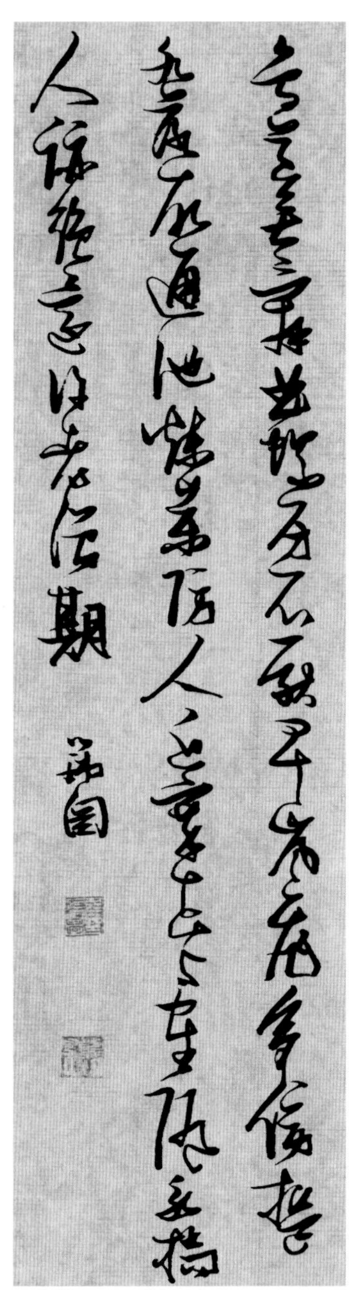

Picture 92 *Five-Character Poem* by Zhang Ruitu, Ming dynasty

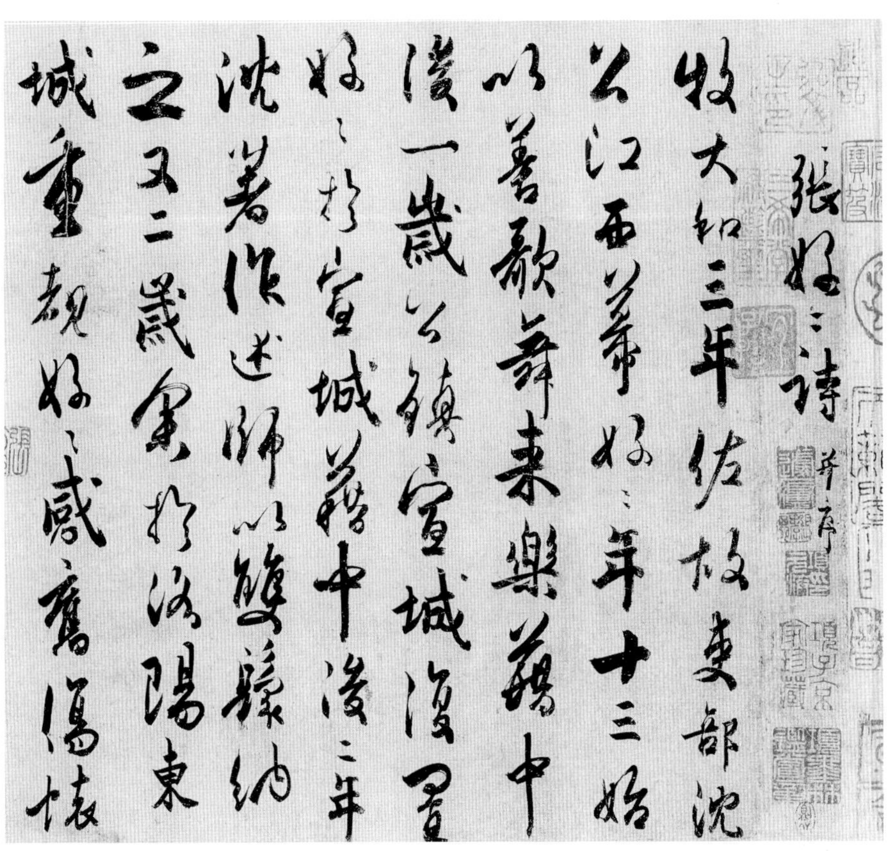

Picture 94 *Poem of Zhang Haohao* (part), Du Mu, Tang dynasty

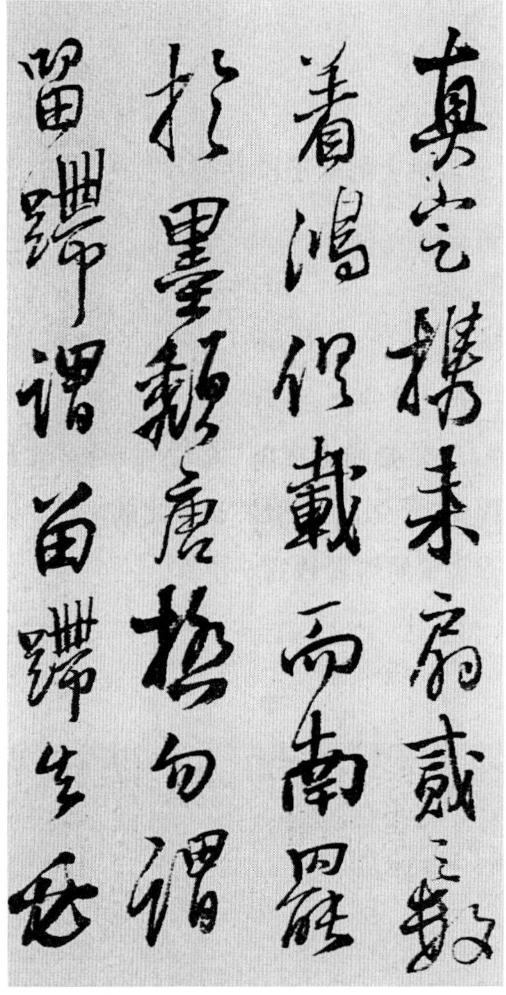

Picture 95 *Scroll of Semi-Cursive Script* (part), Wang Duo, Ming dynasty

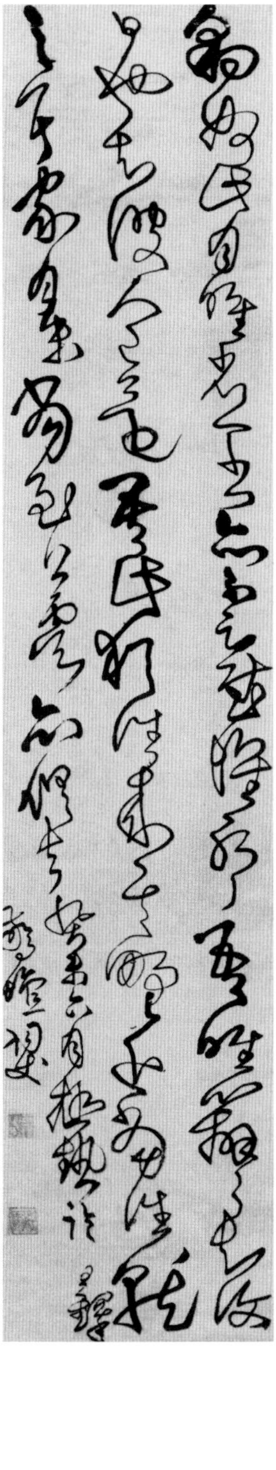

Picture 96 *Note Copying the Work of Wang Xizhi* (part), Wang Duo, Ming dynasty

style (Picture 96). Coupled with the use of raw Xuan paper, the ink in its thick, light, dry and wet forms was as a matter of course, fully expressed. The resulting "ink method" was, to put it bluntly, a response to the texture of raw Xuan paper. There was another possibility, i.e., he used a short-tipped brush without stopping to turn the brush. It was recorded that Wang Duo liked to have the paper stretched and suspended on the ground, avoiding the need to pause at intervals when the paper was too large. This was why there was a continuous flow of ten or so characters.

From the above, it can be seen that different "character-forms" are the result of different penmanship habits of each person. No matter how much you learn, you cannot omit the physiological and psychological differences, just like the difference in "DNA" genetic factors. No two leaves on a tree are the same, let alone two people. That's why there is a field of discipline called graphology.

This is how "unique styles" in calligraphy are formed.

The "uniqueness" in art cannot exist alone without living in the context of "generality." In recent centuries, "uniqueness" or "individuality" has been overemphasized and over-exaggerated, thus neglecting and concealing the "generality" hidden behind, which is inconspicuous but must be observed.

The "fǎ (法, method/standard)" is called "fǎ" because it is "generality." The distortion and alienation of "individuality" results from the loss of "generality."

In the contemporary era flooded with "uniqueness," should we for the time being make light of it for a while?

CHAPTER 38

Correcting the Saying "Envisaging the Artistic Effect before Putting Pen to Paper"

Wang Xizhi once proposed the idea "envisaging the artistic effect before putting pen to paper" yì zài bǐ xiān (意在笔先)." People today like to quote this saying. But their understanding is biased. The truth should be:

"The artistic effect yì (意)" refers to the "desire" of turning the brush, that is, before setting brush to the paper, one should consider carefully about the arrangement of the hand-gesture, whether the brush turns left and then right, or right and then left. They have to be arranged smoothly, clear in "*xiang-bei*" and "avoidingshìbèi (势背)." If the last character is closed at "bèishì (背势)," then the next word must start with "xiàngshì (向势)"; if the "bèishì" at the completion of the character is not exhausted, the next word can use up the remaining shì, or exhaust the shì in the air. Similarly, the changes in the use of the brush can follow this principle to form a line or an entire piece.

Ancient calligraphers had different ways to arrange brushwork, but one tenet is common to all, that is, to be handy and smooth.

This reminds me of the "dot" in cursive script. For example, in the writings of "zé (则)" (Picture 97-1), "bù (步)" (Picture 97-2), and "xián (咸)" (Picture 97-3), the presence or absence of the "dot" is determined by the xiàng bèi and bi-shi of the following characters. The closing of the characters "zé (则)" (Picture 97-4), "bù (步)" (Picture 97-5), and "xián (咸)" (Picture 97-6) is undoubtedly turning right; if the brush still makes the right turn, the brush will have turned to the end. Only by adding a "dot" that helps turn the brush to the left will restore the stroke, aiming to help the stroke turn right again. If the above three characters are completed by linking to the left turn, it will be so handy and smooth that a "dot" is not necessary. Or if there is still room after the right turn when completing the stroke, we could add a dot to turn the brush to the end, so as to prepare for the left turn of the next character.

Song Cao, a calligrapher in the reign of Emperor Shunzhi of the Qing dynasty, said after Wang Xizhi's idea was taken as "the golden rule": "When there is no brush in hand, the empty hand could also make a

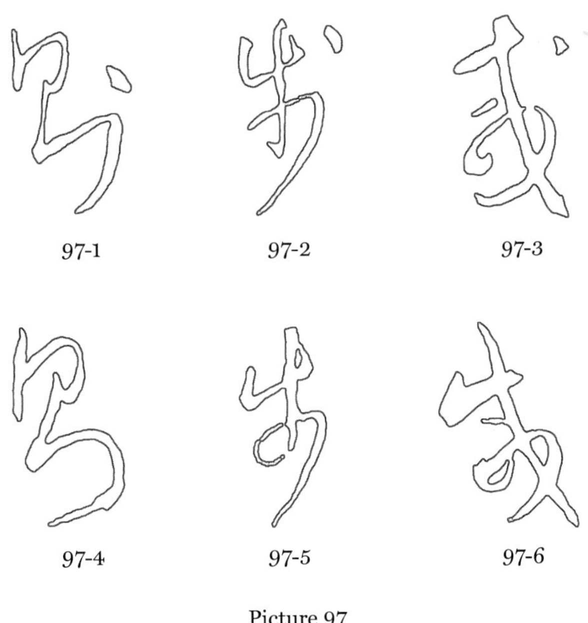

Picture 97

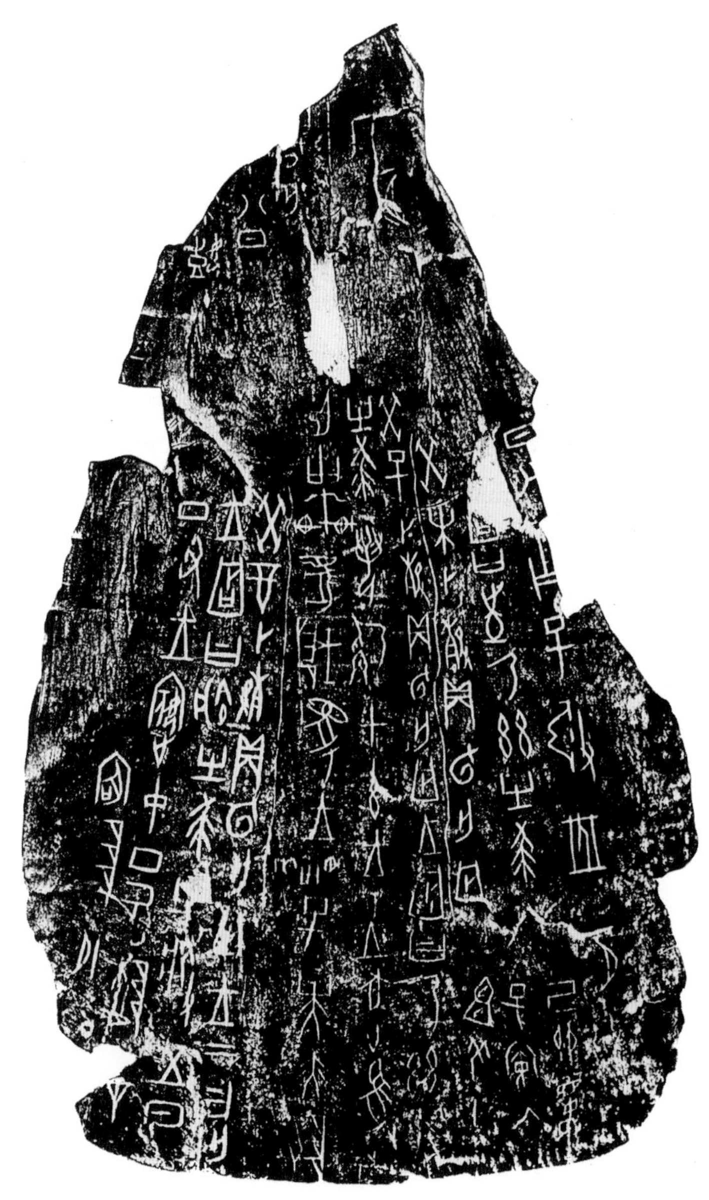

Picture 98 Oracle bone script, Shang dynasty

gesture of holding the brush. Long-time practice makes perfect. One could practice the empty-hand gesture when walking or lying in bed with intention." Song Cao showed to people how to practice the method with "intention." "Shūkōng (书空, writing in the air)" is undoubtedly the best way to refine the smooth brush turning. Even when one is not holding the brush, he could still "express the intention" in his mind. That is what Sun Guoting meant by saying "heart and hand tell the emotions."

In fact, this shūkōng method originated from the Jin dynasty, or even earlier. In *Shìshuō Xīnyǔ* (世说新语, *A New Account of the Tales of the World*), "After Yin Hao (the general of the central army, zhōng jūn jiāngjūn 中军将军) was dismissed, he lived in Xin'an (信安) and spent all day writing in the air with an empty hand."

This process of "intention" requires a long and repeated refinement, practice, and confirmation before it can be wonderfully combined with the strokes.

CHAPTER 39

Brush Turning Determines Writing Vertically from the Right

When I was a child, I couldn't figure out why calligraphy had to be written from top to bottom, and from right to left. It seemed to me not as convenient as writing horizontally from left to right. And by following the old way of writing, I inevitably rubbed ink on my sleeve. In the 1960s–1970s, the Dàzì bào (大字报 Big-Character Poster) was written horizontally, probably because it was not taken as calligraphy. The words on the slip all started from right to left. So if one wrote a long slogan, "One line could not be finished, so he had to follow suit."

I once read an article in *Taipei Palace Museum Monthly* published in Taiwan, which discussed that Chinese custom of writing from right to left and from top to bottom was caused by the fact that the bamboo slips were arranged in such order when they were written upon. It was hardly convincing. The oracle bone script, which was two thousand years older than the bamboo slips, was also written from top to bottom and from right to left on a whole piece of tortoise and animal bones. How to explain that phenomenon?

This form of writing by the ancients should be traced back to the earliest time, when the brush turning was first formed. I have already analyzed the reason why the ancients turned the brush and explained that the brush was turned from left to right in the posture of "xiàngbèi."

As can be seen from the oracle bone script (Picture 98), the writing at that time was balanced and symmetrical. From the perspective of brush turning, this is the earliest "xiàngbèi." A character consists of a restoration of the left and right brush turning. When writing a character, it is obviously from the left to the right, precisely because the right hand is holding the brush. Judging from the structure of the round turn whose both sides are in the shape of wrapping, the ancients were accustomed to first turning the brush to the left and then to the right. If it first turns right and then left, the brush will cover the eyesight, and will prevent the calligrapher from observing the strokes on the right side of the brush to achieve symmetry.

The ancients turned the brush first to the left and then to the right, and when they finished a word, they obviously turned right to complete the stroke, and the next word would start with a left turn.

Imagine this: when the right turn of completing a character is followed by the left turn of starting a new character, which is smoother, to go up to the right or to go down? The latter, of course.

All right, then consider that we follow the brush turning and write down the first line, when we go on writing the second line, which is more convenient for the hand? To go to the right up the first line, or the left up? The answer is still the latter.

So writing habits and procedures all arose from the convenience of brush turning.

I might continue to ask, why did Chinese choose to use a brush and their preference of the skills of hands? This is probably due to the instinct and specialties of human species.

In terms of primitive dancing, Asian dancers are skilled at expressing their emotions with hands, particularly in Southeast Asian countries such as Thailand, Myanmar, and India. The pose of hands is exceedingly fascinating and charming in Chinese opera. In Western dancing, however, dancers express their temperament with legs and feet, as is reflected in their tap dance, ballroom dance and ballet. No wonder Asians choose to turn the brush with their fingers. Because it's been a long tradition.

I am just talking about the current situation, the specialty, and the differences. As for why there is such specialty and differences, Hippolyte Adolphe Taine generalizes it in his *Philosophie de L'Art* to the geographic environment that humans live in.

If we dig and delve into it, it would be left for anthropologists and geneticists to discover.

I take the topic too far. I'd better stop here.

CHAPTER 40

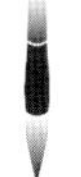

Wrongly Informed "Solid Fingers and Empty Palms"

The illustrious poet Su Shi famously declared: "There is no definite way to hold the brush, but to render the palm empty and relaxed." Ouyang Xiu commented on his words that "You should use your fingers to move the brush without moving your wrist," and Dongpo (the pseudonym of Su Shi) thought "Ouyang's words make the most sense."

It was said that Su Shi held his brush in "single hook (单苞 dānbāo)," using only the thumb, index and middle fingers to turn the brush, which was rarely adopted at that time. However, he thought that it would work as long as the palm was "empty and wide." "Empty (虚 xū)" refers to the main technique of brush turning, namely, the "emptiness" in "solid fingers and empty palm (指实掌虚 zhǐ shí zhǎng xū)." The "empty" hand must be able to "hold the egg." The palm should not be too fixed, because a fixed arm cannot move fingers. "Wide," relative to "tight," meant that the brush should not be held too tight. Ouyang Xiu commented his method by saying "You should use your fingers to move the brush without moving your wrist," which proved that Su Shi's "no definite method" was fully in accordance with the "finger method." He held the brush in "single hook," leaving the brush enough room for horizontal turn, but slightly restricted on the vertical direction, so the structure of "Su character (苏字 sū zì)" was mostly flat.

By analogy, "Mi character" was undoubtedly written by holding the brush in "double hook (双苞 shuāngbāo)." Besides, Mi Fu was adept at using his middle finger, so the word "努" (nǔ) in "Mi character" was prominently longitudinal, and the word was certainly longer.

There is a reason why the ancients stressed the importance of "solid fingers." Since I was little, I've known that when Wang Xianzhi was learning calligraphy as a child, his father, Wang Xizhi, "Tried to take Xianzhi's brush from behind but could not, knowing that his son would grow up to be famous." Of course, this tale is a bit exaggerated, just like the legend of Wang Xizhi's love for geese, which at first only referred to the posture of "stirring the lamp wick," but later went off in digression. "Trying to take Xianzhi's brush from behind but could not" means that the fingers must remain solid and powerful when turning the brush. If the brush is turned with weak fingers, it would easily slip and could not exert force. The "solid fingers" does not refer to gripping the brush using brute force without moving fingers.

Nowadays, however, when people fail to learn well, they make an excuse that "there is no fixed method"; when they fail to copy well, they say "our copy is imbued with our own understanding (意临 yìlín)." Zhang Rong replied to Emperor Gao of Southern Qi's comment on calligraphy, "I don't regret that my characters lack the temperament of Wang Xizhi and Wang Xianzhi, rather I regret that theirs lack the bones and charm of my calligraphy." His words often become the grandiloquence of people today.

In the Spring Festival Gala a few years ago, the host solemnly introduced a "calligrapher" who wrote on the floor with a mop. For hundreds of millions of TV viewers, the "calligrapher" performed his mopping skills, winning a round of applause. It's said his deed has been recorded in *The Guinness Book of World Records*.

There was a book in the Qing dynasty called *Xiào Lín Guǎng Jì* (笑林广记, *A Collection of Jokes in Ancient China*). I was thinking that there should be a new edition considering all the contemporary fuss and jokes.

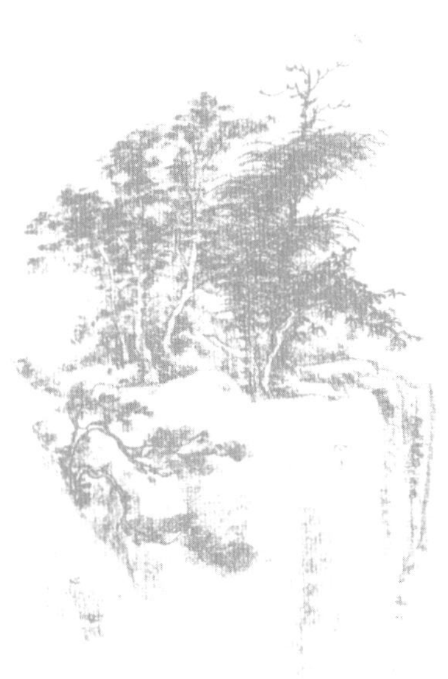

CHAPTER 41

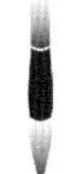

The Blind Do Not Know the Sun

There is a peculiar phenomenon in the history of Chinese calligraphy. What is called the inheritance of brushwork is often hereditary and passed on only to one child. It is mysterious and unpredictable, such as the inheritance of recipes from Chinese medicine family or the secrets of Kung Fu from martial art families.

Xie Jin stated: "The essence of calligraphy cannot be mastered unless it is through oral teaching that inspires true understanding within." Zhang Huaiguan mentioned: "If a man wants to learn calligraphy, he must learn from a teacher." Lu Xie declared: "I've never seen anyone who could learn calligraphy without being taught orally by a teacher at the side." The methods of the ancients learning calligraphy abound in treatise of past dynasties. Although calligraphy academies had been opened since the Tang dynasty, the teaching method remained private. Many popular tales revealed this phenomenon. For instance, Zhong Yao was so eager to obtain Wei Dan works that he successfully robbed Wei's tomb; and Yan Zhenqing invited Zhang Zhangshi (Zhang Xu) several times to teach him brushwork. These examples were quite common in the history of calligraphy.

The calligraphic works of Wang Xizhi and Wang Xianzhi in the Wei and Jin dynasties evinced the perfect stage of ancient brushwork. The ingeniousness, inaccessibility, and subtlety of the brushwork were hard to decipher for later generations. The ancients strived to interpret them in various ways to avoid any whiff of misunderstanding, but their efforts were to no avail.

The process of fingers skillfully working with the brush, if described in words, can be compared to Su Dongpo's *Metaphor of the Sun,* in which the blind man asks an ordinary man what the sun is like, and the ordinary man says, "It looks like a copper plate, and its light is like a candle." The blind man then "knocks the plate and hears its sound"; later he hears the bell ringing and thinks it could be the sun. Afterwards the blind man "touches the candle and feels its shape," and "on the other day he tries to blow up a yuè (龠, an ancient musical instrument shaped like a flute)." A yuè resembles a candle in shape, so he thinks the yuè is the sun too.

Unfortunately, as Sun Guoting said:"The place where the heart could reach cannot be easily expressed in words; the place where the words can touch upon are difficult to be put on paper and ink."

The first thing you have to do in learning the brushwork is to "identify (鉴 jiàn)." Observing with your own eyes might miss the point. To appreciate the beauty and the drawback of brushwork, one must be accompanied by a teacher. This is only the first step. Second, the teacher must personally demonstrate the skills and give a step-by-step guide with a pithy formula. Many ancient formulas on calligraphy are the gist that requires rote learning. The four words "oral and hand teaching (口传手授 kǒu chuán shǒu shòu)" objectively reflect the difficulties and limitations of teaching brushwork.

Then the rest is up to the hard work of individuals. Even Zhang Boying "Learned to write by the pool and dyed the pool black with ink," and Zhi Yong "Climbed up the building and stayed there writing for more than 40 years without going down," showing that the brushwork is not anything that ordinary people can do. Wang Xizhi said frankly: "Calligraphy is a mysterious skill. If the learner is not a man of great learning and understanding, he could not accomplish the technique." When Zhang Zhangshi (Zhang Xu) taught Yan Lugong (Yan Zhenqing), he started the teaching by saying: "Brushwork is mysterious and difficult to pass on. If you are not an aspirant or learned man, how can you learn its subtleties"?

In the ancient times, the word "calligraphy" was the most important subject, and the first thing to learn was to write. Calligraphy was undoubtedly the key to enter the civil service. In the Spring and Autumn Period and the Warring States Period, the Six Arts to be taught were rituals, music-dance, archery, driving a chariot, calligraphy, and mathematics. Calligraphy was one of the six subjects in the imperial examination of the Tang dynasty. The selection of officials was based on "four talents," and calligraphy was one of them.

Therefore, the ancients could not be allowed to undertake official posts if they did not master good handwriting, and vice versa. Just take a look at the writers who authored the history or treatise of calligraphy, they were all officials who enjoyed a good reputation in the court. Only the prominent officials and eminent personages in the court had the privilege to appreciate the authentic calligraphic works that were handed down for centuries. Besides, the nobility enjoyed the priority of learning the first-class calligraphy.

At the beginning of 1998, a *Great Exhibition of Chinese Calligraphy in the Twentieth Century* was held in China. I happened to have a special collection of works from the exhibition. When I browsed through it, a cursive couplet with the ancient style of brushwork suddenly came into

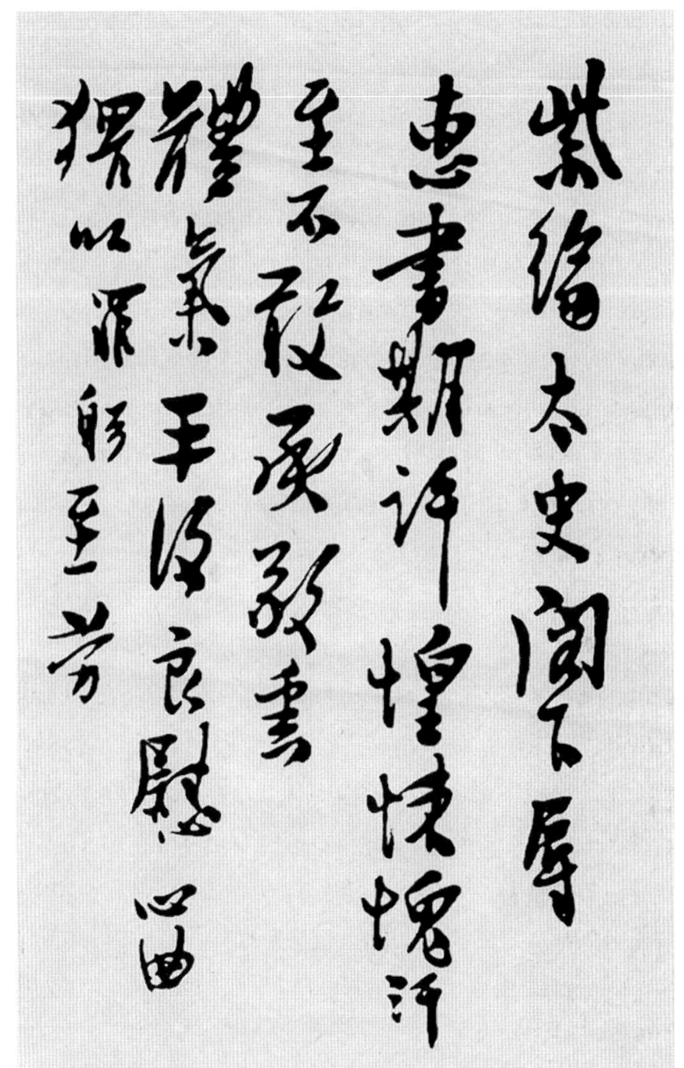

Picture 99 *Three Letters to Zilun Taishi* (official title) (part), Pu Ru

sight. And it turned out to be written by Pu Ru (Picture 99), a royal family member.

In the old days, some real calligraphic works went to private hands. They were cherished as a family heirloom that must be kept secret from others, occasionally shown to a few friends and relatives. Even worse, in ancient China, inconvenient transportation prevented the spread of information and slowed the dissemination of brushwork, making it harder for people to unravel its mystery. "Exquisite craft is hard to spread, so are the adept ones few (工巧难传, 善之者少 gōng qiǎo nán chuán, shàn zhī zhě shǎo)." Things are valued because of their scarcity. Brushwork is undoubtedly a treasure of the ancients, so it is reasonable to have them hidden, treasured, concealed, and inherited in a clan.

This is precisely the important reason for the loss or misinterpretation of brushwork.

CHAPTER 42

Unintentionally "Talking Black into White"

The learning of calligraphy is synchronous with literacy. There is only one way–copying. In retrospect, most of my confusion arose from copying.

Today, not only the rubbings from a stone inscription, but also oracle bone script, jīnwén (金文, inscriptions on ancient bronze objects), shígǔwén (石鼓文, inscriptions on drum-shaped stone blocks) and brick inscriptions fall into the range of copying. These texts are almost named after the texture of the text-carrier. Let's first take an objective look at the formation of the texture of these texts.

Oracle bone script (Picture 100) has been the earliest Chinese script we have seen to date. It was first written on animal bones with a brush and then carved out with a single line by using a sharp tool. To facilitate viewing, the characters had to be rubbed.

There were two types of jīnwén (Picture 101). One type was created by first writing character on the mold with a brush, then engraving the characters, and at last casting the metal solution. The other type was created by writing with a brush on a metal vessel that had already been cast, then engraving the character, and having the characters rubbed.

Brick inscriptions (Picture 102) refer to words written with a brush on a raw brick and then engraved, or characters directly engraved on a raw brick and then fired in the kiln. The words have to be rubbed too.

Tablet inscriptions (Picture 103) mainly refer to Wei steles and Han steles. They were also first written on the stone tablet with a brush, carved, and then rubbed.

Noticeably, the formation of the inscriptions above requires at least three or four procedures. After chiseling, carving, burning, casting, and rubbing, as well as years of wind erosion, the original brush writing has completely disappeared, leaving us with only a vague shape of characters that has endured many-times "re-creation" in a psychologically objective way.

Our initial purpose of copying is to learn the brushwork of ancients and the shape of characters.

We use such tools as the brush, paper, and ink to copy.

And we have to ask ourselves, it would be hard if we dreamed of expressing the traces of multiple "re-creations" only by copying with brush, paper, and ink. And to guess the original ancient brushwork at the time, would have been unintentionally "calling a stag a horse (指鹿为马 zhǐlù wéi mǎ, talking black into white)."

Here the "talking black into white" is precisely what Su Dongpo means in his *Metaphor of the Sun*, in which the blind man mistakes a bell and a flute for the sun.

For example, the single line with two pointed ends on the oracle bone script is entirely created due to carving and engraving, which is not the original writing. Neither do the even roundness of jīnwén and the pale remnants of the Han stele reflect the original handwriting. When I was young, I was confusedly copying almost all the calligraphic styles, such

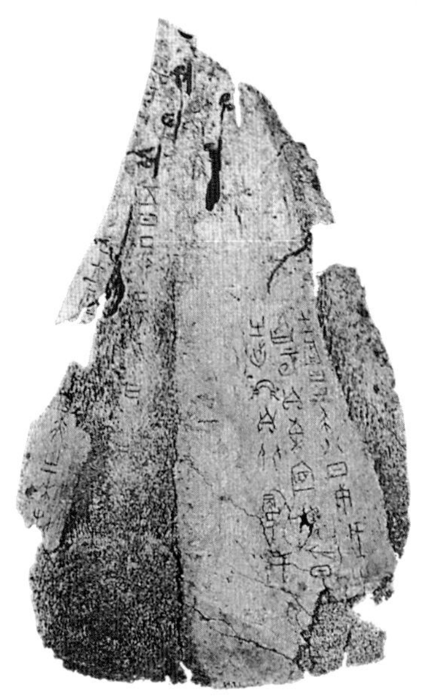

Picture 100 Oracle bone script, Shang dynasty

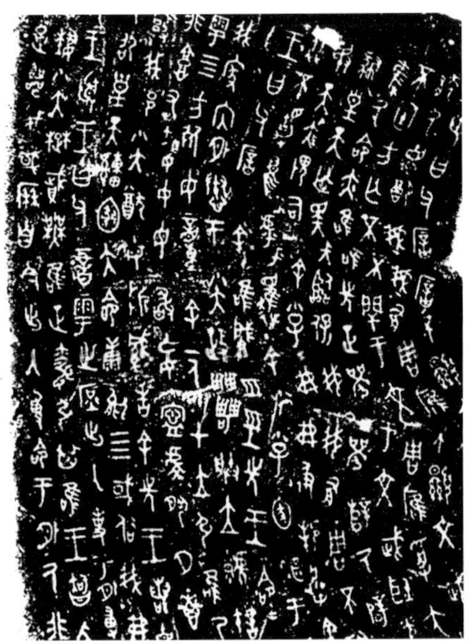

Picture 101 Duke Mao Tripod (part), Zhou dynasty

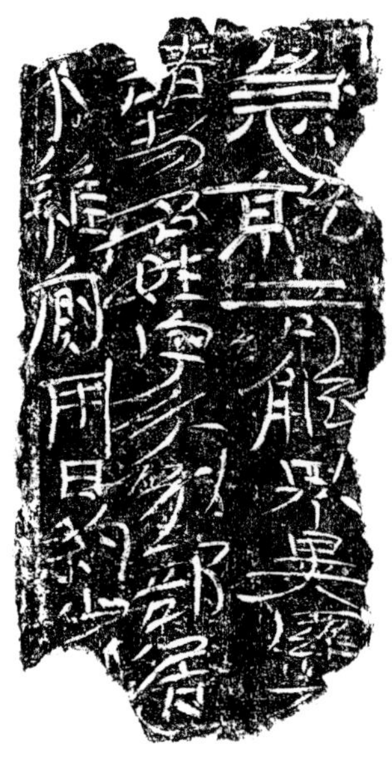

Picture 102 Brick text of *Jijiupian* (*Children's Reading Primer*), Han dynasty

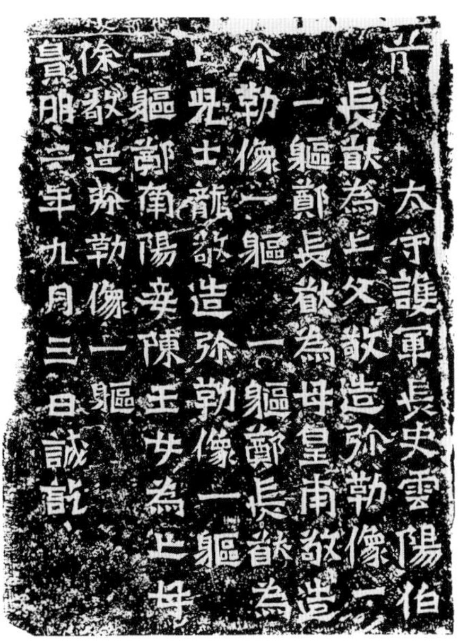

Picture 103 *Record of Statue-Making by Zheng Changyou*, Northern Wei dynasty

as the Great Seal Jīnwén Script, the Han Stele and the Wei Stele, etc. I was full of doubts and confusion, and was never sure of myself.

The reason lies in that I really value the inevitable result of a brush dipping in ink and writing on paper.

As early as the Song dynasty, Mi Fu pointed out that: "One should not learn stone carving, because it was not the real writing of calligraphers, but the carving work of handwriting. One must observe the real writing to find the charm." The tiè (帖, a book containing models of handwriting or painting for learners to copy) resembles the original writing to the largest extent, so we mainly copy the original writing, gétiè (阁帖, the shortened form of *Chunhua Ge Tie*, a collection of model rubbings of well-known calligraphic works of successive dynasties), or steles that are carved in a true-to-life way. Although many of the tiè are copied works, they resemble the original shape of character much better than we could fathom out.

A stone carving that is written randomly with mediocre skill or crudely made by any worker, despite its freshness and simplicity, it cannot be taken as a standard to learn from or to be worshiped. We cannot discuss "individuality" until we achieve "generality" just as a person cannot enjoy his right as an adult unless he reaches 18 years of age.

Truly noble art is like flowers that have been carefully nurtured by men for thousands of years, and definitely not the weeds that sway in the wind on the roadside.

CHAPTER 43

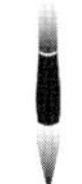

The Collapse of "Tièxué"

When we talk about calligraphy, we cannot forget "tièxué (帖学, the study of tiè; tiè refers to a book containing models of handwriting or painting for learners to copy)" and "bēixué (碑学, the study of steles)." Before the reigns of Emperors Qianlong and Jiaqing in the Qing dynasty, there was no "tièxué," and only after the emergence of "bēixué" was there a corresponding "tièxué."

Let's take a look at their origins.

The earliest "tiè" referred to the words written on the small piece of paper, generally the note, invitation, or gēngtiě (庚帖, the red posts men and women exchanged during engagement in old customs), among others. "Fāshū" in the Wei and Jin dynasties were written on small pieces of paper. After "wánfǎ," the Jin calligraphy had become the fǎtiè (法帖, model calligraphy collections) copied and imitated by generations of calligraphers, so the meaning of "tiè" transformed into a sample for people to copy and learn from. Ruan Yuan in *Treatise on the Northern Stele and Southern Tie* said: "The Jin court migrated south, with xuānshì biǎo (宣示表, an article depicting Zhong Yao's opinion on Sun Quan's *Instrument of Surrender to the Kingdom of Wei*) as the ancestor of the Jiangdong calligraphy, but what they carried with them was the tiè. The tiè began with shǔshū (署书, words engraved on horizontal inscribed board). Later, any treasured handwriting on a piece of silk or paper was classified as tiè."

In the Song dynasty, carving tie was prevalent. Emperor Taizong in the third reigning year of Chunhua took out the collection of fāshū that were restored in the palace. Over half of the fāshū were the handwritings of Wang Xizhi and Wang Xianzhi. He ordered the officials to align them in order, copy the tiè and engrave them on the stone, then rub them in ink, and gave them to officials. The famous tiè was the *Chúnhuà Gé Tiè* (淳化阁帖, a collection of model rubbings of well-known calligraphic works of successive dynasties), which was the ancestor of the fǎtiè (法帖) for future generations. According to this, other tiè were re-carved, including Xìyú Táng Tiè (戏鱼堂帖, rubbings of *Chúnhuà Gé Tiè* and its interpretations on the Fish Playing Hall by Liu Cizhuang in the Song dynasty), Èrwángfǔ Tiè (二王府帖, another rubbing copy of *Chúnhuà Gé Tiè*), *Dàguān Tiè* (大观帖, re-adapted rubbing version of *Chúnhuà Gé Tiè* during the Period of Daguan, the Northern Song dynasty) and Jiàng Tiè (绛帖, rubbings based on *Chúnhuà GéTiè* by Pan Shidan in the Northern Song dynasty), etc. *Bǎojìnzhāi Fǎtiè* (宝晋斋法帖, rubbings by Cao Zhige based on Mi Fu's conserved relics and other famous calligraphic works of the Jin dynasty) and *Qúnyùtáng Tiè* (群玉堂帖, rubbings by Xiang Ruoshui in the Southern Song dynasty, based on renowned calligraphic works of past ages) were conserved among common folks. The numerous tiè laid a solid foundation for the development of tiè studies.

Emperor Kangxi of the Qing dynasty worshiped Dong Qichang, while Emperor Qianlong admired Zhao Mengfu. They accumulated numerous masterpieces and had them carved into *Sānxītáng Fǎtiè* (三希堂法帖; Emperor Qianlong preserved the prominent calligraphic works of Wang Xizhi and Wang Xianzhi in Sanxitang; he ordered officials to inscribe numerous eminent calligraphic works of the past generations on the stone) which was on unprecedented scale. They also had Chúnhuà Gé Tiè re-carved. They advocated the Tang steles, causing Dong and Zhao's calligraphic styles to be popular. Dong Qichang and Zhao Mengfu played the same role in the history of calligraphy, i.e., to restore the ancient style in the decline of gǔfǎ (古法, ancient calligraphic method). For example, Chen Yixi and Gao Shiqi were both masters of gǔfǎ brushwork at that time.

This role of restoration must be played by geniuses.

As future generations continued to recurve the gé tiè, a variety of rubbings mixed the fictitious with the genuine, leaving the descendants

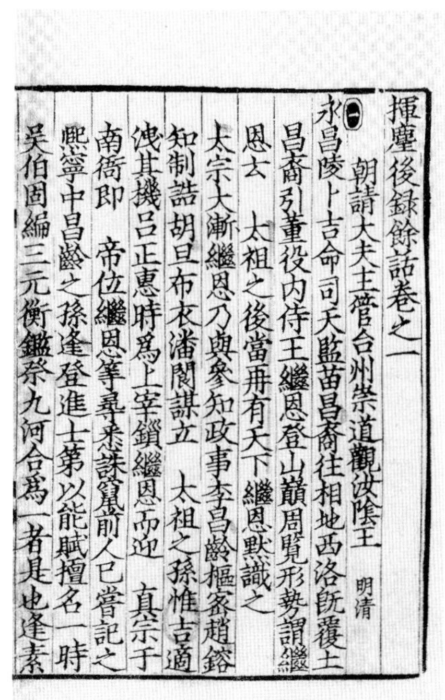

揮麈後録餘話卷之一
朝請大夫主管台州崇道觀汝陰王 明清
一 永昌陵卜吉命司天監苗昌裔往相地西洛既覆土
昌裔引董役内侍王繼恩登山巔周覽形勢謂繼
恩云 太祖之後當再有天下繼恩默識之
太宗大漸繼恩乃與參知政事李昌齡樞密趙鎔
知制誥胡旦布衣潘閬謀立 太祖之孫惟吉適
洩其機呂正惠時爲上宰鎖繼恩而迎 真宗于
南衙即 帝位繼恩等尋悉誅竄前人已嘗記之
熙寧中昌齡之孫逢登進士第以能賦擅名一時
吴伯固編三元衡鑑悉九河合爲一者是也逢素

Picture 104 Lǎosòngtǐ (老宋体, Old Song Style)

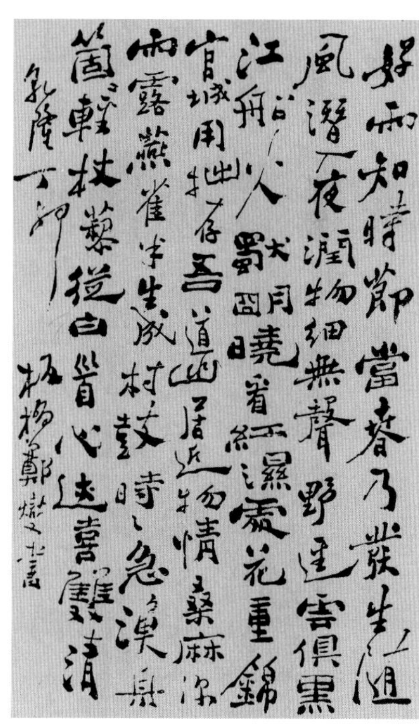

Picture 105 Calligraphy of Zheng Banqiao, Qing dynasty

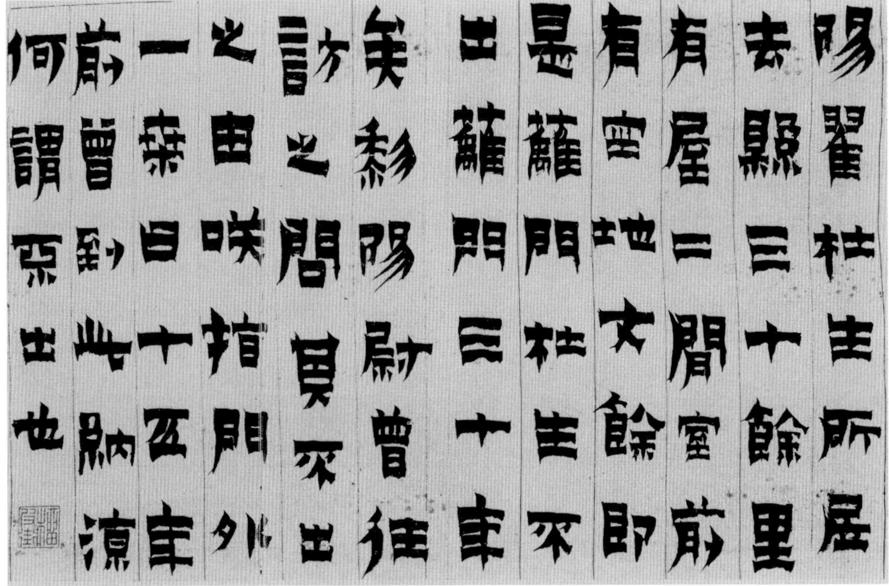

Picture 106 Calligraphy of Jin Dongxin, Qing dynasty

confusion when they copied the fǎshū. As Kang Youwei said in *Enlarged Edition of Sculling in the Boat of Art*: "Paper has a history of one thousand years. By the time now we not only failed to see the remaining work of the Six dynasties, but also couldn't see the rarely preserved *Gouben* (钩本 gōuběn, a book of rubbings in which calligraphers outlined the silhouettes of each character and filled in the outlines with ink) of the Tang dynasty. Therefore, the tiè that are available today, regardless of their type or author, are mostly rubbed or copied versions by people from the Song and Ming dynasties. Though the tiè were named after Wang Xizhi and Wang Xianzhi, the writing in them certainly didn't look like theirs at all, not to mention the spirit and style of the characters."

In addition, another factor should not be ignored.

The movable type printing, one of The Four Great Inventions that China has been proud of, was invented by Bi Sheng in the Song dynasty. The characters engraved in the Song dynasty, which we now call "lǎosòngtǐ (老宋体, Old Song Style)" (Picture 104), were apparently the "artification" of the regular script then. Such neat and tidy regular script originated from the Tang dynasty during which "the regular script was required to be vigorous and beautiful." The imperial examination system then had a stern demanded on how candidates should write regular script. Therefore, it became a must for literati calligraphers to equip themselves with the skill.

In the Ming and Qing dynasties, the style of "*Fang, Guang, and Wu* (a form of square, smooth, and jet-blackcharacters demanded in the imperial examination of the Qing dynasty)" was developed and became prevalent.It was called "táigé style (台阁体, also known as secretariat style, popular among intellectuals in the Ming dynasty" in the Ming dynasty and "guǎngé style (馆阁体, referring to a written style popular among the Hanlin Imperial Academy, an academic and administrative institution of higher learning)" in the Qing dynasty. In addition, the original editions or tiè had been lost after generations of carving. Thus, tièxué (帖学, the study of tiè; tiè refers to a book containing models of handwriting or painting for learners to copy) lost its vitality. Although there were calligraphers proficient in "tièxué," the number was few. And how much difference could a small number of literati calligraphers make?

Then the "Eight Eccentrics of Yangzhou" (扬州八怪 Yángzhōu bā guài) emerged, among whom the characters of Zheng Banqiao (Picture 105) and Jin Dongxin (Picture 106) shocked the world. They were called "eccentrics," contrary to the so-called "orthodoxy" of "tièxué." In fact, the dam of the "orthodox" was collapsing.

The collapse of this "orthodoxy" such as "tièxué," was the collapse of "fa."

CHAPTER 44

Re-examination of "Bēixué (the Study of Steles)"

At the same time, insightful literati and calligraphers attempted to learn the original features of "fǎshū" from the inscriptions before the Wei and Jin dynasties.

Zhao Yiguang's postscript on Zhang Jizhi's *Diamond Sutra* in the Ming dynasty (Picture 107) is now preserved in the Princeton University Art Museum. It is a typical seal script work written in cursive style. Each word is about four or nine square centimeters with fast and smooth brushwork.

This work is obviously written with the ancient method of brush turning. The lines are uneven in thickness. Most of the strokes start and end in a sharp shape. They are not as uniform as bronze inscriptions, nor are they written with similar brushwork used by contemporary folks.

I have observed the seal script of Zhu Da (Bada Shanren) collected in Nanjing Museum (Picture 108). It is the same as Zhao Yiguang's work, with flexible brushwork.

Later, I saw the seal script written by Fu Shan (Picture 109). The way he used the brush seemed eccentric and strange to people today. However, just like Zhao Yiguang and Zhu Da (Bada Shanren), he wrote

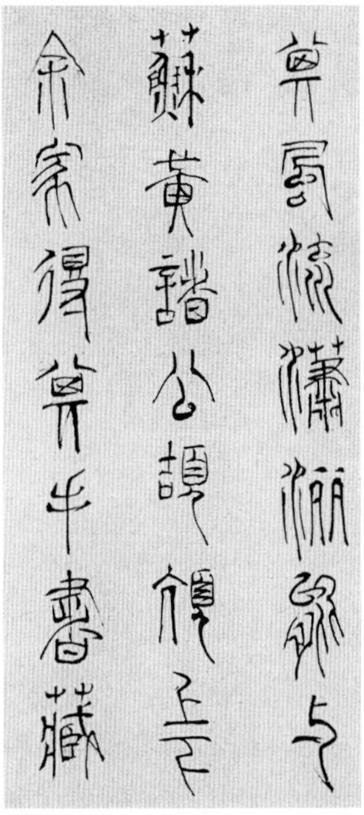

Picture 107 Zhao Yiguang's postscript on Zhang Jizhi's *Diamond Sutra* (part), Ming dynasty

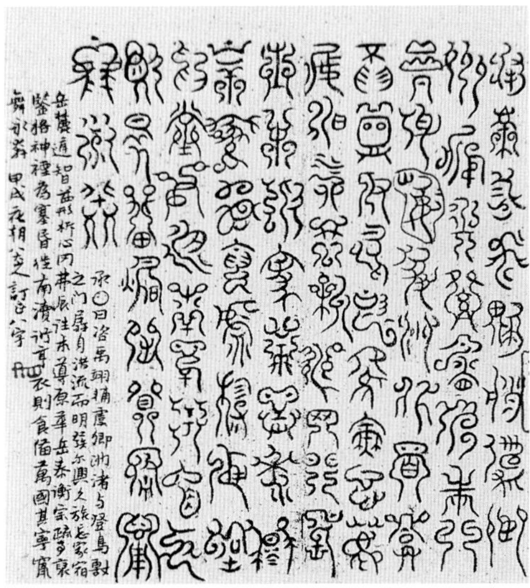

Picture 108 Seal script of Zhu Da or Bada Shanren (part), Ming dynasty

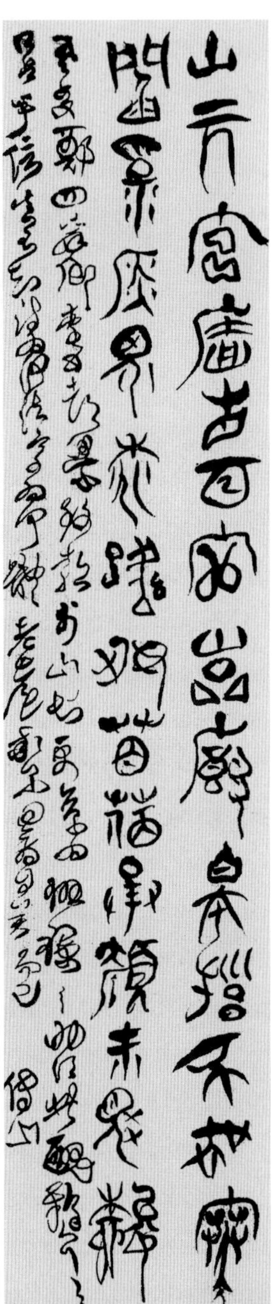

Picture 109 Seal script of Fu Shan, Ming dynasty

the seal characters with the method of turning the brush and moving fingers instead of just writing the seal characters in uniform shape.

Fu Shan's works were usually banners with larger characters, and might have been written by him standing and holding the brush with his wrist in the air.

It can be seen that it was a fashion in those days to practice the ancient method of writing and copy ancient steles.

To discover the origin of a calligraphic form does matter, or this can be understood as the real significance of copying steles.

At the same time, the study of inscriptions and textual criticism flourished, giving rise to the prevalence of recording ancient inscriptions. Ruan Yuan's *Treatise on the Calligraphy Schools in the North and the South* and *Treatise on the Northern Stele and the Southern Inscriptions*, and Bao Shichen's *Yizhou Shuangji* (*Sculling in the Boat of Art*) were successively published, and "bēixué" was greatly promoted.

It was a demanding task to judge the writing style from the stele, and only a few people knew the tricks in it, so "bēixué" gradually lost its original significance.

What I emphasize is that the above is the early stage of "bēixué," which is essentially different from its later stage.

The so-called "stele" is to write the characters on the stone first and then engrave them. However, although "fatie" is carved in stone, it still belongs to "tiexue."

Secondly, there were steles that involved carving skills, the most typical of which were *TwentySteles of Longmen* (Picture 110) and *Stele of Cuan Baozi* (Picture 111). Though there were numerous stone carvings in the Northern dynasty and all kinds of people participated in the writing from the nobility of the court to the common folks, many of the steles were simply written by the engravers, which saved time but were shoddily produced. The engravers omitted many details of the writing and added a lot of personal ideas. The typical square part in Wei steles were chiseled work, rather than the original writing. The reason why modern people are confused in the use of the so-called "square brush" and "round brush" is that they do not clearly know the ins and outs.

There is another kind of stele, which has been eroded for thousands of years by wind and rain. Its writing and knife techniques remain ambiguous, such as *Inscription on Stone Gate* (Picture 112) and *Inscription on Burying Crane* (Picture 113). As it suggested, the scope of stele study (bēixué) broadened. Learners even considered copying the carving skill and the effect of wind erosion and stripping on the steles.

Therefore, when "bēixué" rose during the reigns of Emperor Qianlong and Emperor Jiaqing, seal cutting and seal engraving also flourished, which were closely integrated with calligraphy, making it develop towards pure visualization and involve more painting skills or other craftsmanship.

In *Enlarged Edition of Sculling in the Boat of Art,* Kang Youwei framed the concept of "bēixué" in the steles of the Northern dynasties, excluding the reviving and worshiping of the Tang dynasty steles since the reign of Emperor Kangxi, which laid a theoretical foundation for the later period of "beixue." He insisted that "the ancients wrote calligraphy, without using fingers," criticized the writing by turning brush with fingers as "a mistake made by a wise men among his thousand decisions," and advocated "using the wrist to move the brush," which in theory completely overthrew the "tiexue."

Kang Youwei said: "Everything in the world develops and changes." He said it with a historical context. In the special era of the world bourgeois revolution, the French conquered the Bastille; the Russians overthrew the tsar; Japanese went through Meiji Restoration; and several-thousand-year-old feudal autocracy crumbled fast in China. Ten years after completing *Enlarged Edition of Sculling in the Boat of Art*, Kang Youwei became the leader of the Bourgeois Reform Movement in modern China and the core figure of Hundred Days Reform (or Wuxu Reform). Constitutional reform and modernization were the urgent task, or as he admitted, "the trend was irresistible, and I could not help myself."

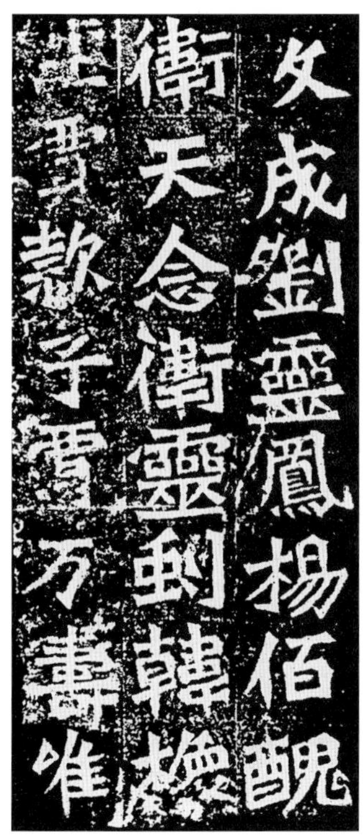

Picture 110 *Twenty Steles of Longmen* (part), Northern Wei dynasty

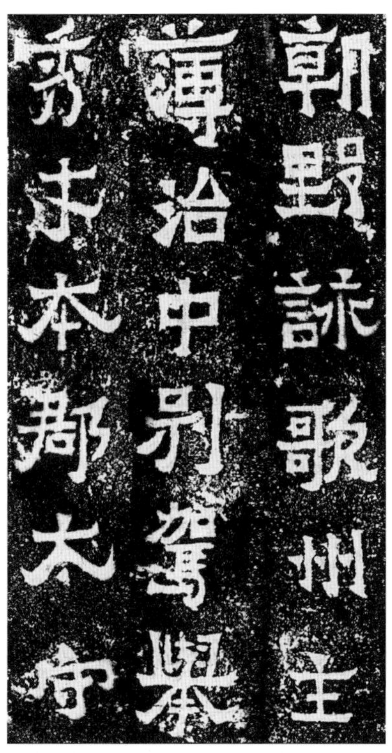

Picture 111 *Stele of Cuan Baozi* (part), Eastern Jin dynasty

Indeed, since the ancient system could be "reformed," why cannot the ancient calligraphy?

I finally had a chance to find *Secret Imperial Edict of Emperor Guangxu* (Picture 114) written by Kang Youwei before Hundred Days' Reform when he was in his 40s. I was surprised by the classic calligraphy tradition inherited in his writing, so rakish and elegant. This is the original and real Kang Youwei!

Interestingly, when reading Kang Youwei's posthumous papers, I found a letter he wrote to a friend in his old age. In it he wrote: "There was a reason then why I wrote the former *Shu Jing* (*My Thoughts on*

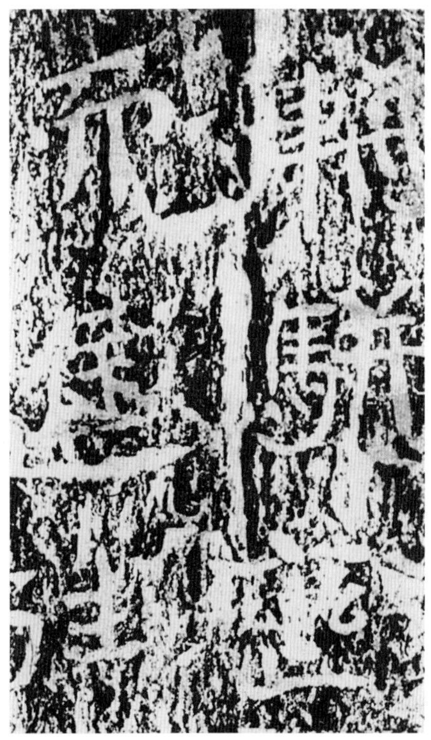

Picture 112 *Inscription on Stone Gate* (part), Eastern Han dynasty

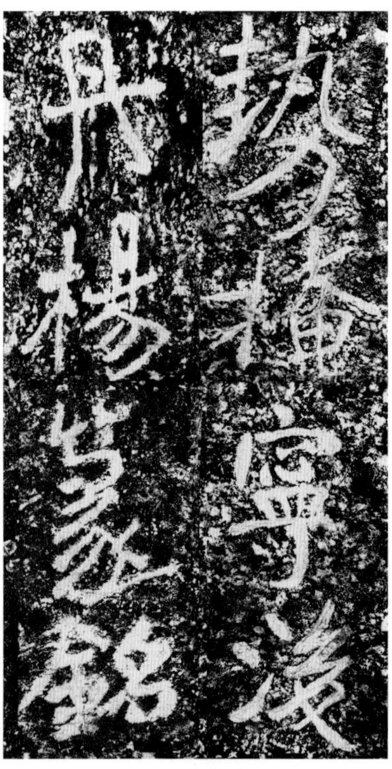

Picture 113 *Inscription on Burying Crane* (part), Southern dynasties

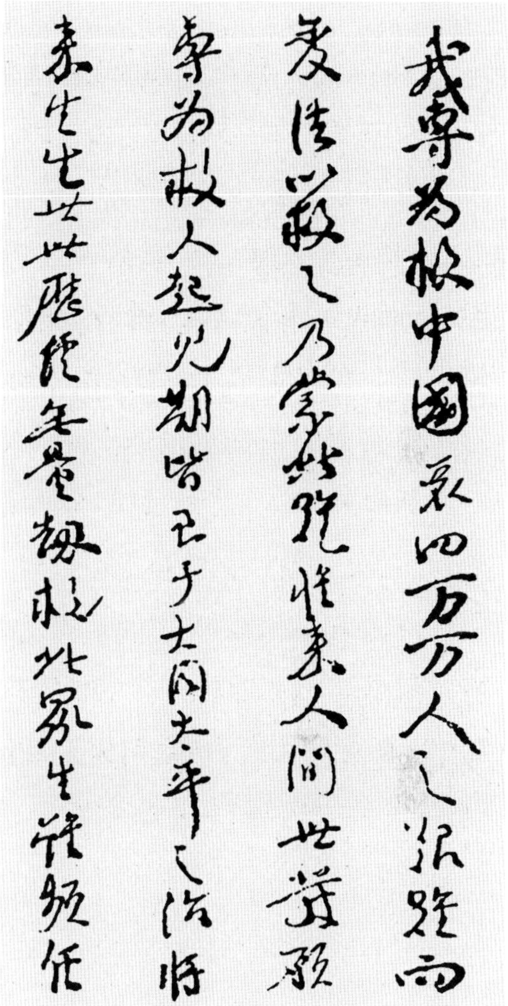

Picture 115 Kang Youwei's calligraphy

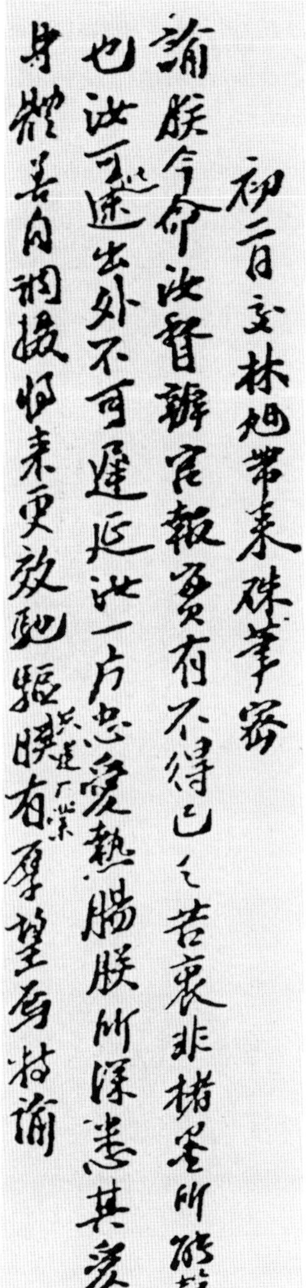

Picture 114 *Secret Imperial Edict of Emperor Guangxu*, Kang Youwei

Calligraphy, i.e. *Enlarged Edition of Sculling in the Boat of Art*). It was not my intention to worship steles. If I had a chance to rewrite it, I would actually worship tiè."

I don't know what people would think about when they see the calligraphy that totally worships tiè (Picture 115) in his letters to his family and friends.

I was only 12 or 13 years old when I lived through the 1960s–1970s in China. I had the best memory at that age.

CHAPTER 45

Seeking Resemblance Inevitably Resulted in "Drawing Characters"

Kang Youwei got the "bēixué" theory off his chest regardless of the consequences of his words in his lifetime. If he had lived another half century, he would have known the repercussions.

I would like to reiterate the rules I mentioned earlier. If the rules were to change radically, the nature of calligraphy would be completely different. If calligraphy were no longer restricted by the fingers and wrist, it would be like dancing ballet and wearing ballet shoes without dancing on the tips of the toes. What would that be called? It would be called "an empty title."

In the previous chapters, I have explained at length the concept of calligraphy as "fǎ." Once it falls into the state of "wúfǎ (no standard)," two conditions inevitably arise.

First, people will, without turning brush or moving fingers, imitate the conventional shape and unique strokes of Chinese characters that the ancients wrote by turning brush and moving fingers. Their aim is to copy the similar form or appearance of the Chinese characters written by the ancients. This phenomenon is called "drawing words or characters."

This was not a rare phenomenon in the ancient times, which was also criticized in calligraphy theory. Zhong Yao, for instance, commented, "The brushwork can be compared to heaven; and the beautiful and moving shape of characters can be compared to earth; common folks cannot figure out the difference." Sun Guoting said, "The category of artistic words, though looking beautiful, involves no real work on the brush." Zhu Lüzhen said: "When delving into the use of the brush, one should not only pursue the resemblance." Although there were calligraphers whose handwriting did "resemble" that of past famous calligraphers, the royal and the literati were all well-acquainted with the brushwork. In the era when authentic brushwork dominated calligraphy, how could "wúfǎ" make a big difference?

However, by the end of the Qing dynasty, the late "beixue" had unconsciously entered the stage of "wúfǎ." Kang Youwei's *Enlarged Edition of Sculling in the Boat of Art* was a formal declaration of "wúfǎ." His book theoretically affirmed the value of "wúfǎ." As a matter of course, calligraphers as a whole consciously and thoroughly entered the age of "wúfǎ."

He Shaoji, a master in the late Qing dynasty, invented "back to the wrist" approach: hukou (part of the hand between the thumb and the index finger) up, palm and five fingers towards the chest, fingers holding the brush handle, both the wrist and elbow hanging in the air. Recently, I visited *The Exhibition of He Shaoji's Calligraphic Career* in Taiwan, which showcased several of his early calligraphic works. The strokes were straight and smooth, different from his later style, and were definitely not written with his "back to the wrist" approach. The small regular script of *Feng Shan Shu* (封禅书, fēngshàn shū) final prose of Sima Xiangru, a litterateur of the Western Han dynasty. It narrates the legend that 72 kings held a ceremony of offering sacrifices to heaven in Mount Tai (Picture 116), which he wrote at the age of 44, was exquisite

Picture 116 *Feng Shan Shu* (封禅书, final prose of Sima Xiangru, a litterateur of the Western Han dynasty. It narrates the legend that 72 kings held a ceremony of offering sacrifices to heaven in Mount Tai) (part), He Shaoji, Qing dynasty

Picture 117 Calligraphy of He Shaoji, Qing dynasty

and complete and the strokes were decisive. But it was clear that he did not follow "back to the wrist" either. Historical evidence showed that he began to adopt the "back to the wrist" approach around the age of 57 (Picture 117), and referred to himself as "the man with the ape's arm," as his poem suggested, "Calligraphy is originally similar to the theory of archery; the most important thing is that the arm is able to circle the air." It remained unclear that He Shaoji took painstaking efforts to create "back to his wrist" approach in his later years.

Interestingly, in the inscriptions to his collection *Epitaph for Prefect Zhang Xuan (Zhang Heru)* in the Northern Wei dynasty, He Shaoji stated: "Every time I did the copy writing, I would go 'back to my wrist,'with my wrist hanging high in the air. Only when I put my entire force into it would I be able to write the word. Before I finished half of the writing, sweat had already soaked my clothes. I thought of how the ancients wrote, they might not be so laborious as I did."

For me, that's true. I grew up in a time of "wúfǎ" and have been fascinated with the shape of Chinese characters since I was a kid, especially these written by the ancients. But I just knew the being as being rather than how the being took shape, as we often brag about our skills in ballet or wear beautiful ballet shoes, yet have no idea that a ballet dancer uses the tips of toes.

To be frank, when we learn "the tradition," we only focus on representing the structure of characters and the thickness of brush strokes. For people born in the 20th century, if they do not learn the knowledge on brushwork, they would have been absolutely ignorant of brushwork and the use of brushwork. Ideally, they can repeat the form of calligraphic copies in an authentic way after 10-years, 20-year practice in their lifetime.

Qian Yong, a Qing-dynasty calligrapher, said earnestly: "Our depth of knowledge is shallow without much insight, and we are intellectually mediocre. It's almost impossible to seek resemblance, let alone similarity in spirit"!

Second, when a calligrapher consciously entered the stage of "wúfǎ," those who still retained logical thinking discovered that the shape of the Chinese characters had become not insignificant. They transitioned from trying to change shape, to exaggeration till the complete elimination of the shape of Chinese characters. "Modern calligraphy" was naturally born overnight.

Japanese have gone ahead of us.

Since the 1970s, China has been engaged in calligraphy exchanges with Japan and influenced by Japanese shodō (书道, way of writing), both ideologically and formally.

Therefore, I will discuss Japanese shodō first and foremost.

CHAPTER 46

A Brief History of Japanese Calligraphy

During the Northern Wei dynasty, Japan directly introduced Chinese calligraphy from Baekje, the king of which received titles of nobility from the Song and Liang dynasties in China. The earliest brush writing in Japan was the works of Prince Shotoku (圣德太子) in the Asuka period (Picture 118), which were close to the style of the Six dynasties.

In Sui and Tang dynasties, China and Japan sent emissaries. In particular, Monk Jian Zhen came to Japan across the sea. The calligraphy of Empress Komyo during the Nara Period (Picture 119) adopted strict and resolute ancient method and exposed "mángjiăo (芒角)" and "yìng dài (映带)," as a loyal fan of Chinese calligraphy.

In Heian period or the glorious age of the Tang dynasty, Sino-Japan Buddhist communication became frequent. Accordingly, Japanese emperor, calligrapher and monk successively came to China to learn calligraphy across the sea, like Emperor Saga (Picture 120), Monk Kukai (Picture 121), Tachibanano Hayanari (Picture 122), Saicho and Monk Enchin. The first three of them were called *Sanpitsu* (三笔, Three Famous Calligraphers). The remaining handwriting was totally Tang style.

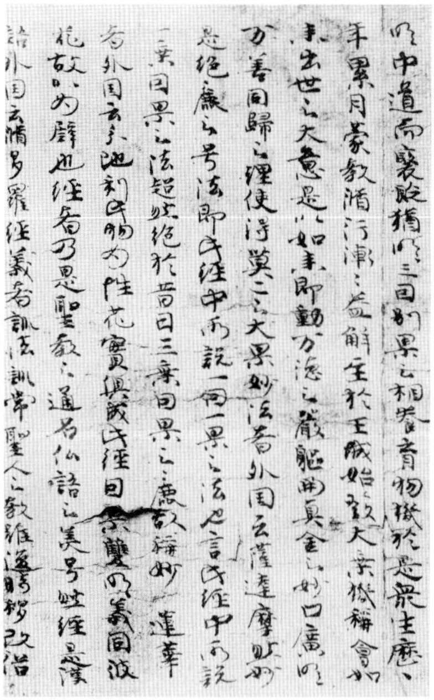

Picture 118 *Expounding Lotus Flower Sutra* (part), Prince Shotoku, Japan

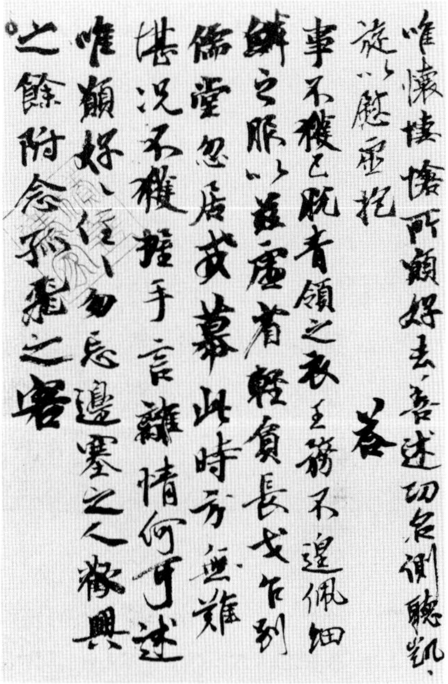

Picture 119 Calligraphy of Empress Komyo, Japan

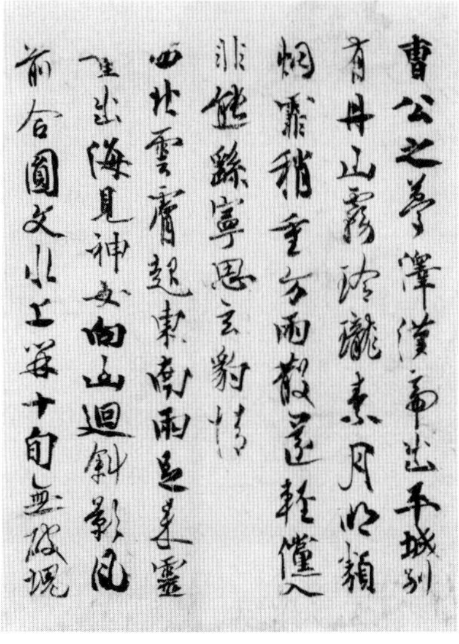

Picture 120 *Remnants of Li Qiao's Miscellaneous Chant* (part), Emperor Saga, Japan

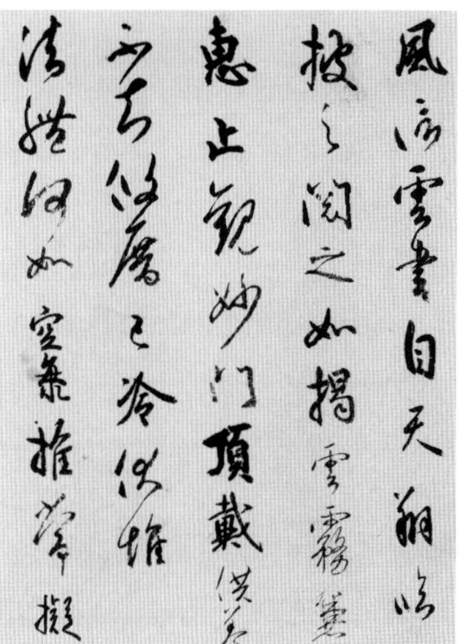

Picture 121 *Fushinjo* (风信帖) (part), Kukai, Japan

The imitation of Tang's calligraphic style in the Heian Period lasted about seven or eight hundred years through the Kamakura period and Muromachi period. From the Five dynasties to the Northern Song dynasty, three Japanese calligraphers, Ono Michikaze (小野道风) (Picture 123), Fujiwarano Sukemasa (藤原佐理) (Picture 124) and Fujiwarano Yukinari (藤原行成) (Picture 125), were hailed as *Sanseki* (三迹) or "three brush traces." They were the representative Pictures of classical style.

The *Sanpitsu* and *Sanseki* were the pioneers and pride of Japanese calligraphy!

This style of ancient calligraphy continued until the Edo period, during which China came to the Ming dynasty. Calligraphers then in Japan were too numerous to name them all.

The later development of Japanese calligraphy was synchronous with that of China.

The most representative calligrapher of Japanese classical calligraphy is by all means Monk Kukai.

He came to China to study the calligraphy of the Tang dynasty at the age of 30, and stayed there for a year and a half. As he noted: "I learned some gǔfǎ (骨法, literally means the "method of bones," but refers to brushwork) while I was in China. Although I have not mastered mòfǎ (墨法, method of ink and brush) to this day, I felt a little more disciplined in writing."

As mentioned above, "calligraphers in the Tang dynasty practiced and advocated fǎ (法, the doctrine or method)," and "fǎ" here refers to the brush turning and moving fingers. The "gǔfǎ" mentioned by Kukai is obviously the "brushwork." Therefore, Japanese classical calligraphy must have incorporated the ancient method of brushwork.

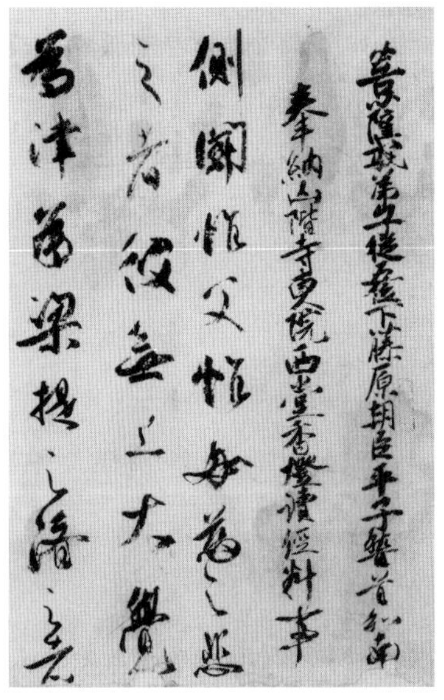

Picture 122 *Ito Naishin'no Ganmon* (伊都内亲王愿文, *Princess Ito's Prayer*) (part), Tachibanano Hayanari, Japan

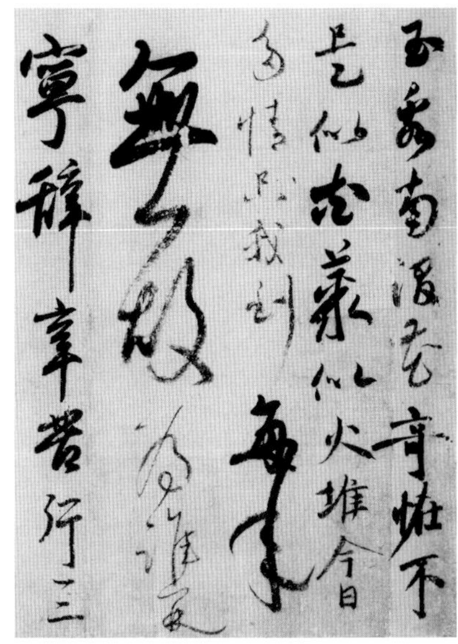

Picture 123 Gyokusenjo (玉泉帖, recording four of Bai Juyi's poems) (part), Ono Michikaze, Japan

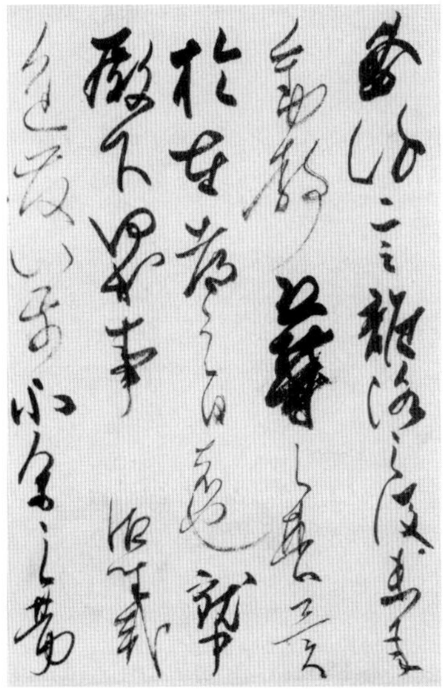

Picture 124 *Touno benjo* (头弁帖, Fujiwara's late piece of work at the ripe age of 55) (part), Fujiwarano Sukemasa, Japan

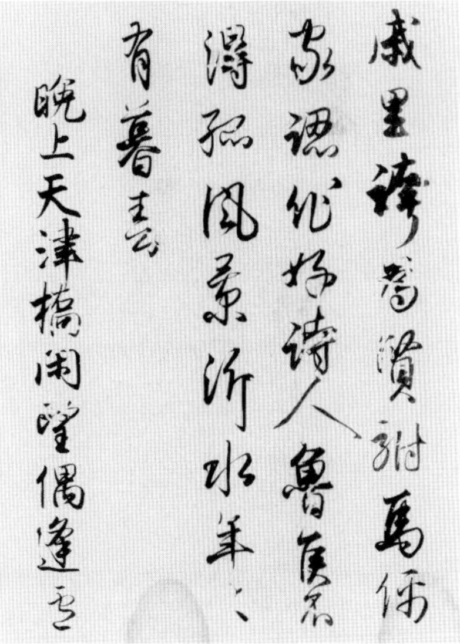

Picture 125 Hakushi shikan (白氏诗卷, Collected Poems of Bai Juyi) (part), Fujiwarano Yukinari, Japan

Looking back to even earlier days, the steles left from the early Yamato period in Japan also went after the calligraphic style of the Northern and Southern dynasties (almost the same time period as Japan) in China, such as *Ujibashi Danpi Monument* (宇治桥断碑, a stone plate on which the origin of the Uji-bashi bridge is described) (Picture 126) and *Hasedera Temple Douban Hokke Sessou Zu* (长谷寺铜板铭, a bronze plaque carved with *Lotus Sutra*) (Picture 127). China then was in the heyday when "no Chinese character was written without fǎ." When calligraphy came into

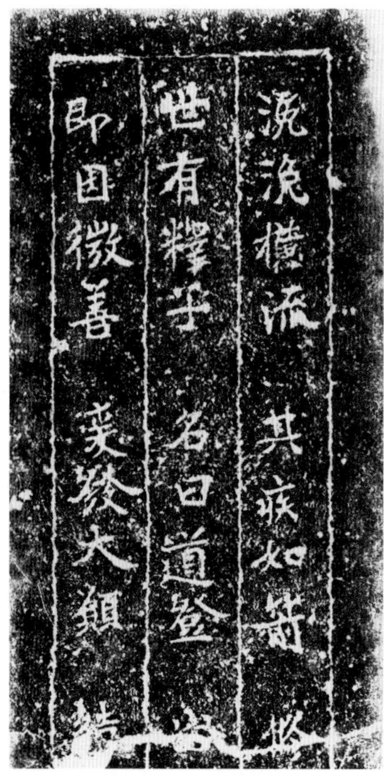

Picture 126 *Ujibashi Danpi Monument* (宇治桥断碑, a stone plate on which the origin of the Uji-bashi bridge is described) (part), Japan

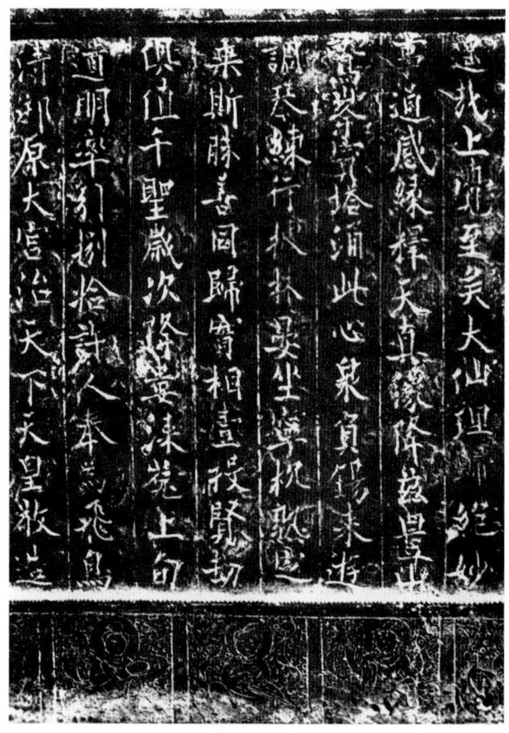

Picture 127 *Hasedera Temple Douban Hokke Sessou Zu* (长谷寺铜板铭, a bronze plaque carved with Lotus Sutra) (part), Japan

Japan, not only the shape of Chinese characters, but also the brushwork of Chinese characters was introduced, which was sufficiently proved by the brushwork shown on the Japanese steles.

The subsequent *kana* script is such an obvious proof, with *hiragana* evolving from cursive script and *katakana* originating from radicals of regular script (Picture 128).

Japanese Kana Script was born in the stage of "shàngfǎ (尚法, upholding the method)." It was wholly written in the hand with the moves of brush turning and fingers twirling the brush. Its advent should be consistent with the historical time when Chinese characters spread to Japan. Therefore, *kana* script certainly resulted from brushwork.

Kana script has long been called *onnade* (女手), "women's writing," which also symbolizes the dominance and rule of Chinese calligraphy. Until now, only a handful of Japanese women have been good at Chinese handwriting. A woman with neat handwriting is sure to impress.

At that time, Japanese people closely followed China no matter in writing posture, the size of paper, or the type of brush. A few years ago, I

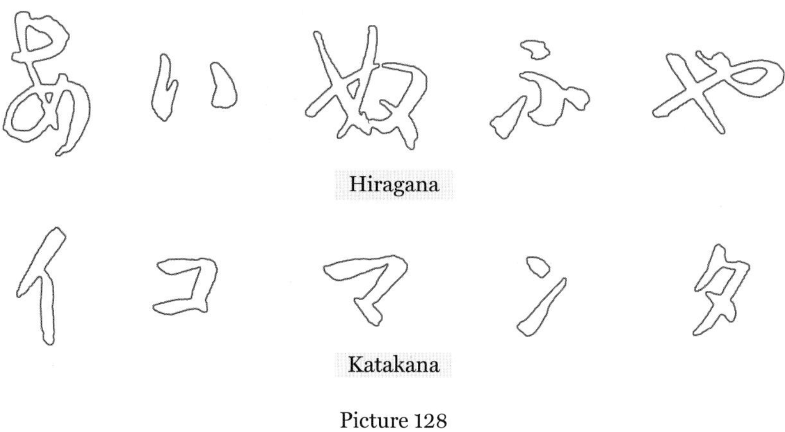

Picture 128

saw in a Japanese magazine a photo of an old man writing with a hand scroll, which was related to the fact that Japanese old men still retained the tradition of "sitting on their knees." Modern Japanese have kept many ancient traditional Chinese habits and customs, such as sumo. Sumo was called "juélì (角力, to wrestle)" in the Western Zhou dynasty in China. It developed into a form of entertainment in the Qin dynasty, and flourished in the Song and Yuan dynasties.

CHAPTER 47

What is Calligraphy and What is Painting?

Modern Japanese calligraphy came out through the Mainichi Shodō (calligraphy) Exhibition (日书道展) and Nitten Exhibition (日展). The earliest works that caused a sensation were *Love* (爱) by Sokyu Ueda (上田桑鸠) (Picture 129) and *Collapse* (崩坏) by Teshima Yukei (手岛右卿) (Picture 130) in 1945.

Japan in the postwar period hoped that calligraphy would enhance national cohesion and promote the "going global" of Japanese culture. Hence, Japanese took the initiative in learning and absorbing Western abstract art, highlighting the visual perception and impact of calligraphy, and considering such factors as mounting, paper color, picture frames, and material related to visual effects as well as the environment where calligraphic works were hung. Simultaneously, Mainichi Shimbun Sha partook in these activities, via which various styles and schools of calligraphy were exhibited and compared on a large scale.

When "new" and "old" calligraphic schools were widely discussed in Japan, Nishikawa Yasushi (西川宁) categorized the modern calligraphy of Sokyu Ueda and Teshima Yukei into "expressionism." As a result, a theory of modern calligraphy arose, which first underscored the expression of lines, the shape of characters, and the role of lyricism.

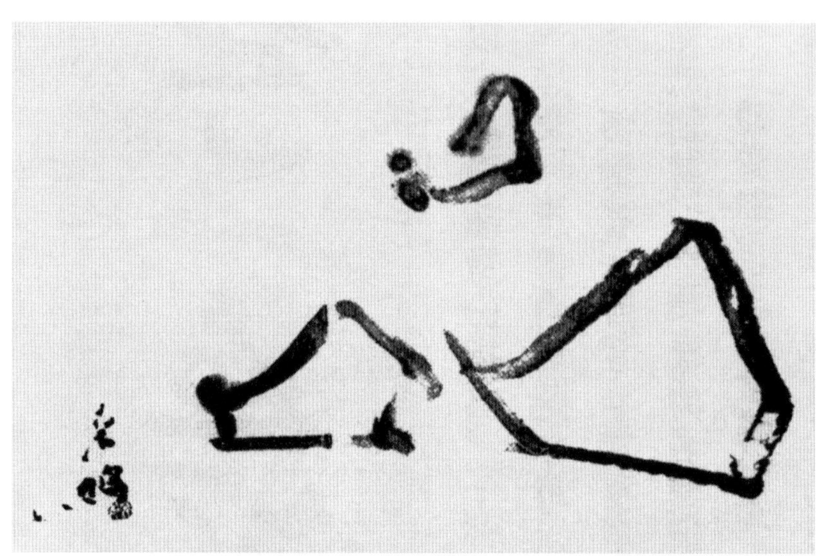

Picture 129 *Love* (爱), Sokyu Ueda (上田桑鸠), Japan

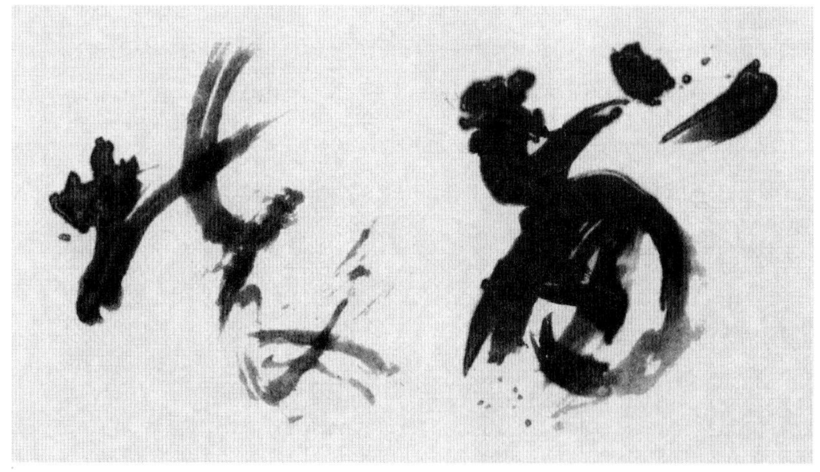

Picture 130 Collapse (崩坏), Teshima Yukei (手岛右卿), Japan

The theory sounds so familiar to us. In fact, it developed from the theory of post-impressionist painting at that time. In the 1980s, the book *Art* (written in 1913) by English art critic and philosopher Clive Bell was well-received in China. In the book, he defines "significant form" as "lines and colors combined in a particular way, certain forms and relations of forms, that stir our aesthetic emotions." His theory has been regarded as the pillar of modernist art theory.

I read the whole book in one sitting and was overwhelmed by it, because I understood a large number of modern paintings, such as the works of Paul Cézanne.

Under the backdrop of modern painting, Japanese calligraphy soon abolished the structure and implied meaning of Chinese characters, and *Bokusho* (墨象, avant-garde Japanese calligraphy drawn with black ink: sumi) emerged. "Significant Form" was immediately used as the most convincing theoretical basis of modern calligraphy. It was at that time that the theories of Western abstract painting and modern calligraphy coalesced. Evidently, Japanese have clearly explained the theories of post-impressionist and abstract painting. If calligraphy were like painting that only left behind visual feelings, and if Clive Bell's theory could be applied to calligraphy, should we get rid of the structure of Chinese characters? As the ancient word of wisdom goes, "With the skin gone, to what can the hair attach itself"?

Don't you find it a big problem?

So what is painting? What is calligraphy?

What is the difference between *Bokusho* and abstract painting? Does the difference lie in the use of oil paints and canvas, and the use of ink and Xuan paper? Have they been integrated ideologically, and the difference simply depends on the variation of materials? If you spray color on Xuan paper and sprinkle ink on canvas, which one is painting and which one is calligraphy? Is there any criterion?

It seems we can't find a single answer for diverse problems.

CHAPTER 48

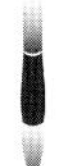

"The Essence of Calligraphy" —A Fruitless Discussion

In the 1930s–1940s, China suffered years of wars and chaos. After 1949, China closed the door to the Western world. Consequently, the understanding and teaching of painting and calligraphy remained *ex parte* and out of date in China.

In the 1970s, China implemented the policy of the reform and opening-up. Chinese's idea of calligraphy was rocked by Japanese Shodō and modernist calligraphy.

I remembered a large number of books on aesthetics were published then in China, which provoked a large discussion on the "essence of calligraphy." Various magazines and newspapers published articles on a range of concepts and had a years-long exhaustive debate with the result no other than "the art of lines." In the end, the debate boiled down to "significant form." Later, when Westerners read Chinese calligraphy theories, they were startled to realize the extent to which "significant form" had been abused by Chinese.

In addition, there was an overemphasis on humanism, spirituality, and artistic accomplishment. I would like to ask: Is there an art that loses contact with the common ground among humanism, spirituality, and artistic accomplishment?

What we need to clarify is not the common ground but the essential difference of art genres.

In recent years, in addition to the *shojisusho* (少字数书, calligraphy of a few characters) and the avant-garde *Bokusho* (墨象, avant-garde Japanese calligraphy drawn with black ink: sumi) that have been freely used by Chinese, the Western "post-modern" painting has also directly influenced Chinese calligraphy. "Post-modern" calligraphy, in which fragments of ancient writing were collaged in a modern and disorderly manner, has been represented at exhibitions. This suggests that after the reform and opening-up, China has strived to learn from the West economically and catch up in the art of calligraphy.

When we go back and attempt to elucidate the "essence of calligraphy," we still disagree with each other. And the more we talk about it, the more confusion arises, straying from the main theme of the debate. However, any argument, positive or negative, must be first based on a thorough understanding of the object.

The West also has clearly delimited classical painting, an art based on "realism," which takes root in the physical limitations of what human eyes can see.

Today, what baffles and vexes Chinese most is that they suddenly are perplexed about how to theorize classical and traditional calligraphy. When they interpret traditional calligraphy, they just prattle on about "keeping the shape of Chinese characters."

In recent years, articles that inquired into the "essence of calligraphy" oddly seem out of sight, probably because authors know better than to toil themselves in the strenuous work.

And the result of the discussion? The matter was dropped.

CHAPTER 49

A Master Key of Calligraphy

In calligraphy and painting, there is a babelism in terms of category and paradigm, because modernist calligraphy and modernist painting "arrived at the same end by different means."

Modern calligraphy is based on "wúfǎ (无法, no method)."

When the rule of calligraphy ("fǎ") no longer existed, that is, when the skill of right-handed brush-turning no longer served as a physiological restriction, and no movement of right-handed brush-turning was involved, and calligraphy became entirely a reflection towards visual sense, then "shūfǎ (书法, calligraphy; literally means the method of writing)" was naturally "huà fǎ (画法, the method of painting)." That's why the ancients had a term known as "huà zì (画字, painting characters)."

To retain the shape of Chinese characters, to put it bluntly, is just writing hard brush characters with soft brushes, and simulating and refining strokes and shapes formed by brushwork. Naturally, "hard-tipped pen calligraphy" walked out from the dark corner and becomes fashionable.

This fundamentally misunderstands ancient traditional calligraphy.

In the two-thousand-year history of immense calligraphy, "brushwork" functions as a master key that can open any kind of lock in treatise and practice on calligraphy.

If I expound brushwork, I would have to start all over again. Please check the previous chapters if you are interested.

CHAPTER 50

An Epiphany on the Bus

Though I started to write and paint when I was little, it was quite late when I came in touch with Chinese painting.

As early as the beginning of 1973, it was the first time that "Worker-Peasant-Soldier-Students" were recruited. At that time, I had just graduated from high school and was less than 18 years old. I was fascinated with Nanjing University of the Arts. Because of my good handwriting, I applied for the major of "Chinese Painting." Under the guidance of kind-hearted people, I scarcely knew what to do but to follow a female teacher who painted "gōngbǐ (工笔, traditional Chinese realistic painting characterized by fine brushwork and close attention to detail)." I repeatedly drew hundreds of "lines" on Xuan paper every day.

I had no idea why I should learn Chinese painting, perhaps only because I heard, with perplexity, others saying that "shūhuà tóngyuán (书画同源, painting and calligraphy share common origin)."

Two months later, I went to the countryside and started working in a production team.

I had deeply buried the question of "common origin of painting and calligraphy" in my heart. Later, I served as a soldier. Afterwards, I went to Jiangsu Traditional Chinese Painting Institute for further study. Though I had practiced and thought for two years, I still did not find the answer.

"Shūhuà tóngyuán (书画同源, painting and calligraphy share common origin)" has been passed from mouth to mouth among the literati for almost a thousand years. It's nearly a "pet phrase." Calligraphers repeatedly elaborated on the term in books. People naturally followed suit and regarded the wording as the "truth."

I often ask myself: Where is the "tóng (同, commonality)"? As I continue my practice and deepen my understanding in calligraphy and painting, I do figure out more differences between painting and calligraphy. I firmly believe that what the ancients considered "tóng yuán 同源 (common origin)" must make sense; it's just that we still don't know the exact commonality or completely misunderstand the original meaning.

I suddenly felt refreshed and enlightened one day.

In the spring of 1988, I went to Xiaguan Wharf to send someone away, and came back taking the number 31 bus. It was drizzling outside. I sat in the left seat by the window, and kept looking at the storefronts and pedestrians that I passed quickly. Without knowing it, the answer to "common origin of painting and calligraphy" suddenly dawned on me, and my heart beat wildly.

That day I paid the price for the epiphany: missing two stops. I was caught in the rain, but I walked lightly all the way home.

CHAPTER 51

Confusion About Traditional Chinese Painting

To be honest, I didn't like traditional Chinese painting in the past because there was so much confusion.

I didn't understand why the ancient Chinese did not create figure paintings in a realistic way. Why couldn't they draw like Westerners do? If it were due to the use of brushes and the limitation of tools, why can modern people use brushes to draw realistic paintings? Was that because the ancients had inaccurate vision? Of course not, as long as you observe the amazing ancient handicrafts with impeccable shapes. Why was it until the Ming dynasty that comparatively realistic portraits appeared? Why did Chinese painters, in two-thousand-year history, avoid using a realistic approach?

I believe many colleagues studying Chinese painting have the same confusion.

Let's start with what we are most familiar with.

What is traditional Chinese painting anyway? The definition that is on everyone's mind must be Xie He's *Six Criteria* (六法 liùfǎ) in the Southern Qi dynasty. Xie declared, "There are six criteria in painting, and what are they? (1) Spiritual nature is conveyed by instilling vitality (qìyùn shēngdòng, 一气韵生动是也). (2) Inner quality is suggested through skillful handling of the brush (gǔfǎ yòng bǐ, 二骨法用笔是也)

(3) Correspondence with reality is achieved through the representation of forms (yìng wù xiàngxíng, 三应物象形是也). (4) Accordance to type is accomplished by application of colors (suílèi fùcǎi, 四随类赋彩是也). (5) Layout and composition are determined by careful positioning and placement (jīngyíng wèizhì, 五经营位置是也). (6) And similitude and accuracy are dependent upon faithful modeling and depiction (chuán yí móxiě, 六传移模写是也)."

Mr. Qian Zhongshu once doubted the punctuation in the paragraph above in his *Guǎn Zhuī Biān* (管锥编, which Qian himself gave the English title of *Limited Views*). He thought that according to correct grammar, pauses should be made as follows: "(1) Qìyùn, Spiritual nature; this is engendering movement qìyùn, shēngdòng (一, 气韵, 生动是也). (2) Gǔfǎ, Inner quality; this is using the brush gǔfǎ, yòng bǐ (二, 骨法, 用笔是也). (3) Yìngwù, Responding to objects; this is making images of their shape yìngwù, xiàngxíng (三, 应物, 象形是也). (4) Suílèi, Complying with categories; this is applying colors suílèi fùcǎi (四, 随类, 赋彩是也). (5) Jīngyíng, Arrangement; this is composition jīngyíng, wèizhì (五, 经营, 位置是也). (6) Chuányí, Transmitting and reproducing; this is copying from a model chuányí, móxiě (六, 传移, 模写是也)." I think Mr. Qian is right.

In the Tang dynasty, Zhang Yanyuan abbreviated the six criteria into four characters in his *Famous Paintings Through History* (历代名画记 *Lìdài Mínghuà Jì,*), which continues to this day. They are "1. Spirit Resonance (一曰气韵生动 qìyùn shēngdòng, the vitality and energy that transmitted from the artist into the artwork). 2. Bone Method (二曰骨法用笔 gǔfǎ yòng bǐ, the way that an artist uses the brush. This refers to both the texture of the brushstroke and the close link between handwriting and personality). 3. Correspondence to Object (三曰应物象形 yìng wù xiàngxíng, refers to how an artist portrays the objects using different shapes and lines). 4. Suitability to Type (四曰随类赋彩 suí lèi fù cǎi, implies to the application of tones, color shades, and layers in the painting). 5. Division and Planning (五曰经营位置 jīngyíng wèizhì, involves placing and arranging objects in terms of space and depth, mainly, picture composition). 6. Transmission by Copying (六曰传移模写 chuán yí móxiě, the techniques of reproducing the look of the models, not only from life but also the works of antiquity). His interpretation also makes sense to me.

The problem is two kinds of punctuation yield two concepts.

In the former, "qìyùn (气韵, spiritual nature or spirit consonance)" equals to "shēngdòng (生动, vitality)"; "gǔfǎ (骨法, personality of handwriting)" is the same thing as "yòng bǐ (用笔, brushwork)." However, to match both pronunciation and meaning in two lines, "suílèi (随类, suitability to type)" should equal to "fùcǎi (赋彩, application of colors)," but the two words seem too far-fetched. In the latter such as "qìyùn shēngdòng (气韵生动, spirit resonance)" and "gǔfǎ yòngbǐ (骨法用笔, the way an artist uses the brush)," four characters form one criteria. According to Mr. Qian Zhongshu, the first, third, fourth, fifth and sixth criteria can still make sense with four characters in one sentence, but the second one "gǔfǎ yòng bǐ (骨法用笔)" in which bone "gǔfǎ (骨法, personality of handwriting)" and "yòngbǐ (用笔, brushwork)" are used in the same sentence, just "like cooking old rice that you can't knead into a rice ball."

Whatever kind of explanation has some truth or ineptness under scrutiny. Although I am talking about two concepts, they are not profoundly different in nature because their contents are exactly the same.

I don't want to linger here for too long, because that is not the key to the question.

CHAPTER 52

"Gǔfǎ (骨法, Personality of Handwriting)" is the Technique of Brushwork

The theory of traditional Chinese painting almost surfaced at the same time as that of calligraphy, and was inseparable from calligraphy at the very beginning.

The earliest systematic theory of painting was Gu Kaizhi's *On Painting* in the Eastern Jin dynasty. At that time, Indian Buddhist painting prevailed in China. Apart from the second criterion of "gǔfǎ yòngbǐ (骨法用笔)," the other five criteria were all derived from standards in Buddhist painting. The third, fourth, fifth and sixth criteria in the *Six Criteria* seem evident at a glance and beyond reproach, while the former two aroused most controversy from the ancient times to the present.

First, let's put aside the first criterion "*qiyunshengdong* (气韵生动)," and turn to the second one "gǔfǎ yòngbǐ (骨法用笔)." Gu Kaizhi mentioned "gǔfǎ (骨法)" and "yòngbǐ (用笔)" early in his *On Painting*.

And what after all is "gǔfǎ yòngbǐ (骨法用笔)"? This is the mysterious and practical key. In the final analysis, the perplexity of modern people in traditional Chinese painting is that this key problem has not been clarified. How to explain the word "gǔ (骨, bone)" in "gǔfǎ yòngbǐ" seems the top priority.

"Gǔ (骨)" refers to (1) bone, undoubtedly; (2) the dictionary says: "gǔ provides an analogy for the frame supporting inside an object," such as "gānggǔ (钢骨, skeleton frame)" and "lónggǔ (龙骨, kneel of a ship)." Whether it is the first or the second interpretation, they both refer to the key hidden within that is invisible to the naked eye.

I am accustomed to reading historical materials which are closest to the time of occurrence, because they are the most authentic and convincing. Materials that dated back too far from the birth of the event will easily cause confusion and misunderstanding.

In the previous chapters, I quoted the words of Japanese Monk Kukai: "I learned some gǔfǎ while I was in China . . ." People in the Jin and Tang dynasties often used the word "gǔ" to portray brushwork. They did so to illustrate the facts that: (1) Bone is hidden in the flesh, which cannot be easily found without pointing out, "a brush stroke in the character, as the eye in Zen"; (2) Bone is the key framework that supports the body.

In the Jin and Tang dynasties, "gǔfǎ (骨法)" was used to illustrate the brushwork within characters, which was pertinent and accurate. Zhang Sengyao in the Southern dynasties was reputed for the so-called "mògǔ" technique mògǔ fǎ (没骨法, boneless), which suggested hiding the lines of "gǔfǎ (骨法)" and directly painting with colors. "gǔfǎ yòngbǐ (骨法用笔)" undoubtedly refers to the use of brush throughout the ages. The question is how to use the brush.

I took this opportunity to carefully read *Treatises on Paintings in Past Chinese Dynasties.*

CHAPTER 53

"Painting and Calligraphy" Share a "Common Origin" Here

Let's first extract some paragraphs from *Treatises on Paintings in Past Chinese Dynasties*.

Zhang Yanyuan's *On Six Criteria of Painting* in the Tang dynasty: "Painting is the art of describing objects, so the foremost thing is to seek similarity of shape; but only similarity of shape is not enough, it must complete the bones and strength inside, and the bones and strength must be based on yì (意, intention of painters); the painting is not a purely objective depiction, but must incorporate the subjective intention of the author, that is, artistic processing; the subjective intention is abstract and must be expressed by means of the brush, so good painters must also be good calligraphers."

"In the past, Zhang Zhi learned from the methods of Cui Yuan and Du Du's cursive script, thus evolving his own handwriting into the present cursive poise. His single stroke laces together several characters that are connected by life-force and not separated by lines. Only Zijing (the courtesy name of Wang Xianzhi) understood the profound truth in it, so the first character of each line often continued from the previous line, which was why Wang's handwriting was called 'one-stroke writing.' After that, Lu Tanwei also created 'one-stroke painting' without breaks in the continuous stroke. Since then Lu realized that the method of brush using was the same in calligraphy and painting."

"Wu Daoxuan (the other name of Wu Daozi) from the Tang dynasty was so unique and was like no one else, before or since. His works were unprecedented, compared with the artistic pieces created by Gu Kaizhi and Lu Tanwei, and he saw no latecomers that could innovate as he did. So, he taught Zhang Xu the brushwork and it became known that the brushwork in painting and calligraphy was the same."

Guo Xi and his son Guo Si in the Northern Song dynasty concluded in "Instructions on Painting Landscapes" of *Lofty Appeal of Forests and Streams* (林泉高致·山水训 línquán gāo zhì·shānshuǐ xùn): "Learning painting is no different from learning calligraphy."

"Brush and ink are men's daily items. If you don't even know how to manipulate them, how could you create wonderful art! This is not hard. Your handwriting is closely associated with it. Therefore, legend says Wang Youjun (alternate title of Wang Xizhi) likes geese. Wang intended to learn from the neck turning moves of geese and combine its posture with handwriting, which is exactly the same as brushwork for painting. People often say that good calligraphers tend to be good painters, because there is non-stagnation in turning their wrists and using brushes." Here, "turning the wrist" is based on the "wrist method" since the advent of the table in the Song dynasty as was mentioned in Chapter 21 and Chapter 22.

Zhao Xihu in the Southern Song dynasty expounded in"An Interpretation of Ancient Paintings" of *Pure Records of the Cave Heaven* (洞天清录古画辨 dòngtiānqīng lù gǔ huà biàn): "Painting shows no trace of handwriting. It doesn't mean the thickness and thinness of ink traces cannot be distinguished. Just as good calligraphers hide their brush tips, such as zhuīhuàshā (锥画沙, painting with an awl on the sand) and yìnyìnní (印印泥, the seal stamping into the clay). Hiding the tip of brush depends on writing with composure and to the heart's content. If one could write well and master the method of holding the brush, he would know there is no trace of handwriting. Therefore, the ancients like Sun Taigu, and the contemporary calligraphers such as Mi Yuanzhang (courtesy name of Mi Fu) are both adept at handwriting as well as painting. Painting and calligraphy are actually one thing."

Yang Weizhen in the Yuan dynasty elucidated in *Preface to the Precious Mirror of Paining* (图绘宝鉴序 tú huì bǎo jiàn xù): "Calligraphy flourished in the Jin dynasty, while painting blossomed in the Tang and Song dynasties. Calligraphy and painting are the same thing. The literati and officialdom that paint well must also write good characters, and their drawing method is where the method of calligraphy lies."

Li Rihua in the Ming dynasty said in *Miscellanea from the Purple Peach Studio* (紫桃轩杂缀 zǐtáo xuān zá zhuì): "I once talked about it in general forms that if one were to draw well, he must first learn good hand writing, only then did he know how to use the brush."

Zou Yigui in the Qing dynasty said in *Painting Treatises by Xiaoshan* (小山画谱 xiǎoshān huàpǔ, Xiaoshan is the courtesy name of Zou Yigui): "When you use the brush, you will adopt the methods of xuán zhēn (悬针, dangling needle), chuí lù (垂露, dropping dew), tiě lián (铁镰, iron sickle), fú é (浮鹅, floating goose), cán tóu (蚕头, silkworm head) and shǔ wěi (鼠尾, mouse tail), and all the methods agree with each other vaguely."

These kind of discussions in *Treatises on Paintings in Past Chinese dynasties* are plentifully available.

The conclusion is crystal clear: the brushwork for painting is the brushwork for calligraphy. The brushwork features turning the brush and moving fingers. Before Xie He's *Six Criteria* came in place, Wang Wei in *Discussion of Painting* (叙画 xù huà) frankly argued: "Painting is not only an activity that only concerns the moving of a painter's fingers and palm, but also a process of instilling the thought of the painter. That's where the appeal and delight of painting come from."

This painting theory of "moving fingers and palm" confirms the ancient calligraphic theory that "the copybooks for calligraphy in the Wei and Jin dynasties all show characters written with the strokes of the palm and fingers."

According to my previous reasoning on the origin and evolution of brushwork, it is not hard to imagine that when the ancients held a piece of silk paper in their hands and drew on the paper, in the absence of support, it is convenient and appropriate to turn the brush just like in calligraphy.

When I was young, I looked at the murals in the tombs of the Han, Wei, and Jin dynasties (Picture 131), and always found the strokes strange. They looked smooth, fluent and casual, exactly the same as the strokes of Chinese characters on the bamboo slips from the Han dynasty (Picture 132). I once painted with a brush on the wall, but the lines were not the same as on the ancient frescoes. Like all the people today, I didn't turn my brush. Presumably, the peculiar lines on the murals in the Han and Wei tombs could only be drawn when turning the brush.

The calligraphy theory and painting theory of the same period all focused on brushwork. Painters drawing for the tomb might not be famous painters, but their method sufficiently reflected the fashion of that time, which was, no brush was unturned.

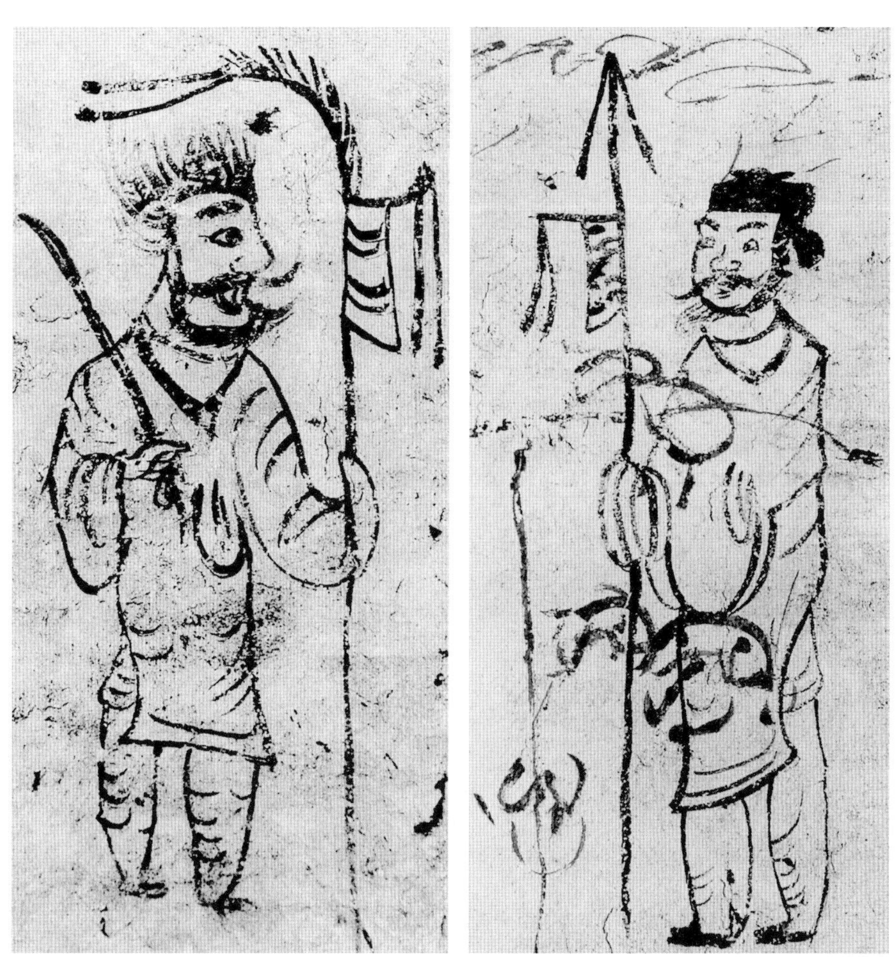

Picture 131 Mural paintings in the main chamber of a Han tomb in Qianmuchengyi Village, Yingchengzi Town, Jinzhou District, Liaoning Province, Eastern Han dynasty

According to clan records, life-size murals in the Tang dynasty were painted by painters who tied brushes to bamboo poles. That's why they could draw a line from beginning to end. If you watch the mural closely, you will find the gliding force is used in the start and end of the stroke.

Once I figured out the brushwork of calligraphy, I've clarified "gǔfǎ yòngbǐ (骨法用笔, the way an artist uses the brush)."

"Common origins of calligraphy and painting" was based on the "same origin" of calligraphic brushwork.

Today, people are confused about traditional Chinese painting, which leads to controversy and a series of problems. In the end, the problems stem from their ignorance of calligraphic brushwork.

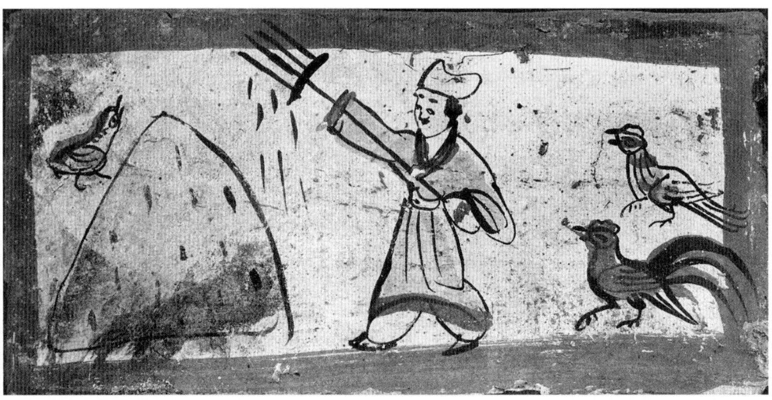

Picture 132 Brick murals in the tombs of the Wei and Jin dynasties unearthed in Jiayuguan City, Gansu Province, Western Jin dynasty

CHAPTER 54

No Brushwork, No Painting

Apparently, "gǔfǎ yòngbǐ (骨法用笔)" is a technical issue, while "qìyùn shēngdòng, (气韵生动)" is an overall feeling. Take calligraphy as an example. Ancient inscriptions are beautiful, indescribable and implicit in the eye of the beholder. It is difficult for practitioners to start with the standard such as "qīngyì (清逸, pure, transcendent and free from vulgarity)," "yōuyǎ (悠雅, carefree, content and elegant)," "duānzhuāng (端庄, dignified and decorous)" and "qiú měi (遒美, vigorous and beautiful)."

Guo Ruoxu in the Northern Song dynasty spoke to the point: "The sophisticated *Six Criteria* is well established and will not be changed for the ages, but the five aspects following gǔfǎ yòngbǐ (skillful handling of the brush, or bone method in employing the brush) can be learned. However, the acquisition of "qìyùn (气韵, spiritual nature or spirit consonance)" requires innate talent, which can be obtained neither by virtue of subtlety and delicacy, nor through long-term accumulation. It can only be achieved by mental conception. I don't know how I made it but I did it without realizing it." That is true, only technique can be learned.

Zou Yigui in the Qing dynasty said, "Qìyùn can only be obtained after completing the painting. How could you start when you are seeking to achieve qìyùn at the very beginning? Only a connoisseur prioritizes qìyùn. It's not what a painter will pursue."

His analysis sounds reasonable and makes sense. And how can we appropriately understand "qìyùn?"

In the previous chapter I mention "one-stroke writing" and "one-stroke painting." I have already elaborated on the concept of the former, which is created by continuous left and right brush turning that result in successive strokes and xiàngbèi (向背) that leads to continuous flow of strokes. It brings about a comforting and vivid rhythm, a feeling which the ancients must also share.

They coined the most exact word to express the feeling, qìyùn (气韵, spiritual nature or spirit consonance).

So is the "one-stroke painting," but only the "xíng (形, shape)" should be relatively taken care of. Whether xing is vivid depends on the overall qìyùn (气韵, spiritual nature or spirit consonance), while qìyùn should be embodied in the use of brush (brushwork). In *On Virtues and Faults in the Use of the Brush* (论用笔得失 lùn yòng bǐ déshī,), Guo Ruoxu said: "Generally, in painting, as spirit consonance originates from pleasing the mind, so spiritual character (神采 shéncǎi) is produced by using the brush. The problems of using the brush properly may be readily appreciated."

Li Rihua in the Ming dynasty explained: "If you want to draw an object or scenery, it's better to possess the shì (势, force or momentum) than to possess the xíng (形, shape); it is better to possess yùn (韵, charm and grace) than its shì; but it's even better to get its xìng (性, temperament and disposition) than its yùn. Xìng, whether it's square, round, flat or oblate, the shape can be painted by the brush. Shì, the trend of turning and changing direction, can be taken by brush. But not all shì can be captured by the brush, and you can refer to the image and object as there will always be beyond the reach of brush. Yùn, the interest of charm, can be figured out with mental conception. It could be obtained unexpectedly but not by racking one's brains. Xìng refers to the nature of things, only to be nurtured and naturally presented with extreme familiarity of skills. Its presence doesn't require taking special care of."

"Xìng" is personality that is innate; "yùn" is acquired in mental wandering by chance, and can be acquired neither through deliberate planning nor lingering thoughts. Only shì and xìng can be taught and learned.

Shì, as I have mentioned earlier, refers to the tendency of turning the brush and generating force. Li said, "Not all shì can be captured by the brush" because "one needs to refer to images," and it is impossible to determine "xíng (form)" completely by "shì" like calligraphy.

Here arises a contradictory yet crucial question.

Traditional Chinese painting adopts the brushwork of calligraphy, that is, turning the brush to gain strength and acquire shì, and xíng is determined by the skill of dealing with the hand, which is in contradiction with the objective "xiěxíng (写形, describing the shape)."

I have painted sketches for many years and also practiced brushwork for a long time. I am fully aware that these are completely two different things. However, traditional Chinese painting abruptly blends these together, and emphasizes calligraphic brushwork.

Zhang Yanyuan once put: "Nowadays when painters draw people, they are good at roughly grasping the appearance, and capturing their shape, but the drawn figures lack *qìyùn*; if the paintings are colored appropriately, they will lose the brushwork. How can they even qualify as painting"!

No wonder, Chinese painting gave up light and shade and three-dimensional viewpoint from the beginning. The gŭfă yòngbǐ emphasized by the Chinese was a shackle that restricted objectivity and accuracy of the vision.

In the Tang dynasty, Zhang Zao famously illustrated: "We learn from nature on the outside and get inspired from within." It is truly so. The word has been used countless times for thousands of years: nature is my teacher; and after taking a panoramic view, I will turn what I learn into the *Six Criteria* in my heart, and should express them with the source of brushwork in calligraphy.

The method of traditional Chinese painting, in fact, is the method of Chinese calligraphy. Strictly speaking, the most essential part of traditional Chinese painting is to turn the brush left and right and generate strength with the flowing trend of xiàngbèi (向背).

I see!

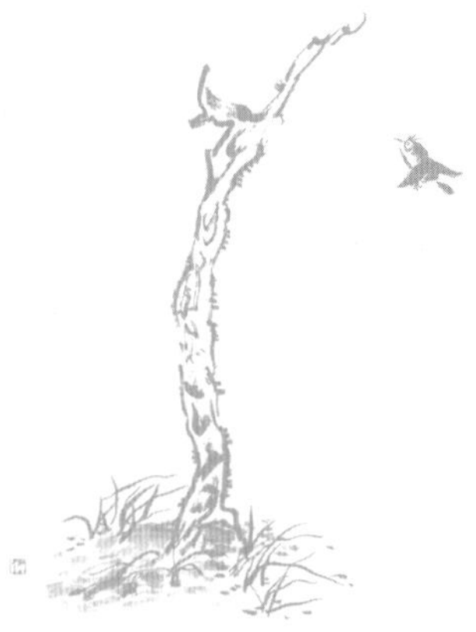

CHAPTER 55

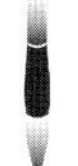

"Only One Route to Reach Mount Hua since Ancient Times"

In view of this contradiction, Chinese have developed their own theory of "conveying the spirit (传神 chuánshén)," first proposed by Gu Kaizhi. Painting is between "likeness and unlikeness," "not to seek likeness of form, but likeness of spirit," "describing the spirit through the form." These words are so familiar to all of us that we can memorize it by heart and recite it fluently, just like a young monk chanting scriptures.

Imagine if you only depict the shape, you will lose the brushwork; if you only pursue the brush, you will lose the shape and form. The most fundamental thing in painting is drawing the lines. It is hard to draw realistic shapes and models with a soft brush, and even harder when Chinese draw the lines using the method of calligraphic "brushwork."

Comparing "xiěxíng (写形, describing the form and shape)" with "using the brush," ancient Chinese always prioritized brushwork, and no stroke was formed without turning the brush. Therefore, we could only take a compromised approach: to get as close to the image as possible without losing the brushwork. How could we get a realistic picture if we depict the shape by brushwork? The best effort we can make is to draw a general picture. To replace the brushwork with the form is an intolerable matter by the course of nature; it's violating the "law" and should be avoided.

Therefore, faced with this great contradiction, Chinese painting can never realistically "describe the form," while it has to "resemble the form" as much as possible. So naturally it could only choose "shénsì (神似, likeness in spirit)"—just as there has been only one route to reach Mount Hua since the ancient times. It took an arduous journey to be a painter in ancient China!

Traditional Chinese painting's "depicting the form" and "using the brush" are like a pair of quarrelsome yet inseparable couple, who have been fighting all their lives. In the gap of formidable survival, "describing the spirit through the form" is the only possible solution.

When the writing brush was invented, Chinese developed the most sustainable method to use the brush as a tool, which resulted in the arts of Chinese calligraphy and painting, like two melons on the single vine of a brush.

And if you think more about it, "describing the spirit through the form" is the aesthetic basis that was naturally born from the ancient method of using the brush.

CHAPTER 56

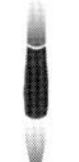

"Literati Painting" Is a Distant Mountain of Bewilderment

Over the past century, traditional Chinese painting has undergone radical and profound changes.

It was mainly influenced by Western art: the introduction of hard-tipped writing tools such as the pencil and pen; the advent of photographic and printing techniques as well as computer graphics; the use of light and dark, three-dimensional space, modernist, and even post-modernist art concepts in Western painting. Thanks to the above changes, Chinese people's long-suppressed and restricted visual sense was liberated as never before.

At this time, a great contrast was apparent between traditional Chinese painting and Western painting, and there were even more irreconcilable contradictions in theories.

I grew up in such a background, satiated with the pleasure of realistic shapes and forms of Western classical painting, while "gulping down" Chinese painting and its theory, which was so "uncomforting."

You must have remembered an article published in the early 1980s, *Chinese Painting as I See It*, which argued that Chinese painting was on the wane and at the end of its rope. The article shocked and caused controversy in the art arena. However, the author spoke out the real status of Chinese painting and boldly acted as the child in Hans Christian Andersen's fairy tale *The Emperor's New Clothes* who watched along with the adults and cried out the truth.

In 1988, a *New Literati Painting Exhibition* was conducted in China.

No matter what is the "new" literati, the "new" must have come from the "old." What is the "old literati painting"?

The explanation in the *Cíhǎi* (辞海, a semi-encyclopedic dictionary of Standard Mandarin Chinese) is as follows: "Literati painting, also known as 'scholarly painting,' refers to the paintings of men of letters and scholar-officials in feudal China, which stands in opposition to the paintings of the folk and palace academies. Su Shi in the Song dynasty proposed 'scholar-official painting"; Dong Qichang of the Ming dynasty coined the term 'the painting of the literati' and considered Wang Wei of the Tang dynasty as its founder and the ancestor of the Southern School. The authors of 'literati painting' generally avoided social reality, and mostly cultivated a more intimate style of landscape such as mountains, rivers, flowers, and trees to express their 'spirituality' or personal grievances, and also contained resentment against national oppression or corrupt politics. The painters were thought to have sought the shìqì (士气, inner realities) and expressed their own yìpǐn (逸品, lofty natures), their interest in brushwork and ink, their disregard for resemblance, their emphasis on atmospheric essence, and their stress on literary cultivation, which had considerablyinfluenced the expression of mood in painting and the development of ink and wash, and freehand brushwork techniques. Yet, the decadent stage of the school often played with the form of brushwork and ink, and their content tended to be empty and spiritually impoverished."

The Japanese scholar Omura Seigai explained "literati painting" as follows: "It is not in the name of a school or style, but is distinguished by the identity of the author." Namely, "literati painting" is a painting by the literati.

In the history of traditional Chinese painting, "literati painting" has always been a supreme, yet distant mountain bathed in murky clouds and mist.

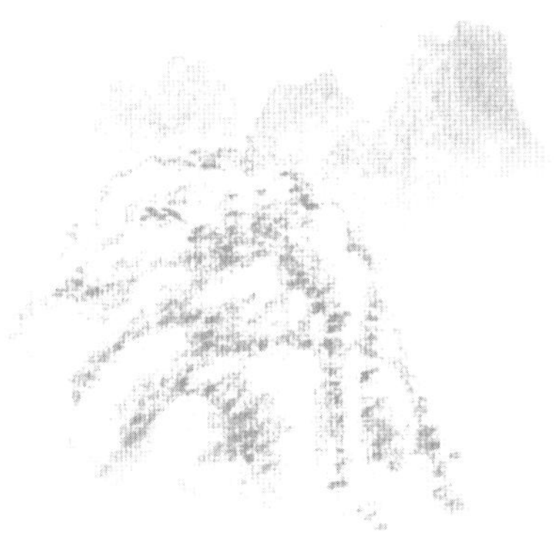

CHAPTER 57

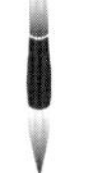

"If We Assess the Merits of the Painting Only by the Resemblance, Then Our Insight Is Similar to That of Children."

When people talk about "literati painting," they talk no more than the requirement of knowing poetry, calligraphy, paintings and yìn (印, an imprint created by the seal). There remain doubts and misgivings in the genre.

Poetry and calligraphy were commonplace to ancient literati, especially those in the Tang and Song dynasties. They know the crafts just as everyone can write vernacular Chinese today. Inscribing a poem on the painting was a favorite of the Song scholars, and it became a rule in the Yuan dynasty that all paintings must be inscribed, which was not exclusive to "literati paintings." Yìn did not become an independent art until the Ming and Qing dynasties. As it suggested, this was how people in the Qing dynasty viewed "literati painting." But it was in the Song dynasty that "literati painting" and "scholarly painting" were formally proposed.

All proposals are established on the contrary basis. "The preciousness of harmony" is upheld because people tend to draw swords and stretch bows. Folks are required to abide by the law because some people run amok. What is the point of emphasizing "Literati Temperament (文人气 wénrén qì)" and "Style of Scholar-Bureaucrat (士大夫气 shìdàfū qì)"? The "Temperament" and the "Style," in addition to venting personal grievances and resentment in spirit, simply play with the skills of brush and ink on paper. What is its opposite side?

Su Shi was the first to put forward "scholarly painting" (Picture 133). He famously said: "If we assess the merits of the painting only by the resemblance, then our insight is similar to that of children." I couldn't understand his words before. In common sense, the unlikeness between painting and the real object is the level of children. How could a genius without peer in his generation say something in reverse?

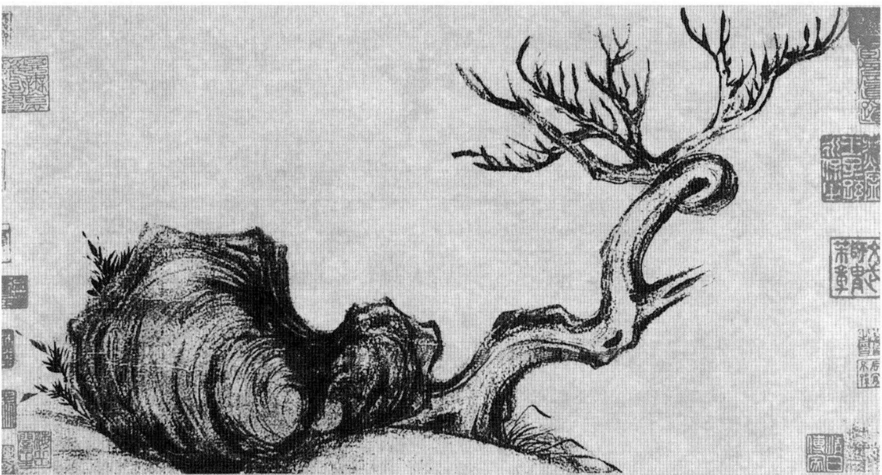

Picture 133 *Withered Tree with Odd Rock*, Su Shi, Song dynasty

How famous sayings are alike in their first line! It turns out that other ancients also talked about calligraphy as Su Shi did.

Cai Xiang said: "The crucial thing of learning calligraphy is to convey the spirit. The spirit is greater than the resemblance. If only the shape and form are well imitated but the spirit is lacking, then it cannot be considered good calligraphy." Liu Xizai praised those who were good at learning Wang Xizhi's writing: "If you are not proficient in strength and brushwork, but only imitating the shape of the characters . . ." It is clear that the opposite of "likeness/resemblance" is "brushwork." Calligraphers easily fell into the trap of "likeness of shape and form," let alone painters!

Su Dongpo went on to say, "Poetry is also like painting. If you only pursue the portrayal of the external features, you do not really know poetry. Poetry and painting are both arts, and are essentially of the same origin; if poetry and painting are not wonderful workmanship excelling nature, they must exhibit freshness and originality." The so-called "paintings with poetry, and poetry with painting" implies many wonders and beauties hidden in the art forms. Similarly, poetry contains level and oblique tones (tonal patterns in classical Chinese poetry). "Brushwork" is incorporated in "describing the form," just as Zen Buddhism has mental discernment.

Therefore, Dong Qichang explained "scholarly painting": "Scholars should paint with the methods of writing cursive script, clerical script, and script on the bamboo slips and silk of the Warring States Period. Trees should be drawn like zhéchāigǔ (折钗股, literally means twirling the hairpin; a calligraphic technique that requires the brush hair to remain flat on the paper with the tip of brush round but not twisted); mountains should be drawn like painting with zhuīhuàshā (锥画沙, literally meaning an awl on the sand; when the tip of the awl is drawn into the sand, there forms a concave middle line). And get rid of the cheesy and vulgar taste in painting. This is what I call the temperament of scholars." No wonder Su Dongpo regarded those who didn't understand this truth as near-children.

Historical facts are very important:

After the Five dynasties, large paintings appeared, depicting court landscapes, figures, flowers and birds. These works are exquisite and relatively lifelike, which were closely related to the use of tables. Before tables were put into use, the ancients painted with silk paper in their hands. They could hardly exploit their brushwork at will because their ability was limited by long and narrow paper, so there were very few large paintings. Sometimes they drew on the wall, or the unprocessed silk, both of which hindered their display of "ingenuity." When the writer's wrist touched the desktop, due to the support, he would use the brush in a smoother manner, which was suitable for drawing large, meticulous, and delicate paintings.

The traditional Chinese realistic paintings of flowers and birds (Pictures 134, 135, and 136) and landscape painting (Picture 137) in the Song dynasty came beyond reproach from sketching. Whether in depicting shape, coloring, composition or proportion, the artists made a giant leap forward compared with previous generations.

The Song dynasty was undeniably the peak of the Chinese painting history.

As with calligraphy, when a table served as a support, painters couldn't help depicting the form realistically and neglecting the brushwork.

In this historical context, the literati and scholars underpinned the calligraphic use of the brush and did not mind the likeness of the form. This point of view was reflected in Liang Kai's painting (Picture 138).

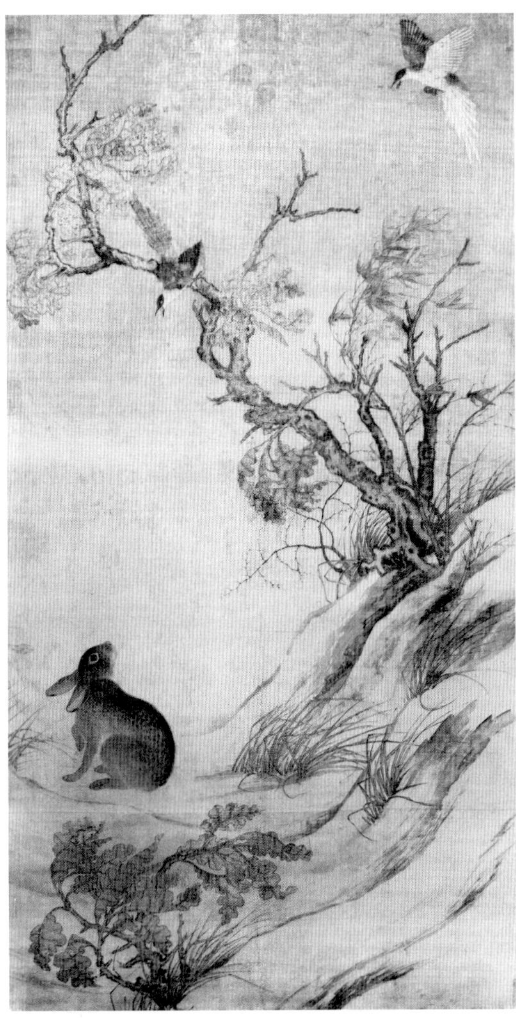

Picture 134 *Double Happiness: Magpies and Hare* (part), Cui Bai, Song dynasty

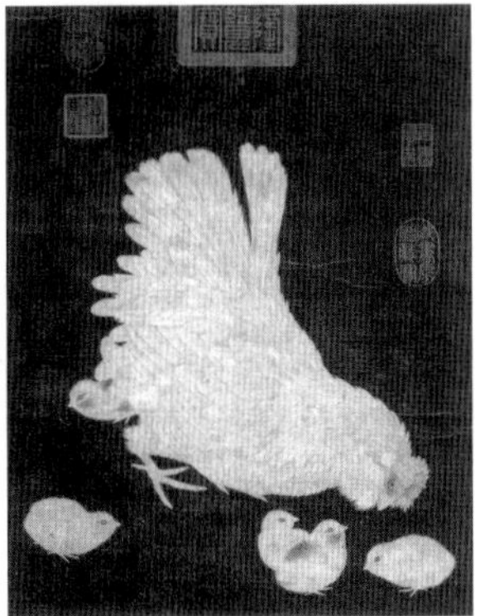

Picture 135 *Mother Hen and Chicks* (part), Song dynasty

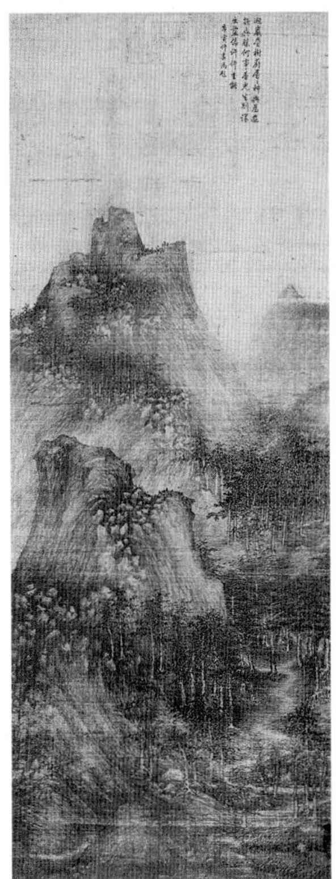

Picture 137 *Storied Mountains and Dense Forests*, Ju Ran, Song dynasty

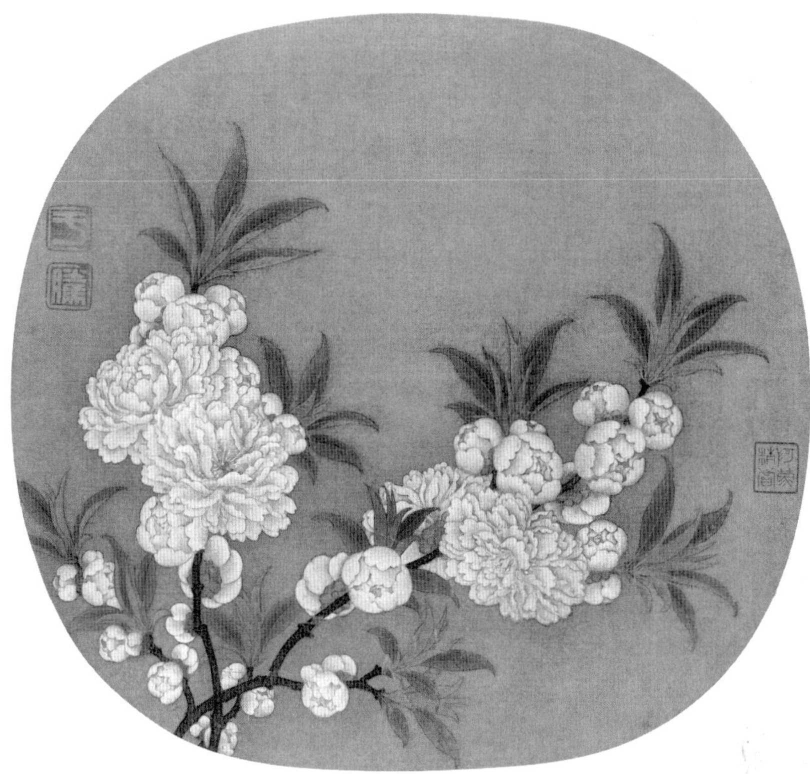

Picture 136 *Flowering Peach*, Song dynasty

This is how "literati painting" came into existence.

But the comparatively realistic path continued to expand. In the Ming dynasty, realistic portraits of people appeared. But the drawing of clothing was more superficial, and the head and the clothing were said to be painted by two kinds of painters. By the early Qing dynasty, the Italian missionary Láng Shìníng (郎世宁 Giuseppe Castiglione) was the first to incorporate Western chiaroscuro into Chinese painting (Picture

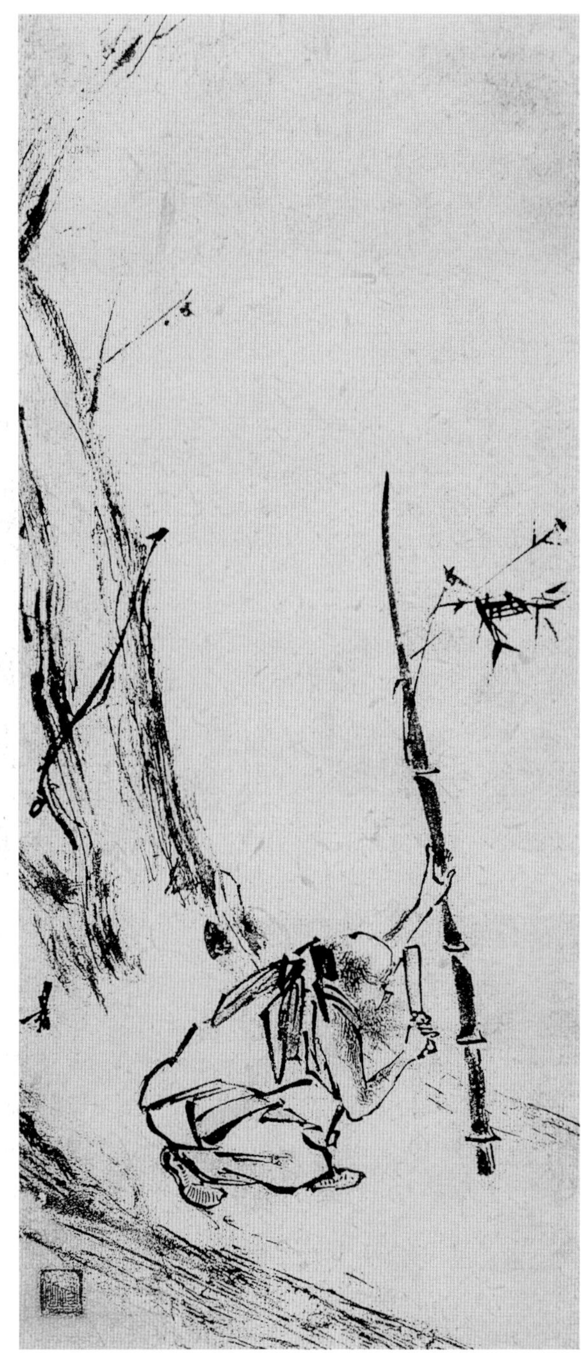

Picture 138 *The Sixth Patriarch (Hui Neng) Cutting the Bamboo*, Liang Kai, Song dynasty

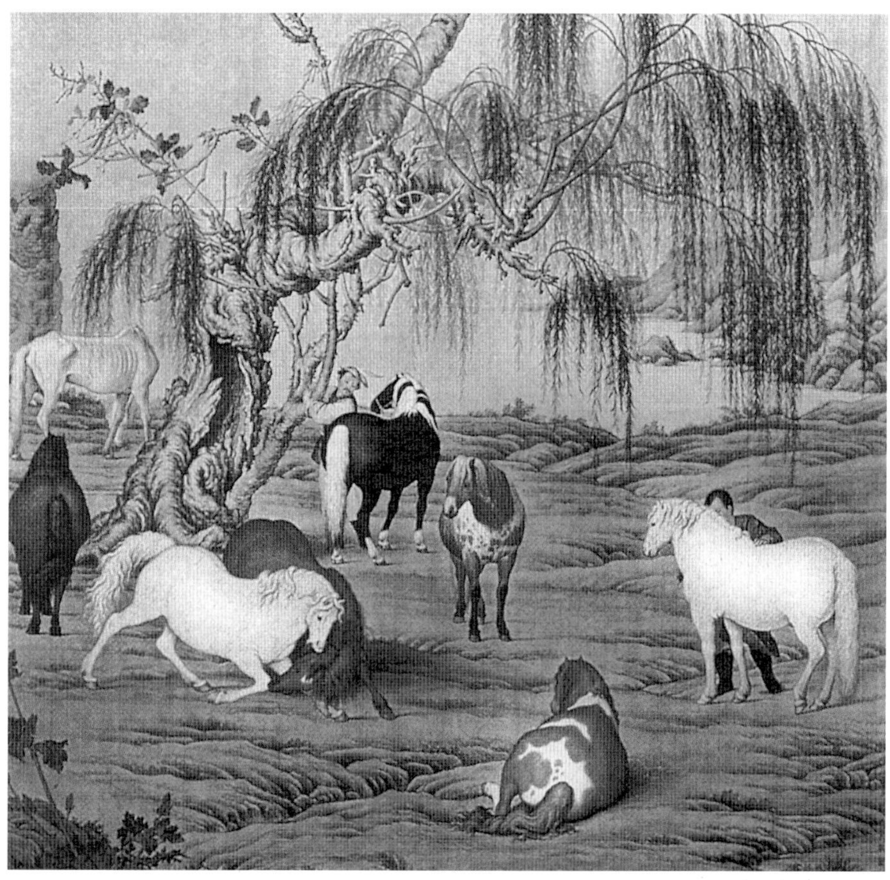

Picture 139 *Eight Horses* (part), Giuseppe Castiglione, Qing dynasty

139), which was a significant chapter in Chinese art history. Although the emperor was startled at first: "Why did you paint half of my face black"? He still granted the title of court painter to Castiglione.

When the great painter Huang Binhong taught his students brushwork in private (Picture 140), he put a thin strip of paper on one side of the brush and showed them the direction of the paper's movement when he used the brush.

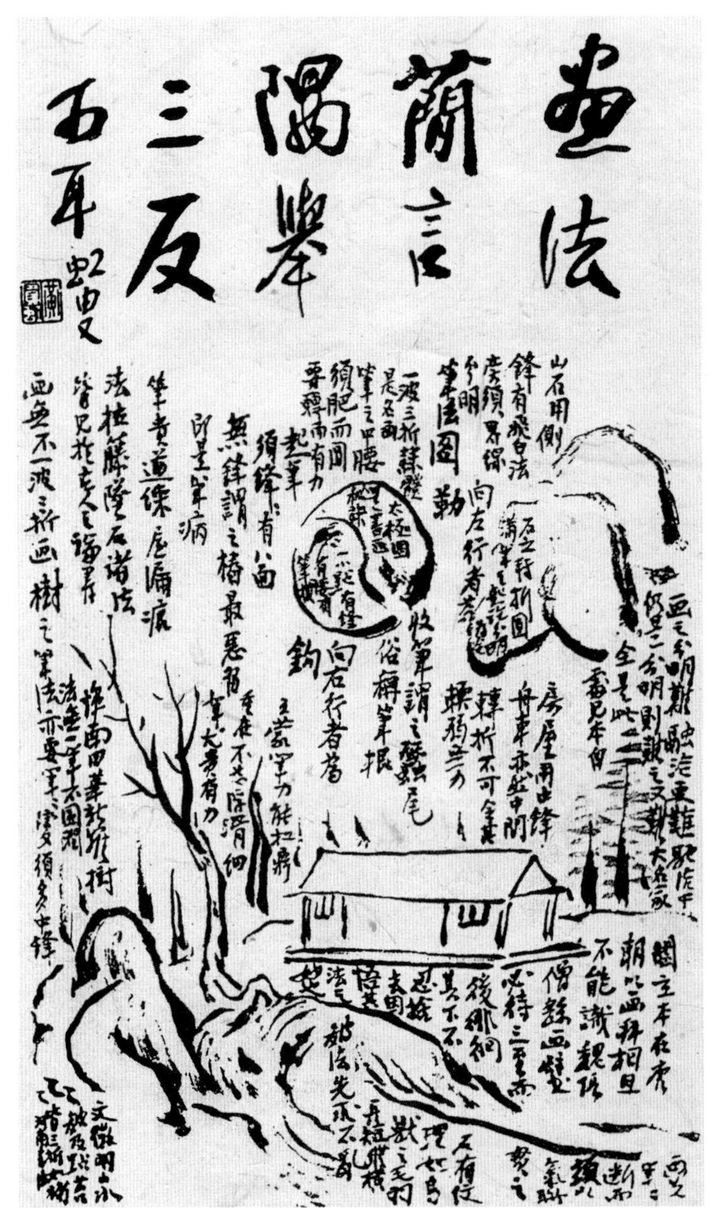

Picture 140 Huang Binhong's rough sketch

It turns out that Mr. Huang was showing the secret and knack of moving the brush.

Here is a procedure diagram of Huang Binhong's brushwork when he painted *Tai Po Market to Fanling* (粉岭大埔墟 fěnlǐng dà bùxū) (Picture 141), which I found in *Huang Binhong Talks About Art* (黄宾虹谈艺录 Huángbīnhóng tán yì lù). We can follow the sequence of numbers next to the strokes from 1 to 36, and apparently every two strokes are a complete reversion of turning the brush to the left and right, with clear xiàngbèi (向背, backward and forward) directions. That's why Huang often affirmed that "painting goes before calligraphy, and the trick lies in the brushwork," and "seeking painting method in calligraphy, and applying calligraphy method to painting."

The painter Huang Zhou once earnestly and secretly told his best friend's child: "Do you know? Qi Baishi turned his brush when he was drawing shrimp feelers." Huang was twirling three fingers as he imparted the knowledge.

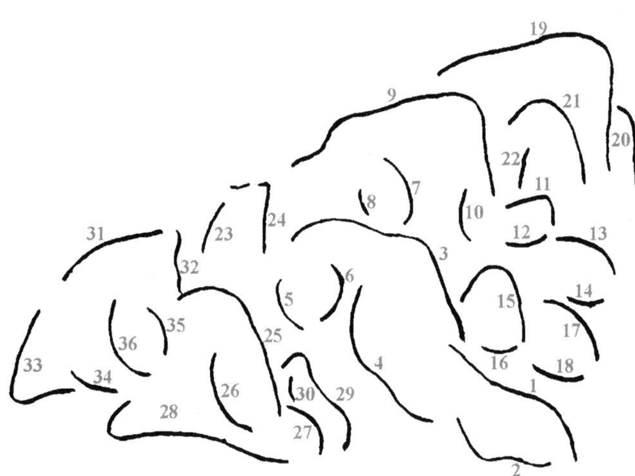

Picture 141 A procedure diagram of Huang Binhong's *Tai Po Market to Fanling*

CHAPTER 58

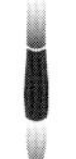

"Paper Copying Paper"

Gōngbǐ (工笔, a careful realist technique in Chinese painting) and xiěyì (写意, the interpretive and freely expressive style of "sketching thoughts") were first proposed in the Song dynasty. Generally speaking, gōngbǐ is the opposite of xiěyì. Tang Yin put them in this way: "Gōngbǐ is like regular script; xiěyì is like cursive script; both involve turning the brush in a dexterous and nimble manner." In other words, both xiěyì and gōngbǐ require turning the brush and brushwork, but gōngbǐ uses regular script and xiěyìadopts cursive script.

When I first came in touch with traditional Chinese painting, I had little understanding of the procedural drawing method of *The Four Gentlemen* or *Four Noble Ones* (四君子 sìjūnzǐ, a collective term referring to four plants): the plum blossom (Picture 142), the orchid (Picture 143), the bamboo (Picture 144) and the chrysanthemum (Picture 145), and *The Three Friends of Winter* (岁寒三友 suì hán sānyǒu, an art motif that comprises the pine, bamboo and plum). They are ubiquitous on the folk stalls. Later that it dawned on me that *The Four Gentlemen* and *TheThree Friends of Winter* were important expressions of xiěyì in "literati painting" in the Song dynasty, and their origin was another matter. Zhao Mengfu (Picture 146) and Ke Jiusi, the representative painters of "literati painting" in the Yuan dynasty, distinctly proposed

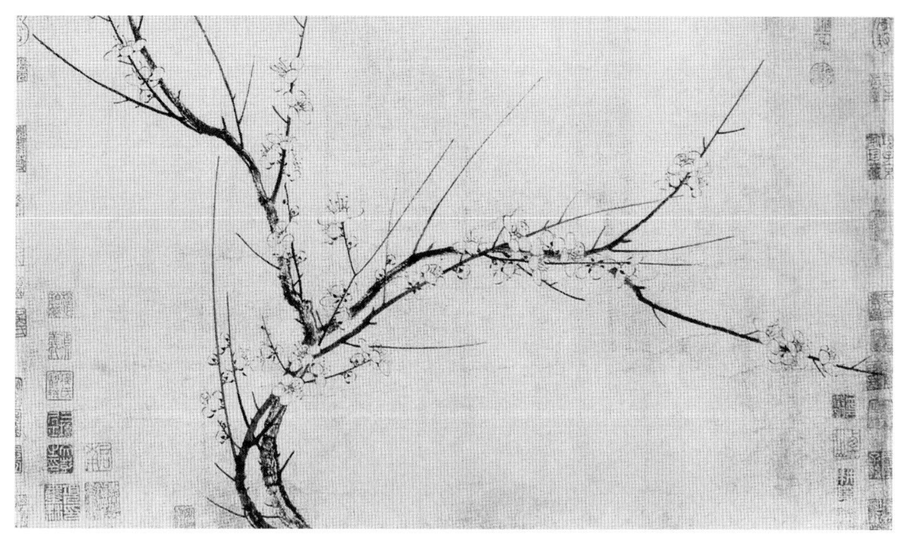

Picture 142 *Four Stages of Blossoming Plum* (part), Yang Buzhi, Song dynasty

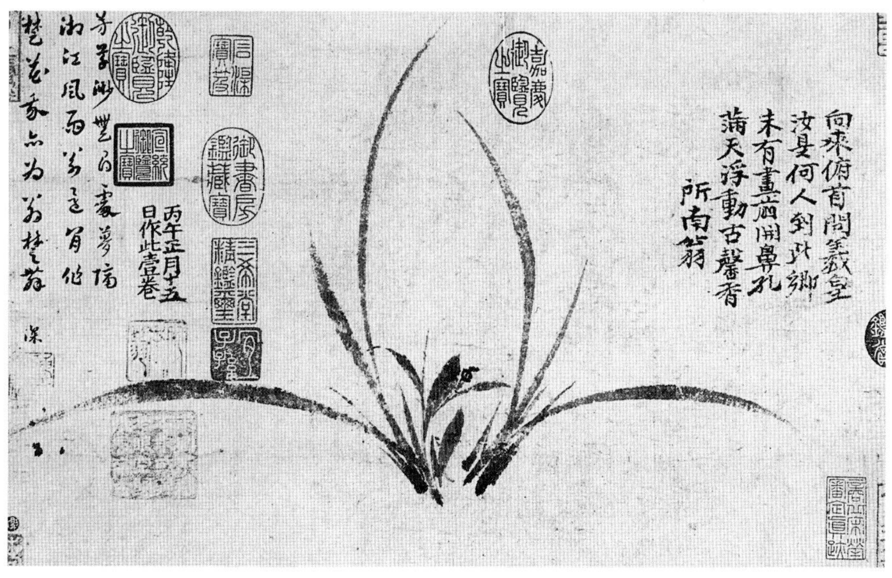

Picture 143 *Ink Orchid* (part), handscroll, Zheng Sixiao, Song dynasty

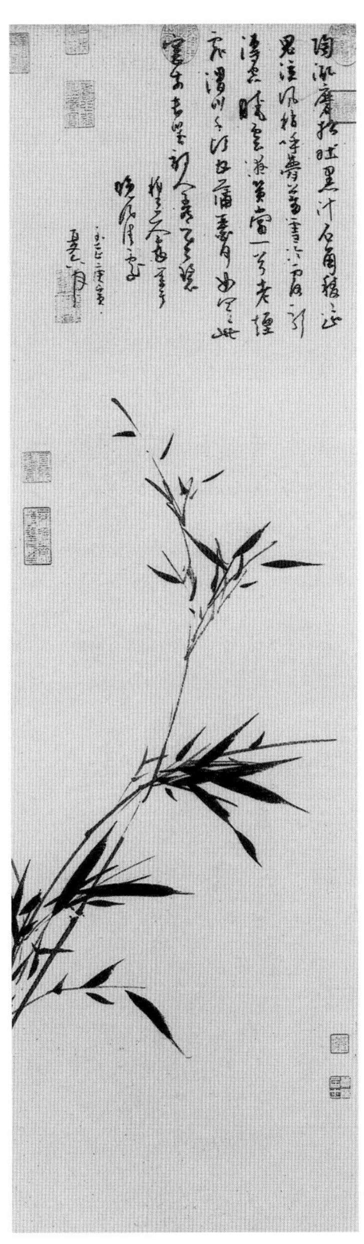

Picture 144 *Yundang Valley Slanted Bamboos* Wu Zhen, Yuan dynasty

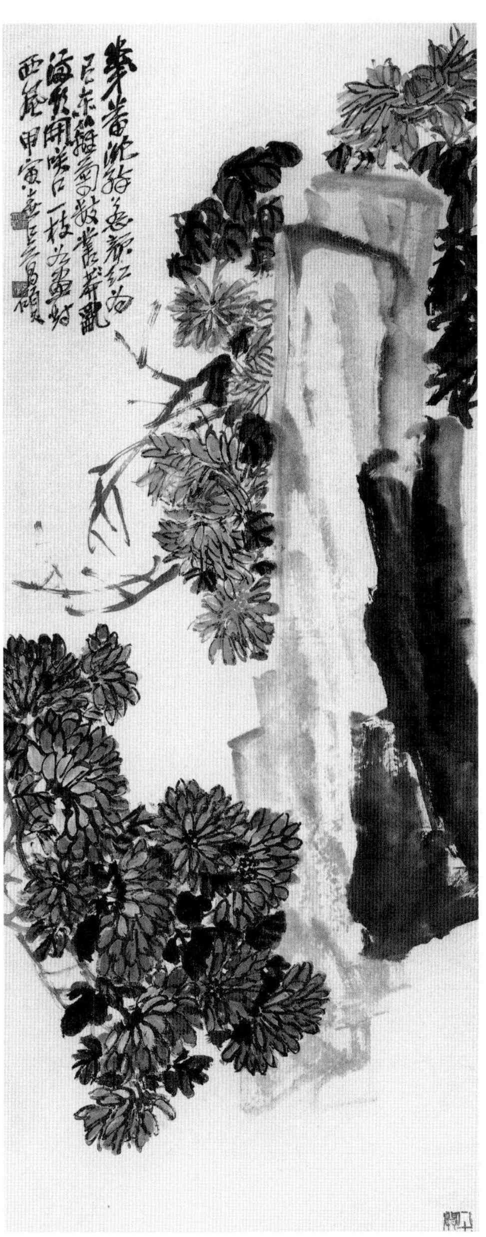

Picture 145 *Chrysanthemums*, hanging scroll, Wu Changshuo, modern China

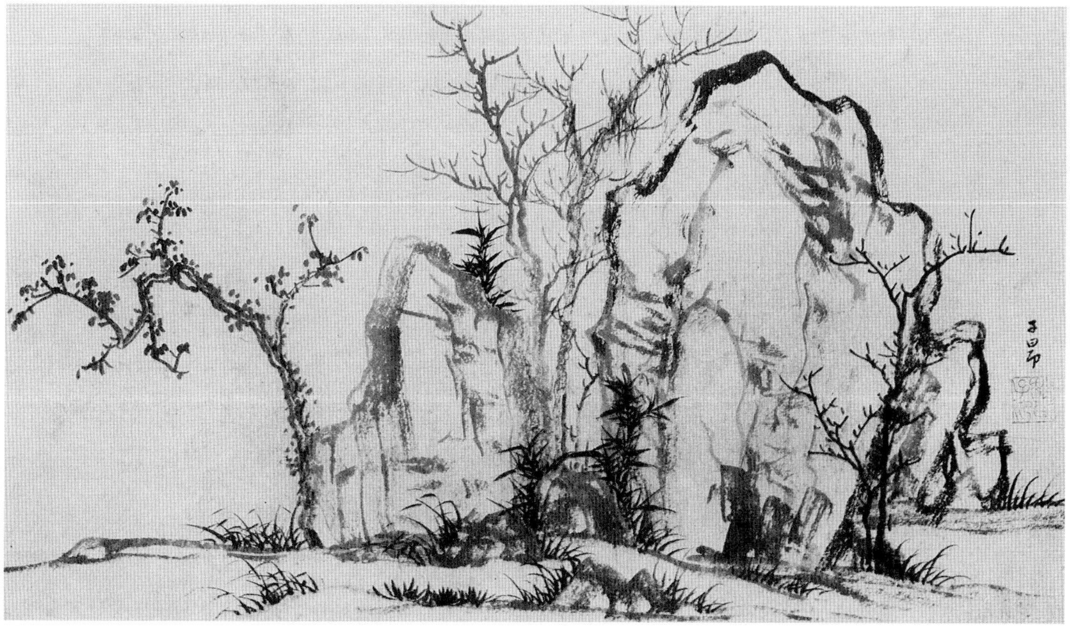

Picture 146 *Outstanding Rocks and Sparse Grove* (part), Zhao Mengfu, Yuan dynasty

integrating and articulating calligraphy brushstroke techniques to pictorially "write" the bamboo. Their advocacy of this approach can be explicitly seen in the following inscriptions, which state: "Rocks are like fēibái script (飞白, also termed cursive seal, which features white parts exposed in strokes as if they are written with a dry brush) and trees are like the large seal (籀 zhòu); drawing bamboo goes back to mastering bāfēn (八分, Broad Chancery Style). If people understand this, they will know calligraphy and painting come from the same root." "Use seal script for writing bamboo stems, cursive script for branches and official script (bāfēn) for leaves. Or use the left-downward stroke of Yan Zhenqing, the techniques of zhé chāi gǔ (折钗股, literally means twirling the hairpin; a calligraphic technique that requires the brush hair to remain flat on the paper with the tip of brush round but not twisted) and wū lòu hén (屋漏痕, literally means water Stains on the Wall; comparing the brushwork to the rainwater running down the wall of the house) for writing on wood and rock."

Chen Jiru in the Ming dynasty summarized the theory by saying: "The ancients wrote jīnshí金石 (ancient, engraved texts that extol the merit of people or events) or zhōng dǐng 钟鼎 (inscriptions on ancient bronzes and stone tablets), seal script and clerical script just like painting; while painters depicted water, orchids, bamboo, plum blossoms, and grapes with calligraphic techniques, which was precisely the combination phase of Zen Buddhism."

In other words, the strokes used in the xiěyì (freehand, "sketching thoughts") painting can be found in the corresponding calligraphic brushwork. For example, the bamboo stems in the painting were drawn with the "vertical" method of regular script; the bamboo leaves were drawn with the "left-downward stroke"; the plum blossom petals were written with the cursive script on hanjian (bamboo slips of the Han dynasty); the orchid leaves were written with hanging arm and wrist and the turning of the brush, etc. To put it bluntly, a large xiěyì painting lives up to the force-generation tendency of calligraphy's left and right turning strokes without caring too much about the exact resemblance; conversely, it applied the general image indiscriminately to different calligraphic strokes. *The Four Gentlemen* and *TheThree Friends of Winter* provide the most objective and comprehensive schema expression of the brushwork style forxiěyì painting.

Does it sound like the *Eight Principles of Yong* (永 yǒng)?

Later generations overexerted or even completely expanded the spiritual factors of xiěyì, overemphasizing the superficial and visible composition and main idea, and the comprehensive learning of poetry, calligraphy, painting, and sealcarving, to the point of completely ignoring the implied brushwork which was the most quintessential part in literati painting. However, the original presentable pattern used to illustrate the problem was widely circulated among later generations. The *Eight Principles of Yong*, for instance, has been printed on the front of each model copybook for practice. Another instance is Zheng Banqiao's *Nándé hútu* (难得糊涂, Where ignorance is bliss, it's folly to be wise), which is hung in numerous households.

What "literati painting" ultimately wants to deliver is, as the great painter Ni Zan in the Yuan dynasty suggested, "What I call painting is only sketchy brush strokes. I am not seeking resemblance, just to amuse myself"! This sheer game of brush and ink is purely playing with brushwork. Dong Qichang in the Ming dynasty alleged, "Paint with the methods of writing cursive script, clerical script and qí zì (奇字, literally strange characters, script on the bamboo slip and silk of the Warring States Period)," in which the word "qí zì" is pertinent and intriguing. It boils down to the idea that "literati painting" is nothing more than using brushwork to write bizarre and exaggerated characters, and multiplying them.

"Literati painting" has dispensed with "Suitability to Type and Application of Colors (随类赋彩 suílèi fùcǎi)" and simplified "Correspondence to Object (应物象形 yìng wù xiàngxíng)" and "Division and Planning (经营位置 jīngyíng wèizhì)" in the *Six Criteria*. The only Criteria left to be implemented is "the Skillful Handling of Brushwork (骨法用笔 gǔfǎ yòng bǐ)" and "Transmission by Copying (传移模写 chuán yí móxiě)." Thus, the brush and ink game of "literati painting" had developed to be the same as calligraphy, and could be done behind closed doors. The latecomers did not seek resemblance; they created the painting by using brushwork, or directly copied the painting of predecessors (as a matter of fact, copying their brushwork), which was the same as copying the calligraphy of forefathers, imitating the copybook, and writing with the brushwork.

This was the so-called "common origins of calligraphy and painting."

A friend told me that in the late 1970s, when Liu Haisu gave a speech at the Central Academy of Fine Arts, he declared, "Chinese painting used to be 'paper copying paper,' namely, copying from predecessors. Now, we are going to do sketches."

My friend later recalled, "Yes, Chinese painting was really 'paper copying paper.'"

"Literati painters," without seeking resemblance, painted behind closed doors. They used "Skillful Handling of Brushwork (骨法用笔 gǔfǎ yòng bǐ)" and "Transmission by Copying (传移模写 chuán yí móxiě)." Are they just practicing "paper copying paper"?

Calligraphy is typical and pure "paper copying paper."

CHAPTER 59

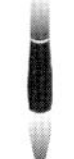

Truth and Helplessness

I often read comments saying that a certain calligrapher "innovated in his declining years" or "changed the method in his old days." Well, this is my take on this phenomenon.

Before one's genetic heritage could be defined through a DNA sample, people were most convincingly identified by their fingerprints and handwriting. Because calligraphy is the closest to human physiological response. Due to my years of experience, I can tell the age and personality of a person from his or her handwriting based on the natural physiological response.

Some years ago, I deliberately kept a tally of the dates of birth and death of calligraphers who have left authentic handwriting in history, and compared their works at various ages, from which I reached a conclusion: the process of art is a process of physiology; the life of art is a true record of a person from young to old.

Smooth, fast, detailed and meticulous characters were written by the young, while trembling, sluggish, stagnant, large and careless characters belonged to the old. For calligraphers whose whole lives were observed by the world, none of their writings had gone unchanged as they got older. I compared the characters of Wang Duo, Zhu Yunming, Dong

Qichang, Lin Sanzhi and many other calligraphers in their early and later years, and discovered their clear physiological trajectories.

Therefore, "biànfǎ (变法, change of method)" is actually the change of physiology, which even the calligrapher himself was unaware of. "Biànfǎ" might have been a self-deprecating and self-explanatory expression, and later generations just blindly followed their self-mockery.

Most of the writings of Wang Xizhi and Wang Xianzhi impress us with beautiful vigor and strength, because they both died in their 40s or 50s, before their physiology had declined. No wonder their ink marks are filled with ease and grace of the young and middle-aged. It also makes sense that all of Wang Chong's writings are beautiful and sensitive, for he lived less than 39 years.

I have been a fan of old people's handwriting since childhood, and I could do a good imitation. In 1985, when I was 30 years old, I attended the first National Women's Calligraphy Exhibition. The judges unanimously thought that my handwriting was a forgery, ghostwritten by an old man. After confirming my identity, they surprisingly found out that it was written by me. The jury even published my work in *Wen Wei Po*, a Hong Kong-based newspaper.

However, I soon grew bored of this state and thought myself contrived and hypocritical. I was not old. I could write agilely and fluently. Why should I insist on pretending to be an old calligrapher and behaving in an affected way?

So stupid! Did I not know that I would get old one day? Of course, the day would come when my eyes are blurry and my hands shaky.

The works of the ancients in their old days are not to be learned at my age. Although, the charm of being thoughtful and reckless, naive yet calm, refined and "doing as one pleases without breaking the rules" from time to time moves me and appeals to me.

But the physiology-related change in writing has not yet happened to me. I should only honestly walk on my own path, step by step, because one day I will be old and write that way too. I'm just afraid that when I have my unique writing in old age, I might not cherish that capability.

Of course, there are exceptions. Wen Zhengming was a legend for he could still write tiny clear letters in his eighties. I wish I could do the same. But the prospect is bleak. My mother started to have trembling fingers in her fifties. She said it was hereditary, because my grandfather and grandaunt both trembled from their hands to lips when they got old. My father is nearsighted and has senile cataracts. Whichever side I inherit from, I will hopelessly have either trembling hands or cataracts.

So, I understand what to do in the present and the future.

CHAPTER 60

The Story of Jizi

I've written quite a bit, and everything that needs to be said has already been said.

So, what should I do now? The question was my ultimate confusion back then, and became the ultimate meaning of my subsequent thoughts. It was from then onwards that I unconsciously pushed the first domino.

History is moving forward; people are being born from generation to generation; words are being written; paintings are being drawn; and life will still go on. Fortunately, nowadays we see various genres and forms of art. Art has never been so free and democratic as in contemporary times. The national treasures of painting and calligraphy that were hidden in the palace or in private hands can be appreciated by every civilian, and the authentic ancient paintings and calligraphy scanned by Japanese Nigensha are clear even to the grain of the paper. You can choose to admire at your will the art back to thousands of years, the East or the West, classical or modern, rigorous or romantic. Everyone is entitled to this freedom.

If things were really as what I said and discussed, people would still do what they intended to do.

It will take a long time to put into practice any form or concept.

I simply want to provide my readers with one more perspective, to "follow the roots," and keep a clear head, knowing what Chinese calligraphy and Chinese painting were all about in the past, and not get confused in "zǐ fēi yú (子非鱼, you are not a fish)," "zǐ fēi wǒ (子非我, you are not me)" and "wǒ fēi zǐ (我非子, I am not you)," which limits their cognition to watching "minnows swimming over the Haoliang River."

Not long ago, I had a chat with a friend. We talked about the original opening of wéiqí (also known by the Japanese name of Go). It used to have four starting stones. But when Japanese learnt to play Go, they abolished the starting stones. The opening of China's current rules of Go adopted the Japanese style. It is said that Japanese experts who study Go openings suddenly found that the most ideal opening, that can both take care of one's territory and keep an eye on the rival's formations, is to start with four stones.

That sounds interesting.

To the reformers who abolished the starting stones, is it bliss or remorse? Is it pleasure or pain? Is it a curse or a blessing?

I do not know either.

It was recorded in the ancient legalist treatise *Hán Fēi Zi* (韩非子): "King Zhou of the Shang dynasty drank all night long, and once forgot the date after days of carnival. He asked the minister of civil and military affairs around him, but none of them knew the date either, so Zhou sent someone to ask Jizi, one of his relatives. Jizi told his attendants that "As the king of a country and the people around him do not know the date, the country will be in danger; and the people of a country don't know the date, and only I know the date, then I will be in even greater danger." So Jizi asked the doorman to tell the visitor that Jizi was too drunk to know the exact date."

In *Records of the Grand Historian* (史记 shǐjì), Jizi was imprisoned for remonstrating against King Zhou's misrule. One later version states that he pretended to be mad after Bigan (a loyal official) had been killed by King Zhou. After Shang was overthrown by the Zhou dynasty in the mid-eleventh century BC, Jizi was released by King Wu, to whom he gave advice on how to rule the new polity. Jizi was said to have escaped to Goryeo. Chinese texts from the Han dynasty onwards claimed that King Wu enfeoffed Jizi as ruler of Cháoxiǎn (朝鲜, pronounced "Joseon" in Korean).

This happened 3,100 years ago.

I suddenly remember a poem written by my uncle a long time ago, but unfortunately, I only remember the last two lines.

"An art career is like a dream.

Ten years have gone by when you wake up from the dream."

Jan.–Aug. 1998, Nanjing (first draft)
Aug.–Sept. 2002, Nanjing (second draft)

Postscript

I added nearly 10,000 words and more than twenty pictures to the latest edition published by the Encyclopedia of China Publishing House. In addition, I revised relevant chapters and adjusted some pictures to refine the book. As I am about to deliver the manuscript, I continue to find places for revision, and there will always be regrets. If readers can be inspired, solve some puzzles, raise questions, and offer criticism to this book, that will be my greatest pleasure.

I would like to take this opportunity to thank the enthusiastic editors of the Encyclopedia of China Publishing House and all those who have helped provide, collect, and make pictures and materials and proofread the manuscript.

Sun Xiaoyun
December 27, 2002, Beijing

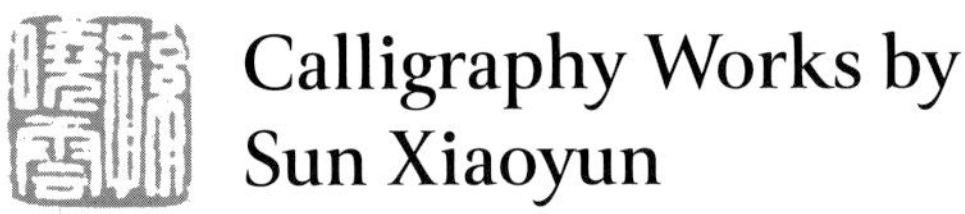

Calligraphy Works by Sun Xiaoyun

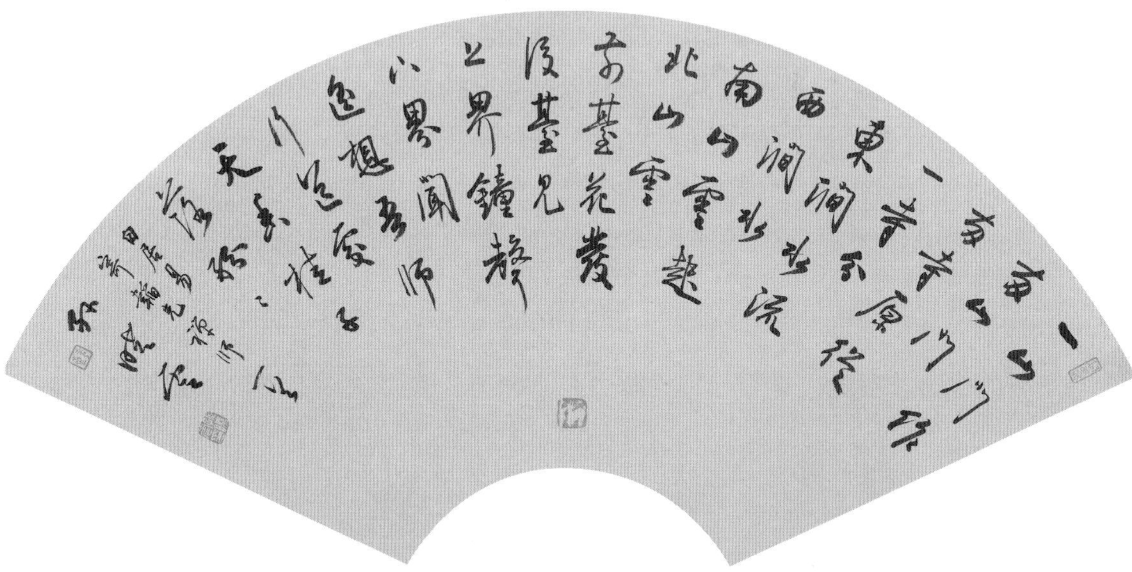

A poem by Bai Juyi in semi-cursive script, 28 cm × 56 cm, 2012

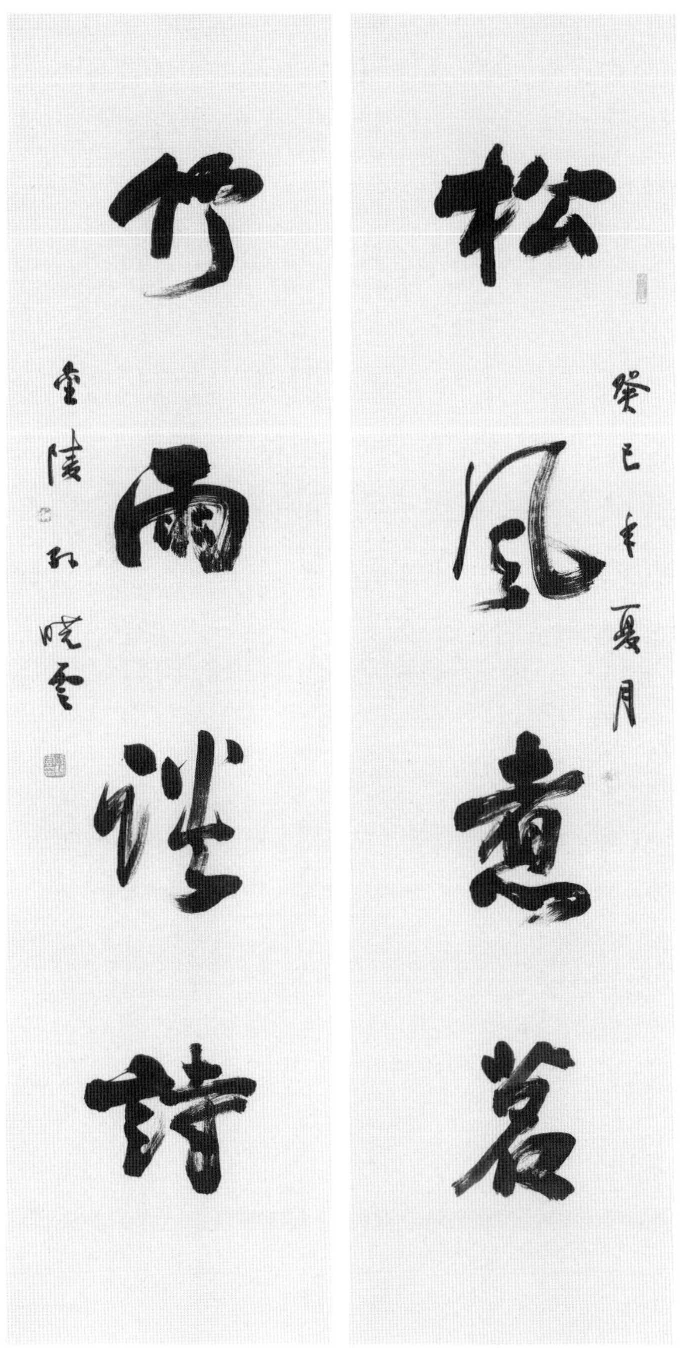

Couplet *Windswept Pine Tree and Bamboo Woods in the Rain*,
137 cm × 34.3 cm × 2, 2013

浮圖文瑛居大雲庵環水即蘇子美滄浪亭地也亟
求余作滄浪亭記曰昔子美之記記亭之勝也請子
記吾所以為亭者余曰昔吳越有國時廣陵王鎮吳
中治園於子城之西南其外戚孫承佑亦治園於其
偏迨淮南納土此園不廢蘇子美始建滄浪亭最後
禪者居之此滄浪亭為大雲庵也有庵以來二百年
文瑛尋古遺事復子美之構於荒殘滅沒之餘此大
雲庵為滄浪亭也夫古今之變朝市改易嘗登姑蘇
之臺望五湖之渺茫羣山之蒼翠太伯虞仲之所建
闔閭夫差之所爭子胥種蠡之所經營今皆無有矣
庵與亭何為者哉雖然錢鏐因亂攘竊保有吳越國
富兵强垂及四世諸子姻戚乘時奢僭宮館苑囿極
一時之盛而子美之亭乃為釋子所欽重如此可以
見世士之欲垂名於千載不與澌然而俱盡者則有
在矣文瑛讀書喜詩與吾徒遊呼之為滄浪僧云
丁亥元月錄歸有光滄浪亭記孫曉雲

A central scroll in regular script featuring Gui Youguang's *The Records of the Canglang Pavilion*, 81 cm × 61 cm, 2007

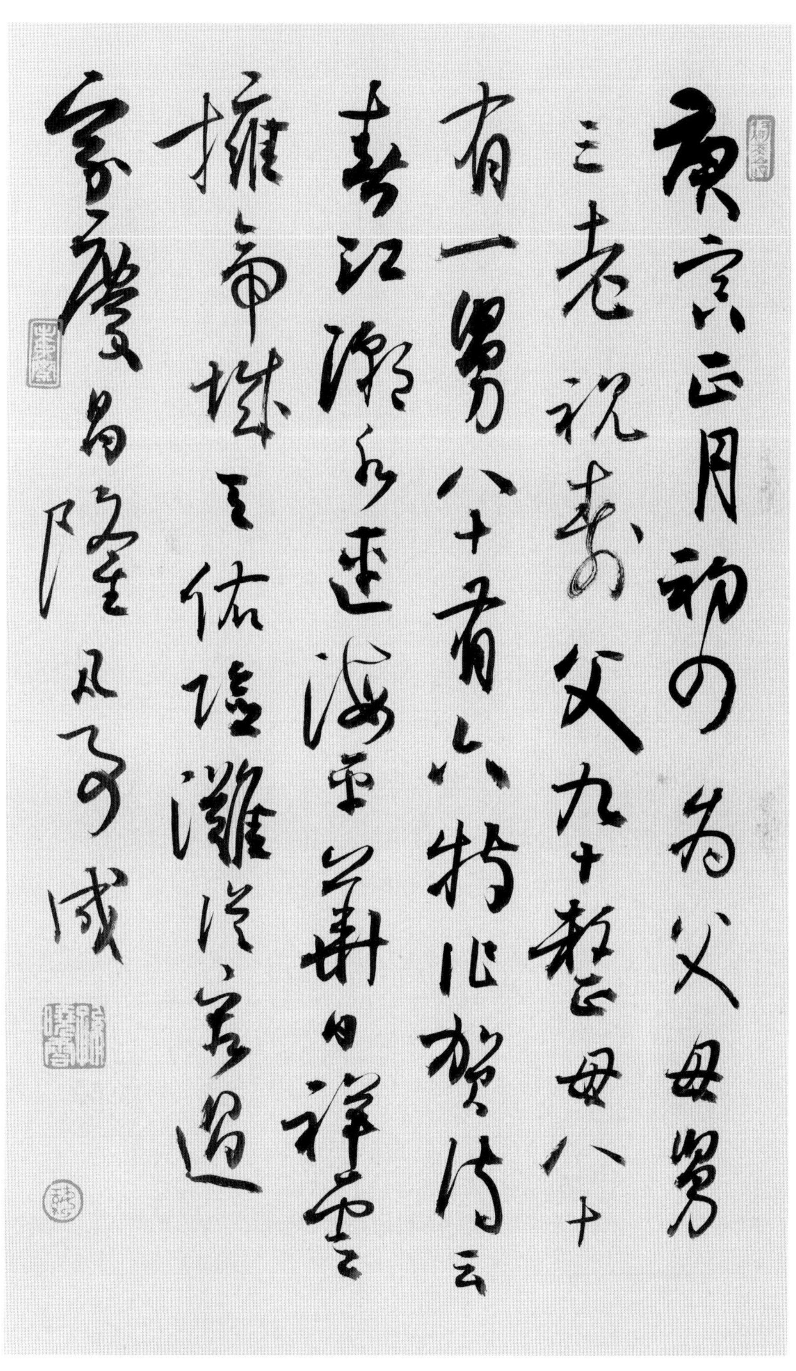

A Letter Named Geng Yin (the Year of Metal Tiger) in semi-cursive script,
34 cm × 22 cm, 2010

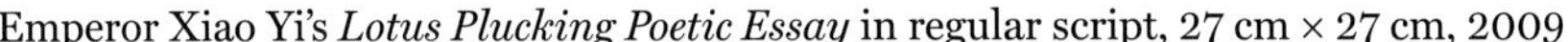

Emperor Xiao Yi's *Lotus Plucking Poetic Essay* in regular script, 27 cm × 27 cm, 2009

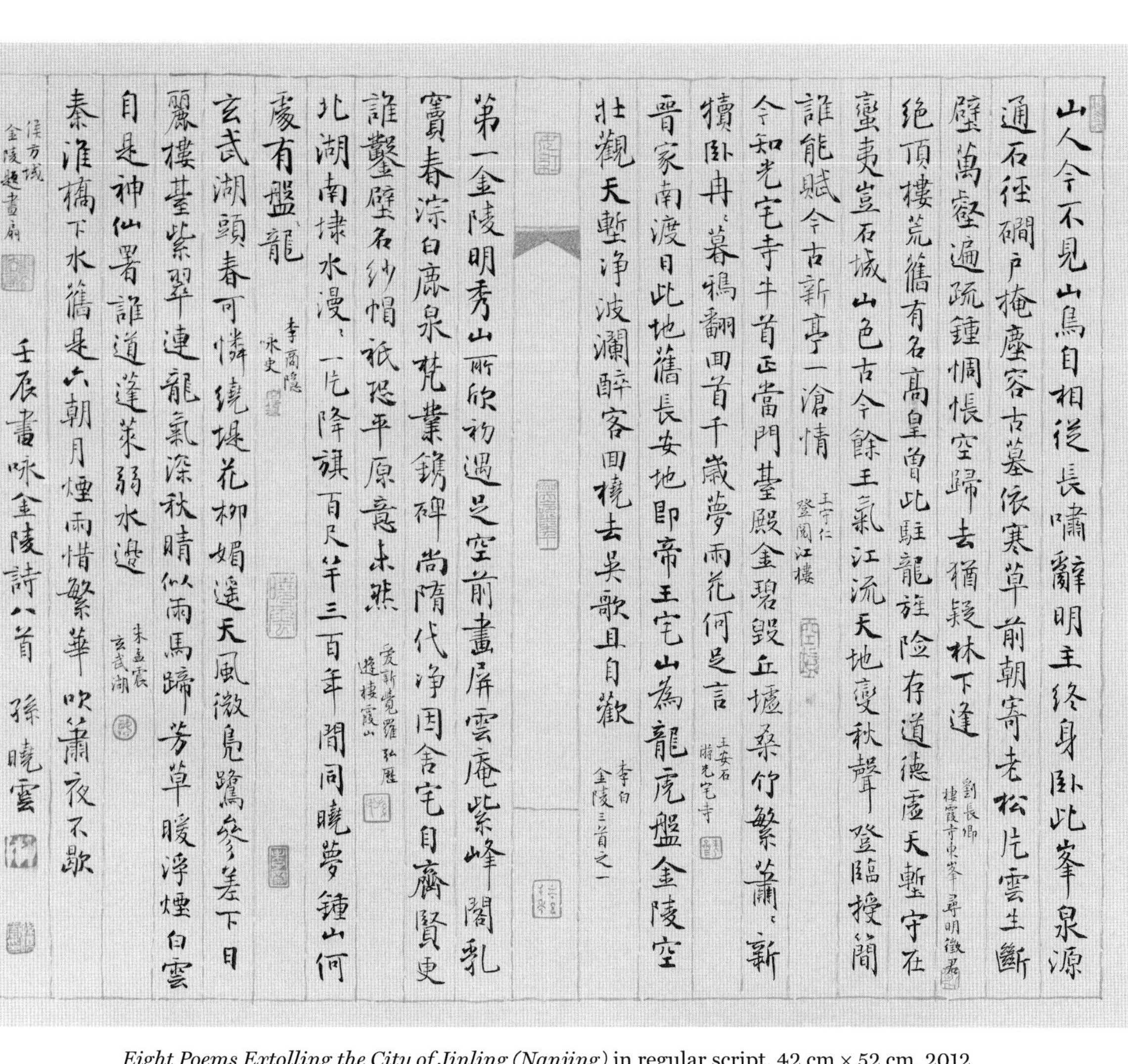

Eight Poems Extolling the City of Jinling (Nanjing) in regular script, 42 cm × 52 cm, 2012

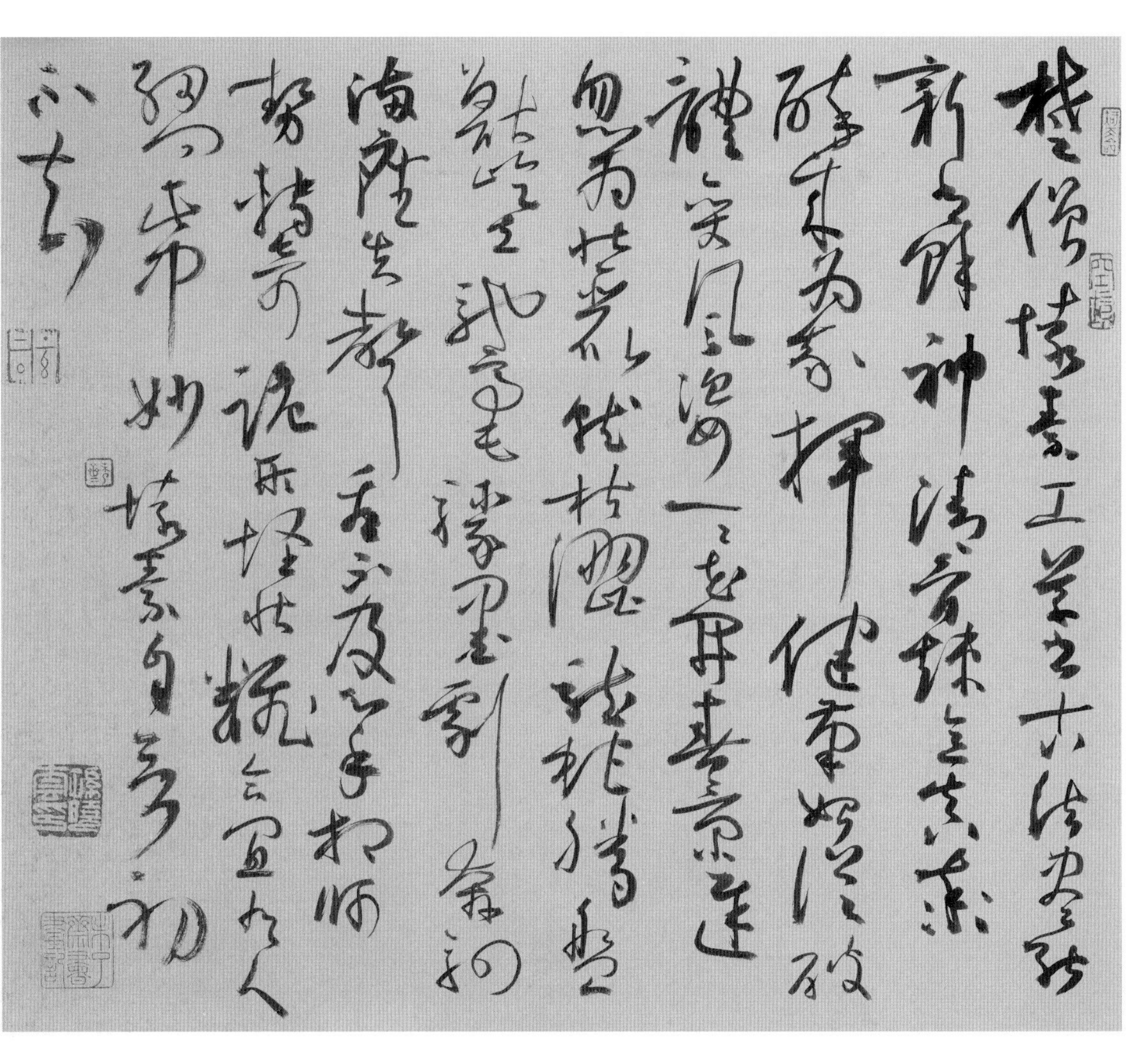

Work in cursive script featuring Dai Shulun's *Poem on Huai Su's Cursive Script*, 35 cm × 41 cm, 2010

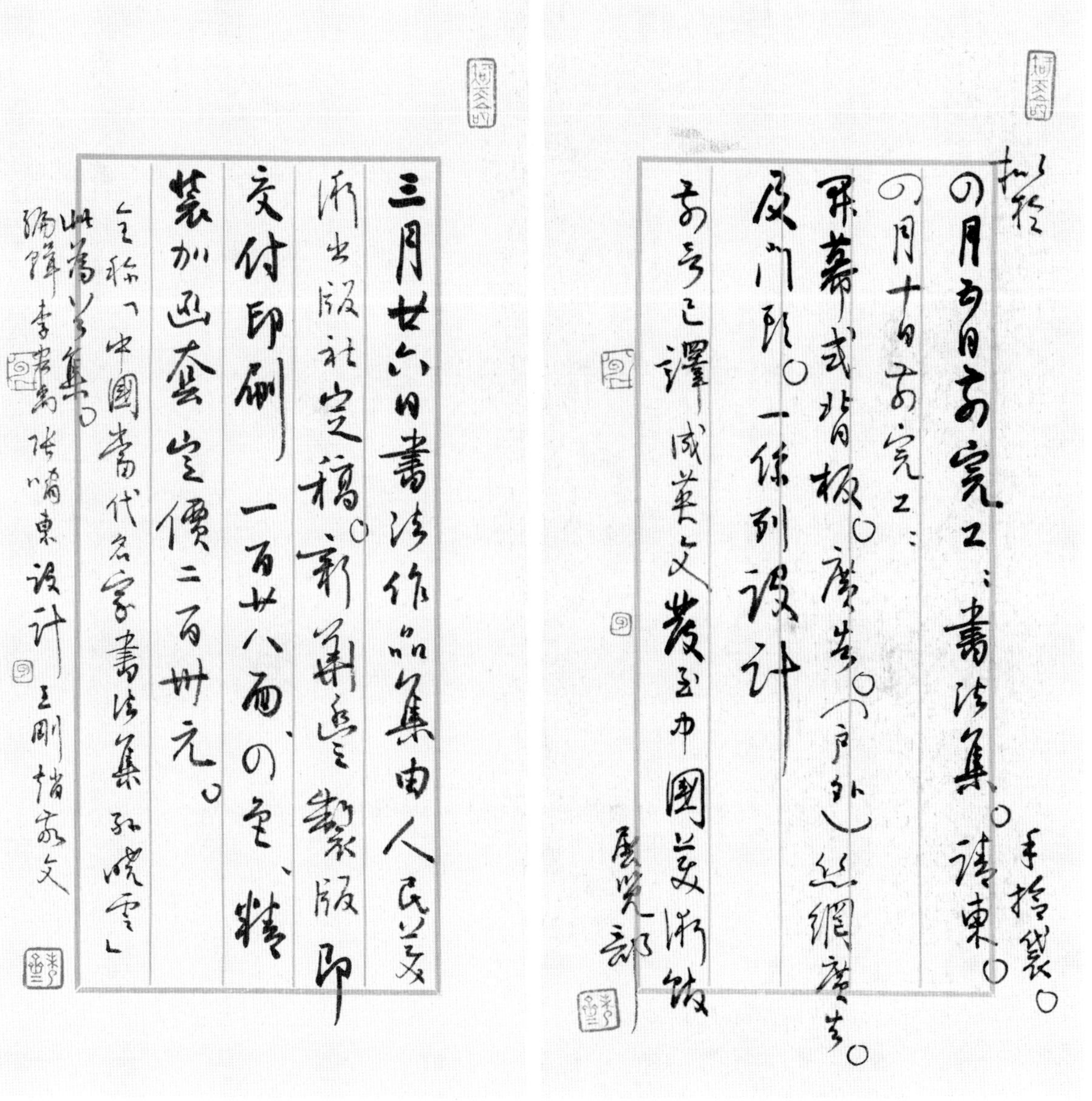

A letter in cursive and semi-cursive script, 20 cm × 10 cm × 2, 2010

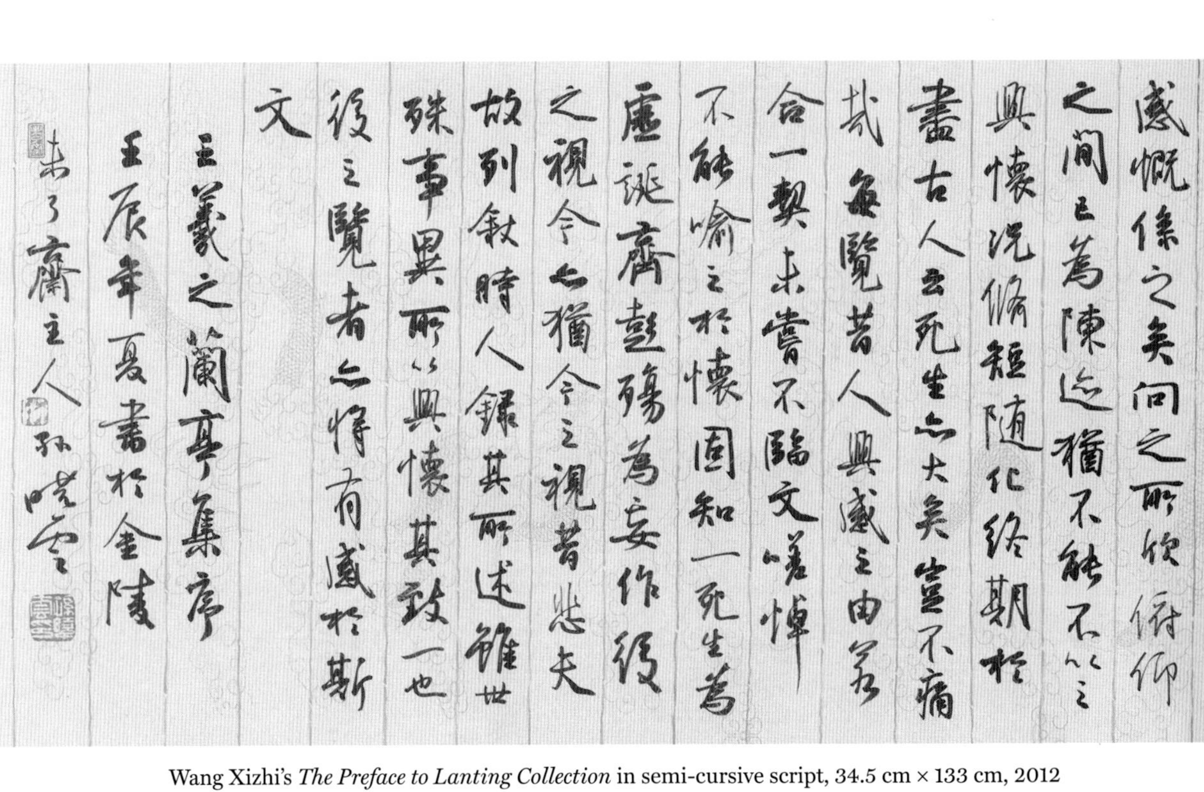

Wang Xizhi's *The Preface to Lanting Collection* in semi-cursive script, 34.5 cm × 133 cm, 2012

永和九年歲在癸丑暮春
之初會于會稽山陰之蘭亭
脩稧事也羣賢畢至少長
咸集此地有崇山峻領茂林
脩竹又有清流激湍映帶
左右引以為流觴曲水列坐
其次雖無絲竹管弦之盛
一觴一詠亦足以暢敘幽情
是日也天朗氣清惠風和暢
仰觀宇宙之大俯察品類之
盛所以遊目騁懷足以極視聽
之娛信可樂也夫人之相與
俯仰一世或取諸懷抱晤言
一室之內或因寄所託放浪
形骸之外雖取舍萬殊靜躁
不同當其欣於所遇暫得於

古公亶甫積德垂仁思弘一道哲王於豳太伯仲雍王德之仁行施百世斷髮文身伯夷叔齊古之遺賢讓國不用餓殂首山智哉山甫相彼宣王何用杜伯累我聖賢齊桓之霸賴得仲父後任豎刁蟲流出戶晏子平仲積德兼仁與世沈德未必思命仲尼之世王國為君隨制飲酒揚波使官

曹操善哉行其一 庚寅正月書於金陵 曉雲

Cao Cao's *Shan Zai Xing (part one)* in clerical script,
59 cm × 33 cm, 2010

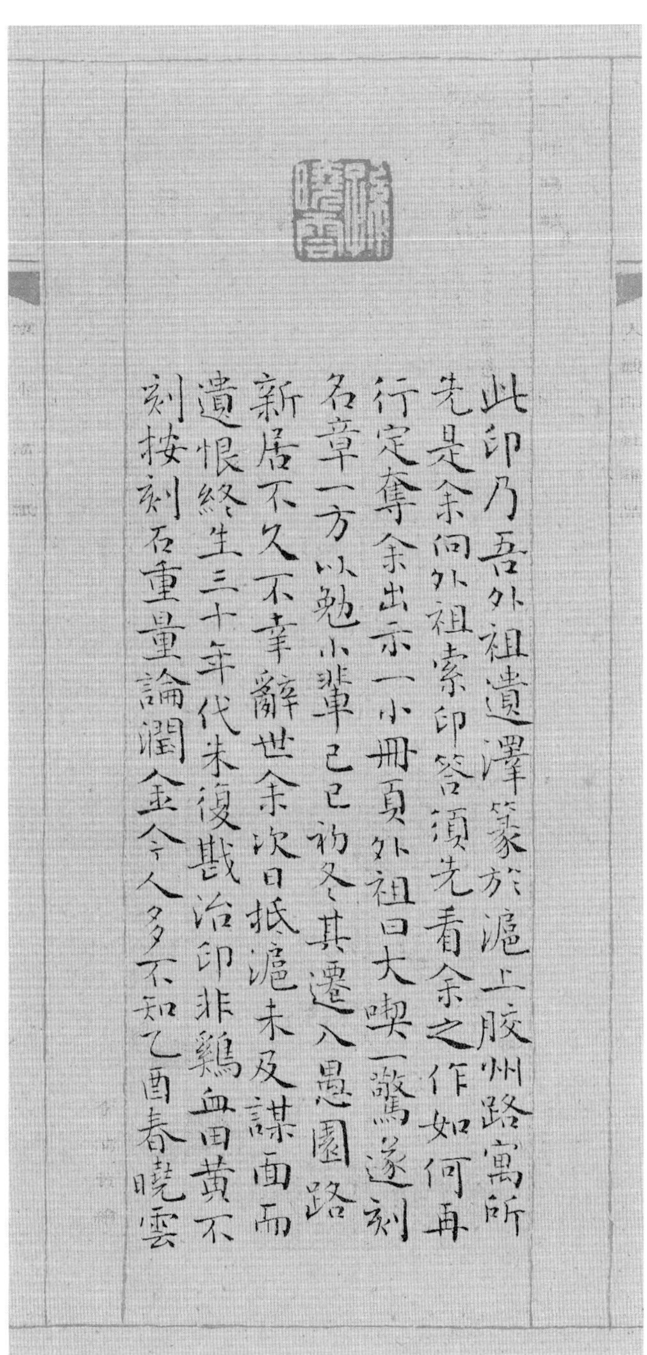

An impression of seal in regular script on how the author's maternal grandfather made a seal, 21 cm × 10 cm, 2005

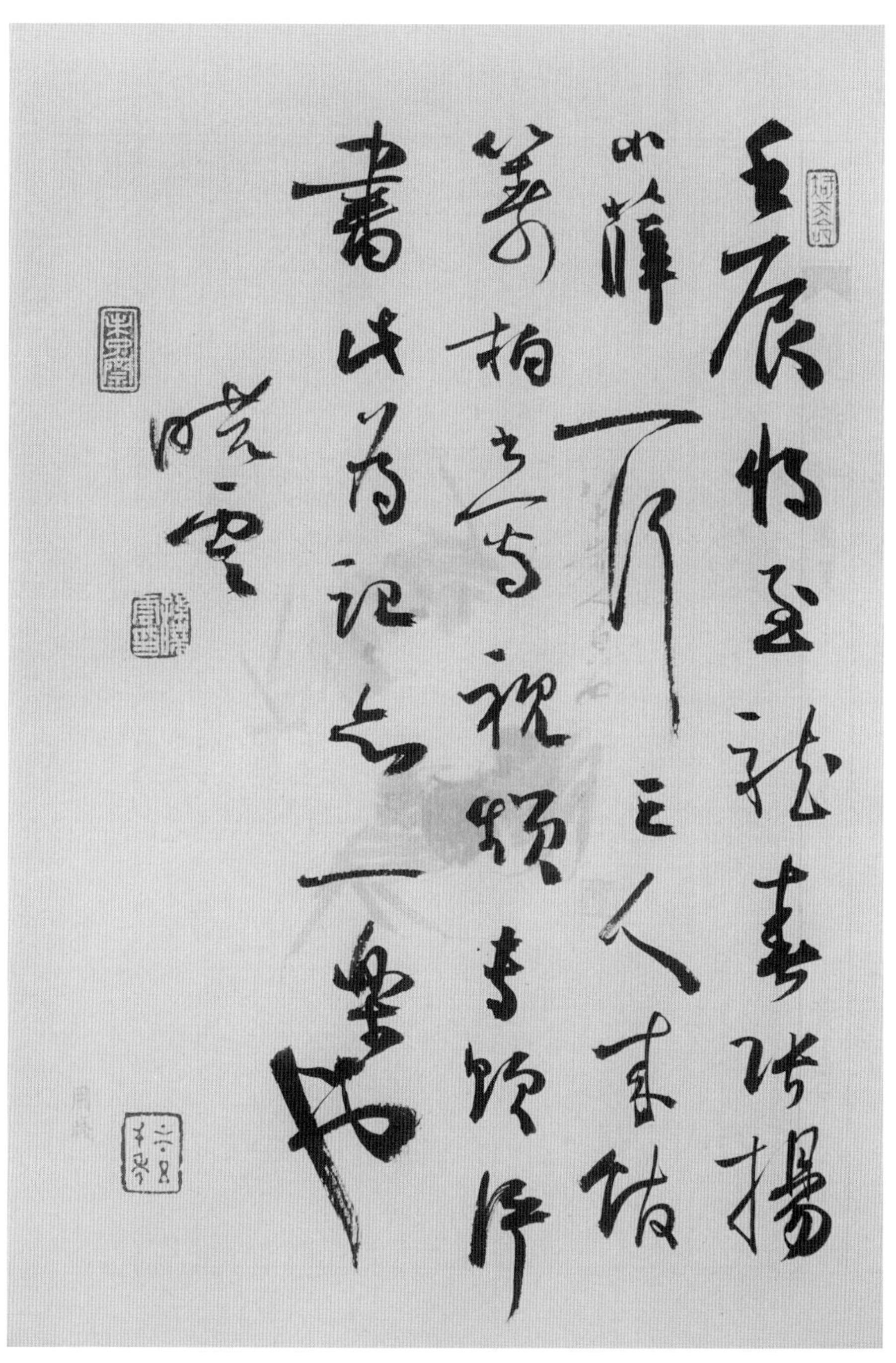

A Letter Named Ren Chen (the Year of Water Dragon) in cursive and semi-cursive script, 27 cm × 17 cm, 2012

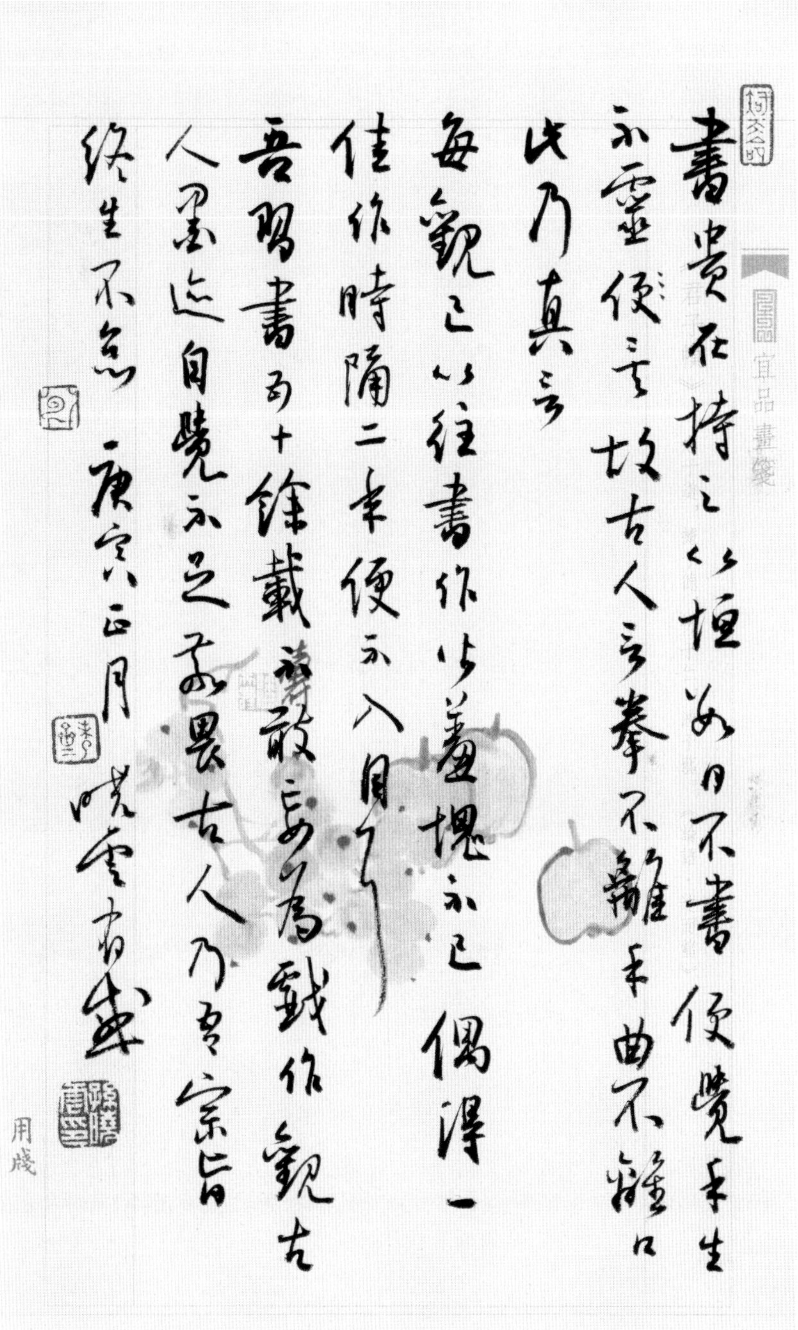

A *Letter Named Shu Gui Zai (Practicing Calligraphy Lies in Perseverance)* in cursive and semi-cursive script, 27 cm × 17 cm, 2010

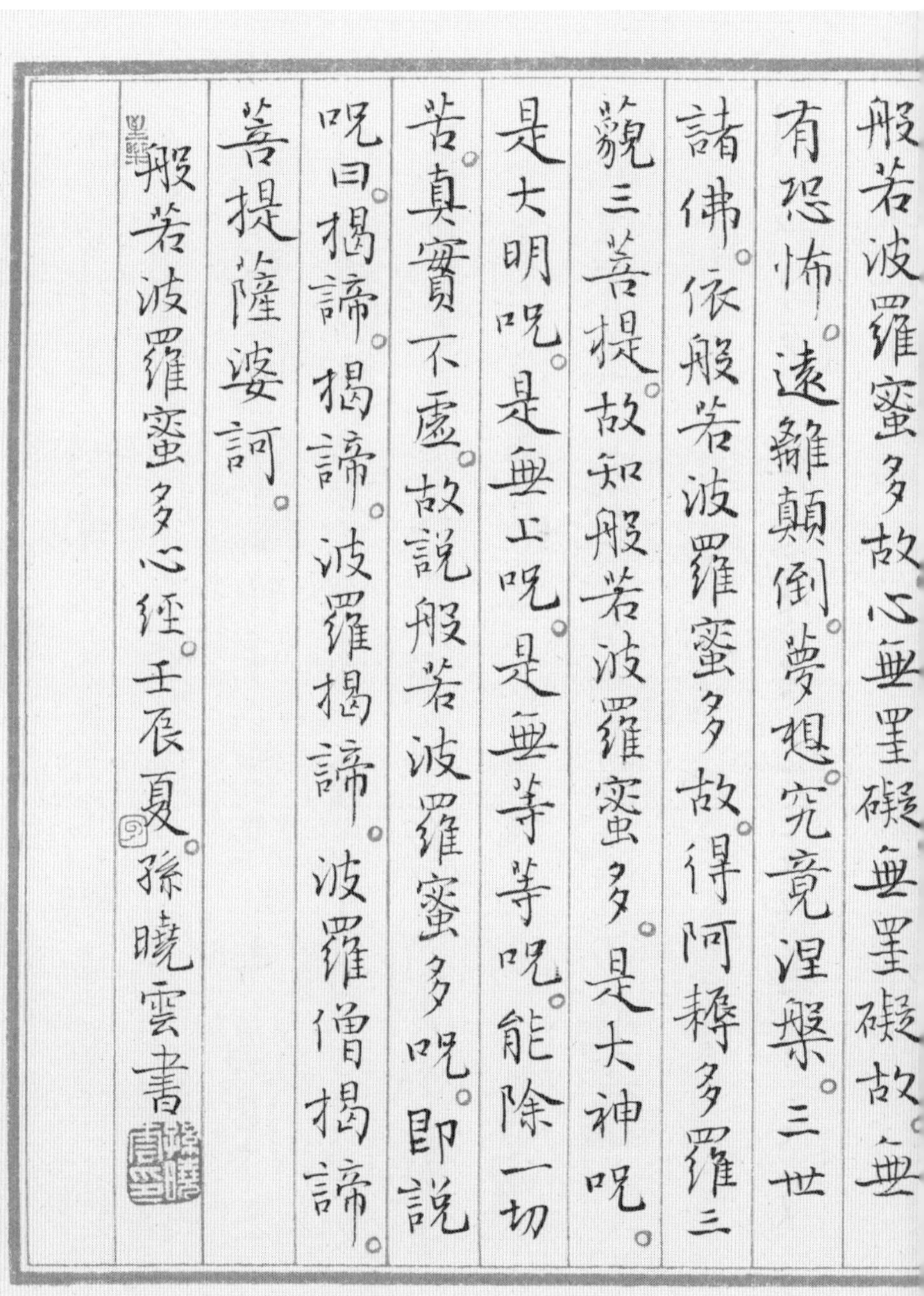

Prajna Paramita Heart Sutra in regular script, 36 cm × 52 cm, 2012

觀自在菩薩行深般若波羅蜜多時照見
五蘊皆空度一切苦厄舍利子色不異空空
不異色色即是空空即是色受想行識亦
復如是舍利子是諸法空相不生不滅不垢
不淨不增不減是故空中無色無受想行
識無眼耳鼻舌身意無色聲香味觸
法無眼界乃至無意識界無無明亦無無
明盡乃至無老死亦無老死盡無苦集滅
道無智亦無得以無所得故菩提薩埵依

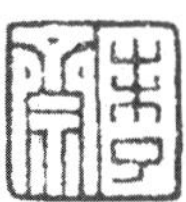

Index